THOMAS JEFFERSON
AMERICAN HUMANIST

THOMAS JEFFERSON
Portrait in the manner of an ancient coin, by Gilbert Stuart.
Fogg Art Museum, Harvard University

THOMAS JEFFERSON

AMERICAN HUMANIST

by

KARL LEHMANN

UNIVERSITY PRESS OF VIRGINIA

CHARLOTTESVILLE

To

PHYLLIS

THE UNIVERSITY PRESS OF VIRGINIA
Copyright © 1985 by the Rector and Visitors
of the University of Virginia

Third paperback printing 1991

Foreword by Dumas Malone Copyright © 1965 by
The University of Chicago. Reprinted by
permission of the publisher.

Library of Congress Cataloging-in-Publication Data
Lehmann, Karl, 1894–1960.
Thomas Jefferson, American humanist.

Reprint. Originally published: New York: Macmillan,
1947.
Bibliography: p.
Includes indexes.
1. Jefferson, Thomas, 1743–1826—Knowledge and
learning. 2. Presidents—United States—Biography.
I. Title.
E332.2.L4 1985 973.4'6'0924 85-13479
ISBN 0-8139-1078-1

Printed in the United States of America

FOREWORD

THE PROTEAN character of Thomas Jefferson has evoked such a variety of responses in the last two centuries that we are not warranted in saying that any one of these was exclusive at any time. Yet, because of the fact that for upwards of forty years he was a public figure and more than ordinarily controversial, it would have been surprising if the view of him as a political man had not generally been dominant. This seems to have been the case during most of the century after his death, when he was less widely recognized as a man of science and learning than in his lifetime. Our generation has witnessed his renaissance as an omnivorous mind and humane spirit.

If I may report on my own experience, I am sure that when I began as a teacher and serious student of American history, just after the First World War, I thought of him primarily as a father of our democracy and an apostle of political freedom. If I was not already aware of his advocacy of religious liberty, I soon became so, but I doubt if I quickly or sufficiently recognized his identification of this with intellectual freedom. At first, I certainly would not have thought of describing him, in Karl Lehmann's words, as "one of the greatest humanists of all time"; and while aware that his intellectual interests were broad, as a fledgling scholar I probably thought them rather superficial. I do not remember precisely when or under what external stimulus it was that, while going over some one of his papers, I became aware of his kinship of spirit with that of all devotees of learning and honest seekers after truth, but to me this was a real and an important discovery.

The present book, first published in 1947, was not then available. Since Karl Lehmann did not come to the United States from Germany until 1935, he may not yet have thought of writing it. This work of a distinguished humanist would have been welcome at any date, but actually the process of broadening the view and deepening the understanding of Jefferson's extra-political activities was well under way in the 1920's, though, ironically, it was at this time that Claude Bowers, with dramatic brilliance, was presenting him anew as a party chieftain. In his own time he was undoubtedly that, but a number of his other activities and interests were beginning to attract the attention and arouse the enthusiasm of scholars in the twenties. These fell within the fields of architecture, agriculture, invention, science in numerous branches, religion and philosophy, languages and linguistics.

Without entering upon a bibliographical essay, I deem it sufficient to say here that Professor Lehmann's book, besides being an admirable synthesis of the findings of scholars in our generation, is a fresh treatment—marked by rare perceptiveness—of a multi-faceted personality. There are stimulating suggestions in every chapter and on almost every page. Before presenting Jefferson's view of the ancient world, he says that, while necessarily dated, this has the timelessness of any portrait of a great subject by a great artist. Designating it as a dialogue between the American and the Greeks and Romans, Mr. Lehmann describes it in detail, thus enabling us to gain a better understanding of both Jefferson and the ancients. The figure which emerges on our side of the Atlantic is not that of a master politician but of a universal man.

In scope and duration this dialogue is amazing. As a schoolboy in his native hills and as a student in colonial Williamsburg, Jefferson acquired and sharpened his linguistic tools. He was unusually fortunate in his teachers, and in his maturity he needed no interpreter or intermediary. When President of the United States he said that he never read translations. Since the observation applied to French, Italian, and Spanish, as well as to Greek and Latin, he could read modern treatises as well as classical texts. Though he took up Anglo-Saxon and collected Indian vocabularies, he never learned German. Mr. Lehmann emphasizes Jefferson's admiration for the copiousness and beauty of Greek, and has much to say about his attitude toward languages generally. This unusual linguist was an advocate of linguistic growth and a foe of grammatical rigidity. He read works in Greek and in Latin (which he did not admire as a language though some of his favorite authors used it) until his dying day. In this author's opinion, he was primarily a Hellenist, though not entirely so; in architecture, for example, he was a Romanist. Though curtailed during his most active years as a public man, his dialogue with the ancients was never wholly interrupted. It was most active in the seventeen years after his retirement from the presidency. In this period, as Mr. Lehmann says, the amount of his reading was incredible. Much of the freshness of the present book is due to the fact that the author drew freely on the records of these last years, which are far more extensive than those of his young manhood and have been considerably less exploited than those of his public life. For Jefferson the delightful pursuit of knowledge was unending, and in terms of the mind and spirit these were the richest of all his years. His correspondence with John Adams alone is proof of that.

Mr. Lehmann's standing as a classicist makes his testimony to the breadth and depth of Jefferson's classical scholarship most impressive, but in describing him as one of the greatest of humanists, he is not thinking merely of learning. And he emphatically denies that the "Sage of Monticello" adhered to any cult of antiquity. Jefferson was no desiccated antiquarian. As shown here, he was a man of the past, present, and future, transcending in his own person any differences there may have been between specialist and amateur, while reconciling science and humanism in his own mind. Actually, there was

relatively little specialization then, and the various fields of
knowledge were far less sharply differentiated than they became later; when he used the term "science" he meant all
knowledge. What is more, he agreed with the ancient Greeks
that man is the measure of all things. Herein lay the essence
of the humanism of one who recognized no barriers to the
operation of the mind, who abhorred pedantry of any sort,
and who sought incessantly to make knowledge useful. Mr.
Lehmann does not, I believe, quote Jefferson's highly significant saying: "The earth belongs always to the living generation." He clearly perceives, however, that the dead hand of
the past did not blindly direct the actions of this friend of
human freedom and happiness.

In the realm of the arts Jefferson was weakest in sculpture
and painting and made his chief personal contribution in
architecture, where utility and beauty could, and in his opinion should, join hands. Perhaps none of his non-political
activities has received so much expert attention as his work in
architecture. Here, more than in any other field, he went back
to ancient sources for guidance. While manifesting his eclectic spirit in choosing Roman models rather than Greek, he
was not averse to copying ancient monuments precisely. This
was especially true in his efforts to have monumental public
buildings erected in the young Republic. In domestic architecture he was much more flexible. The degree of originality in his own work can be endlessly argued, but Mr. Lehmann has no hesitation in describing him as creative and
there can be no doubt that he put the stamp of his artistic
personality on his dwelling at Monticello and on his academic
village at the University of Virginia. One cannot rightly assume that if he were living under the very different conditions of our day he would proceed as he did then; but in his
own time, when trying to improve architectural taste in a
young country and to prepare the way for future developments, he turned back to the purest and noblest models that

he knew and made them the starting point. Repudiation of the past is no sure sign of creativeness in architecture or anything else. Jefferson would have been the last to apologize for his eclecticism, and his buildings still speak eloquently for themselves. Mr. Lehmann, for one, regards the Rotunda at the University of Virginia as more beautiful than the Pantheon on which it was modeled.

Jefferson did not regard the ancient world as something which could not be improved upon. He viewed it critically and commented sharply on its limitations. This was notably true in two fields: ethics and government. As a young man he valued the precepts of the classical moralists, but with the passing years he became increasingly aware of their inadequacy. These writers were superb with respect to man's relationship to himself, inculcating noble ideals of self-control, moderation, and equanimity in the face of adverse fortune. In this area he accepted them as very great teachers and from them learned his lessons well. He found them deficient, however, in dealing with man's relationship to others: they failed to inculcate the social virtues. In his dialogue with the past he also talked with the Jews, though unfortunately he did not understand Hebrew, and he charged them, too, with ethical inadequacy. To him the idea of a peculiar people was deplorably anti-social. The necessary supplement to the ethics of the ancient Greeks, Romans, and Jews he found in the moral teachings of Jesus, which he studied in the Greek as few American public men ever studied them in English. Fully aware of their beauty and convinced of their superiority, he followed them to the best of his ability. In this connection it may be noted that Mr. Lehmann, while comparing Jefferson to Goethe as a "universal man," describes Jefferson's attitude as Christian and that of the great German man of letters as pagan.

Christian he undoubtedly thought himself, but he took no stock whatever in doctrinal orthodoxy of any sort. Basically an empiricist, he thoroughly disliked systematic philosophy, and in that sense of the term was no philosopher at all. He honored the Greeks for the freedom they granted their thinkers in pursuit of truth and their artists in search of beauty, and he valued the moralists of both Greece and Rome because of the practicality of their teachings; but he profoundly distrusted the builders of complicated systems of thought and the glorifiers of abstractions, especially detesting Plato. Mr. Lehmann says that when Jefferson used the term "philosophy" he meant the "comprehensive result" of the search for knowledge. Quite clearly he did not mean metaphysics. Literally, a philosopher is a lover of wisdom and for Jefferson wisdom was based chiefly on experience.

Viewing the political record of antiquity with a respect for original sources and a critical spirit which would be deemed creditable in any historian of today, he found in the experience of the Greeks and Romans few positive guides, if indeed he found any. His admiration for the ancients did not extend to their governmental and social systems. What the Greeks called democracy—that is, direct democracy—was practicable in only a limited area, and they knew no alternative to this but tyranny since they had no notion of a system of representation. Apart from New England towns, and the "wards" of which Jefferson talked so much as units of government, the models for American institutions of government must be sought elsewhere. Actually, they were derived in colonial times from those of "Mother England," and were progressively adjusted to American conditions. The political history of the ancient world offered Jefferson little beyond warning of dangers which confront any government—public inertia and the lure of wealth and power, for example. Another was the strife of parties, which he accepted as a necessary evil. He found the political experience of the distant past deeply discouraging, and his predominant optimism about the American experiment in self-government is the more striking by contrast. His hopefulness was partly congenital, but it could hardly have survived had he not had enduring faith in the basic good sense of the people and been aware of the extraordinarily favorable environment provided by the North American continent.

If Jefferson was not the best example of the "universal man" which his times afforded, as Mr. Lehmann believes, we should be hard put to find a better. But he operated most conspicuously in the field of public affairs, into which the present book does not enter. In that field he often appeared as a partisan. The charges against George III in the Declaration of Independence are those of an intense patriot pleading a particular cause; they are not an example of scholarly judiciousness. And in his long and bitter struggle with the Federalists, though generally counseling moderation, this individualist was very much a party man. How, then, can he properly be described as universal? Did he not, as a man of science and learning on the one hand, and as a political man on the other, operate under different standards?

No attempt will be made here to resolve such contradictions and inconsistencies, real or apparent, as marked his long and varied career. I will suggest, however, that his political thinking and political actions become more understandable when viewed in the light of Mr. Lehmann's admirable presentation of him as an empiricist who was skeptical of formal systems of thought and of abstractions. Certain maxims which he regarded as timeless and universal he undoubtedly clung to; nowhere are they better summarized than in the most famous passage in the Declaration of Independence, where they are designated as "self-evident." Here he was talking of "rights," and the very term suggests that their basis was moral; they were natural rights arising from the very nature of things. They might be further summarized by the statement that man is the measure of all things. It may be claimed that Jefferson's consistency lay in his loyalty to these "self-evident" truths which he proclaimed. Beyond them, one who was distrustful of all systems of thought and never himself developed one, might have been expected to be guided by experience. In the ripeness of his years he declared that nothing is immutable but "the inherent and inalienable rights of man." With this may be coupled the judgment of Mr. Lehmann that, when studying the past, Jefferson recognized that human efforts could never be expected to conform to any absolute standard.

To claim impeccability for any statesman is quite absurd, but a strong case can be made for the third President of the United States, as a political empiricist and as an enlightened realist engaged in the actual conduct of government. Opinions about his statesmanship, however, are much more likely to differ than those about his humanism. As a political figure, furthermore, he cannot be detached from his own era, while his appeal as a universal spirit is timeless.

DUMAS MALONE

September 1, 1964

PREFACE

THIS BOOK deals with the meeting between a genius and a great subject. The wide range and deep penetration of Jefferson's studies and ideas regarding the "Ancients" will, I hope, emerge with sufficient clarity to show that they are of considerable importance—more than hitherto acknowledged—for a correct appraisal of his personality, his life, thought and art.

But at the meeting of a genius and a great subject, something happens to the latter, too. Whenever a man of the stature of Jefferson looks steadily and curiously, throughout a long life, on a great period of human civilization, a picture emerges that is timeless—like a portrait of a great man painted by a great artist. However dated, limited and conditioned this eighteenth century man's picture of antiquity may be, its unity and vitality lend a permanent value to it.

Consequently this work attempts to reconstruct that picture and to exhibit the breadth and depth of Jefferson's Humanistic thought. His own statements and various other documents form the basis of this reconstruction. I have limited myself to published sources, because they are extensive and eloquent enough to allow the drawing of this outline. And such limitation seemed advisable, since an exhaustive investigation of all the details cannot be undertaken until after the publication of the voluminous documentation now being edited at Princeton University.

Given the theme of this book, I have not attempted to trace or point out the parallelism of Jefferson's ideas with those of other men of his age. Even if it could be proved that

each individual statement of his has analogies in those of
other men of his century, and even if definite contemporary
sources for many of them could be exposed, Jefferson's re-
casting of such ideas would clearly emerge. The eighteenth
century style of Jefferson's mentality and the all-pervasive intellectual climate of his age make it difficult, if not impossible, to say in each case whether the articulation of a specific
viewpoint was borrowed by him from an antique source
or whether he simply found confirmation in such sources.
Wherever I have pointed out and documented the relationship between Jefferson and such sources, I mean to leave this
question open to discussion.

Critical readers will note that the author has refrained
from discussing the gradual change of emphasis in regard to
certain issues during the various periods of Jefferson's life.
I do not mean to deny or to obscure such change and the impact of actual experience in an agitated age and career on
the formation of his ideas. But in the present stage of our
knowledge and for the present purpose, I felt justified in
attempting to draw a comprehensive picture. From the
material submitted, I have gained the conviction that, fundamentally, Jefferson's Humanistic "philosophy" remained
astonishingly constant, though it unfolded and branched out
with enriched experience.

It is in the nature of any such study concerned with a
single aspect, however important that aspect may be, that the
resulting picture is one-sided. I must leave it to others to fit
this picture into a more general framework and thus to as-
sign to Jefferson's Humanism its appropriate place in his
biography.

I am indebted to many friends for encouragement and
helpful interest. Above all I have to thank her to whom these
essays are dedicated for inspiring and fundamental participation in plan and execution. Douglass Adair and Allan Nevins
have granted me the benefit of expert criticism that has led

to revisions and improvements. Fiske Kimball, the great explorer of Jeffersonian architecture, has read the manuscript critically, and various corrections and suggestions of his have been incorporated. I have also had the privilege of having it read by Jane Bradley, Marie Kimball, and Edgar Sturtevant. Bolton and Florence Love's hospitality in Virginia has been invaluable to me.

For assistance in securing the illustrations I am indebted to Fiske Kimball, O. W. Larkin and Clarence Ward. Wayne Andrews, I. T. Frary, and Frank Roos have generously allowed me to reproduce some of their own fine photographs. The Hillyer Gallery of Smith College and the Metropolitan Museum of Art have permitted reproduction of certain items of their photographic collections.

Finally, this book could never have been written without the untiring assistance of the staff of that magnificent institution of learning, the New York Public Library.

K. L.

NEW YORK, January 1947

CONTENTS

ILLUSTRATIONS

Frontispiece: Thomas Jefferson—Portrait by Gilbert Stuart (courtesy Fogg Art Museum, Harvard University; gift in memory of Thomas Jefferson Newbold, from Mrs. Newbold and their family).

INTRODUCTION

THE GIGANTIC FIGURE of Thomas Jefferson stands midway on the road which leads through what is commonly called the modern age. He was born two hundred years after the heyday of the Renaissance, of the Reformation and of Humanism. And two hundred years more have passed since his birth. Like every other man of his age, he was an heir of the Renaissance tradition. He consciously applied its basic creeds in the specific form of rational enlightenment. But more than any other man of the eighteenth century he led that tradition toward a new world that is ours.

It has been said that "Jefferson was the most universal as a human being of all of his American and perhaps European contemporaries also." If in that respect he had a counterpart —only vaguely known to him—in Goethe, with Goethe he emerges as one of the few truly universal men known in history.

His universality in action and reflection has animated the writings on Thomas Jefferson. Biographers and students of special aspects of his ideas and activities have submitted to the public a glittering variety of facts. Anthologists have attempted to select what seemed to them the most important statements he made. The details of his life have been described and documents referring to them have been published. And again, in its bewildering assemblage of the great and the minute, the literature on Jefferson resembles the unceasing avalanche of writings about Goethe. His political career and its impact on American history have naturally been major objects of historical investigation.

His ideas about government and organized society have been of the foremost interest to most of his biographers, and their character, the connection with their true or alleged sources have been studied and appraised.

His educational plans and activities occupy the next place in general interest and special research.

The architect Jefferson, whose work is of outstanding quality in his country and in his age, has been the subject of thorough and scholarly studies.

Aside from these three areas of political history, education and architecture in which Thomas Jefferson has left the most obvious and tangible stamp on our culture, his remarkable mental and practical achievements in many directions have been investigated.

There is the great array of books, pamphlets, articles with titles such as "The Philosophy of Thomas Jefferson," "Thomas Jefferson's Views on Religion," "Thomas Jefferson, Man of Letters." There are more or less penetrating studies on the mathematician, anthropologist, archaeologist, linguist, jurist, classical scholar Jefferson. His interests in art, in gardening, in cooking have been exposed. His personal contacts with specific men of his age have been the matter of special monographs and articles: his correspondence with John Adams, Du Pont de Nemours, George Ticknor, French ladies, American Jews.

His biographers have more or less referred to all these various aspects. They have tried to give a fair picture of his basic character and of his genius; the eulogists and the unfavorably biased critics have not been as numerous among them as one might expect, in view of the radical position of Jefferson's political, religious and social views.

In recent decades, attempts have been made to find a common denominator of his thoughts and actions. He has been called an apostle of Americanism, and his primary concern has been defined as the promotion of civilization. And while some writers have taken the rather cynical attitude that he wanted to achieve everything and failed in almost every direction, or that one could more easily define what he was not than what he was, the opinion that there existed a basic approach to the world at large in Thomas Jefferson seems to gain more and more followers.

His immortality, it has been said, "does not lie in any one of his achievements, but in his attitude toward mankind."

But to Thomas Jefferson mankind was not an invariable species of nature. He did not believe in species. He believed in individuals. Mankind was neither to be grasped as a physiological unit nor to be apprehended as a mystic society or community. It was an infinite sum of individuals in time and space. To grant freedom and happiness to the greatest possible number of individuals should be the common concern of all of them. Each individual was an independent unit, and the formation of his personality was the free development of his natural gifts.

The appraisal of man as the measure of things was first brought into the world by the Greeks. The cultured Romans deserve the name of Humanists because they chose to make this Greek sense of civilized personality their own. The Humanism of the Renaissance was the soil in which Thomas Jefferson grew. However much we may today appreciate subconscious tradition from the Middle Ages which pervaded the Renaissance, the concept of the human individual as an independent, free and self-reliant genius was a continuation of that line of antique Humanism. And whatever subtle overtones from different directions the listening historians may perceive, in all those respects in which the "modern age," from the Renaissance through the eighteenth century, was modern, it is rooted in and has exploited basic ideas of that Humanist tradition. Even Romanticism as it emerged around 1800 was consciously or unconsciously an offspring of that self-assertion of the human individual which is an inheritance of ancient and Renaissance Humanism. Only the later nineteenth and twentieth centuries' collectivisms in practical life, politics and sociology have deliberately and definitely deviated from that tradition and created, in large sections of the cultured world, a fundamentally different outlook.

Humanism was not a gift of nature, though Jefferson believed the recognition of the supremacy of individual personality sprang from a natural desire of man. To him as to other Humanists, civilization meant fulfillment of what God or Nature had intended of man against barbarisms of early and oppression of later phases. History had started this development in Greece, it seemed to the Humanists, and the classical world in its entirety was to become the source of modern civilization.

The dialogue with the ancient world in thought and in the arts was thus to Jefferson, as it had been to other Humanists, the natural means of individual development. If he was an apostle of Americanism and civilization, his idea of what civilization in future America—even of what humanity—might be was unthinkable without his Humanistic experience.

Again, the parallel with his great contemporary Goethe occurs in this deliberate Humanism of Jefferson. Both men were outstanding classicists in their time, the one in poetry, the other in architecture; both in reflection. Yet, if both Goethe and Jefferson combined that classicistic Humanism with progressive and advanced scientific ideas which led into our world, there was a profound difference between these two great figures. It was not primarily a difference in emphasis between the poet who was also a naturalist and minor statesman among many other things, and the statesman, builder and educator who was also a naturalist, mathematician and linguist. Nor was the difference between a predominantly artistic genius in Goethe and a fundamentally scholarly genius in Jefferson what ultimately mattered.

Their profound divergence in Humanistic outlook is defined by an opposition of ethical standards. Goethe chose to live his life as a poet and to exploit all his other activities for the sake of self-realization in imaginative works. Jefferson, though conscious that nature had intended him to be a scholar rather than anything else, dedicated his life to his fellow men.

Goethe was fundamentally truly pagan in his selfish concentration on his own personality and creative work of thought. Jefferson was fundamentally—and consciously—truly Christian in his fulfillment of duties to humanity which to him were first in order.

In his synthesis of social sense and Humanistic tradition, Jefferson was different from his forerunners, his contemporaries and those who have called themselves Humanists in more recent times. It implies neither an apology for "the classics" nor a eulogy of Jefferson to call him one of the greatest Humanists of all time. This title is not in the nature of an overstatement. It is justified by his own unceasing preoccupation with ancient civilization, the nerve of Western Humanistic tradition. It is justified by the stature of the man and by his impact on American ideals. It is, above all, justified by the humanitarian and social direction which he gave to Humanistic thought.

If Humanism has any future in the sense of a living connection of past and present, it will not be rooted in a nostalgic longing for lost beauty, nor in the dreams of an ivory tower, nor in an attempt to dress the ancients up for modern shopwindows. It will be in the concrete grasp of broad human experience, in the records and works of the ancient world, in its integration in individual, progressive personalities who are aware of their duties toward the human society of their time.

Scattered in the writings of Thomas Jefferson are the stones of a mosaic picture of the ancient world which was a unit in his mind. It was a picture of humanity, of its character and behavior, of good and evil, of justice and cruelty, of greatness and deceit, of sublime thought and its expression, of passions and their function, of the music of sound and the beauty of form, of the value all these things might have to modern man. To attempt a reconstruction of this picture may be of some avail.

PART I

Conversation with the Ancients

CHAPTER 1

The Search for Knowledge

THOMAS JEFFERSON was a lawyer, politician, revolutionary, the author of the Declaration of Independence, wartime governor of his native state, writer of epoch-making bills, American minister to France, secretary of state, vice-president and, for two terms, President of the United States, founder and directing spirit of the University of Virginia. He was an assiduous farmer in the extensive manner of big eighteenth century landowners, supervising not only agriculture but also a sprawling home production of almost everything needed in a community of several hundred people. He was a great builder and creative architect, a manufacturer of nails, an enthusiastic gardener who gave much of his time to procuring plants and experimenting with them. He was a student of mathematics, an inventor of practical devices and gadgets, a naturalist, a meteorologist who made observations year after year, a collector of records about the Indians. He assembled the biggest private library in America and possibly of his age, and gave much time to its organization and cataloguing. He wrote so many letters that those hitherto published fill a score of volumes; he estimated that in one year their number amounted to twelve hundred. He was, in addition, a devoted head of his family, paying much attention and dedicating much time to the minutiae of the education of its younger members. He loved society, enjoyed good and long conversations, and indulged in a hospitality so extensive that it contributed to the growing financial difficulties of his later life. All this is the record of only part, though a major part, of his interests and activities.

It was a marvelously rich life, a long one of more than fourscore years—a life, it would seem, that must have been filled to overflowing. And men of his age who disliked him for one reason or another, as well as those of a later age who could no longer grasp the full strength of this vigorous man of a vigorous era, said that he was a superficial amateur who did a bit of everything, and nothing thoroughly. If this were true, men of a period of professional specialization might be induced to question seriously the value of doing things thoroughly and professionally rather than in an amateurish way. The paradox is that the alleged amateur Jefferson shows a record of contributions to human civilization, knowledge, and outlook which made this life more valuable to his contemporaries and to posterity than that of most other men. And these contributions are not only in the nature of inspired and inspiring expressions of thought, reflection and emotion, such as he gave in the *Summary View of the Rights of British America* and in the Declaration of Independence.

They are not only in the nature of beautiful buildings, individual practical innovations, laws, the Louisiana Purchase, the establishment of the University of Virginia. In many spheres of "science," to use the term in its eighteenth century sense, as inclusive of any and every scholarly search, he actually was a pathfinder. Running ahead of his time, he anticipated or even directly inspired later developments. Competent scholars of our time have shown this to be true in numerous instances. The paradox, thus fairly stated, is that Jefferson's personality and activity transcended the customary contrast between the specialist and the amateur as did the personality and activity of his great contemporary counterpart Goethe. Unconsciously, he was himself aware of this. He was as critical of the attitude of those who see "a little of everything and the whole of nothing" as of scholars who write in a specialized lingo intelligible only to their professional colleagues.

Jefferson's approach to understanding the entirety of the intelligible world, natural and human, and each in relation to the other, was an eighteenth century phenomenon, to be sure. It was encyclopedic, in the original meaning of the word; that is, it aimed at an all-inclusive knowledge of facts related to each other within a continuum of natural and historical life. But unlike the typical "encyclopedists" of the eighteenth century, Thomas Jefferson abhorred the system and the scheme, the mental shelf full of ordered pigeon holes. Systems and schemes were only practical devices, necessary and tedious evils which one had to use as he did, conscientiously and meticulously, making records in his account book, day after day, year after year. He kept his affairs in order, those of his mind as well as those of his practical life. He had a garden book, and commonplace books, and collections of laws in mansucript. He kept his library in shape according to a rigid scheme based on Bacon's division of the three faculties of the human mind, reason, memory, and imagination, with appropriate subdivisions for putting every book in its proper place so that he could easily find the sources of knowledge. That was what systems and classifications were for, Linnaeus's classification of flora, for example. But they were mere devices and aids to memory.

True knowledge was a progressive dynamic penetration of the world. Seeing, listening and reading—reading above all. In this way one got more and more facts and included them in one's own personality until they became part of it. The unity thus achieved was a personal unity. Things seen and heard and read—read above all—became part of a man, and in each stage of his life they grew with him. Jefferson penetrated more and more. He formed his judgment about anything as it came along, relating past experience, thought, facts that stuck in his memory, looking things up again in a scrapbook, in records, going back to the original source once more.

Thomas Jefferson—again like Goethe—had a naïve, strong mental vitality, the source of courage for a task which, even in the eighteenth century, seemed to be beyond the reach of any individual. It was already an age of specialization that tried heroically to keep the growing mass of facts together in rigid encyclopedic classification or to order it in philosophies of reason. In this age, Jefferson's vital and dynamic approach to the ceaseless acquisition of factual knowledge which was to be kept together by personal "wisdom" has the flavor of the vigorous curiosity of those early Greek thinkers who inaugurated the line of civilized reflection on the intelligible world. This flavor is strangely blended with the exact recording, the scientific spirit, the awareness of the extent and methods of the scholarly approach characteristic of the eighteenth century.

The strength of an aboriginal genius cannot be explained by any trend of a century. Jefferson himself once remarked that it would be foolish to attempt an explanation of why there was a Homer in a given age. It would be equally foolish to try to explain from the circumstances of his time the incredible mental strength and daring that were his.

This strength and this daring necessarily led to a readiness for physical and mental exertion far beyond the standards of the average man of our or his or any time. If Jefferson's genius, like all genius, remains an unfathomable mystery, this readiness for exertion which was its natural complement explains part of the amazing range and intensity of its objectives. Those who have seen in Jefferson a superficial busybody and amateur have failed to measure the degree of exertion of which he was capable or have lacked the imagination of what that exertion implied and could achieve.

Jefferson's amazing readiness to labor and his ability to stretch time beyond its natural limits have not escaped his biographers. It is known that, when a youth, he had a clock in his bedroom and he got up as soon as he could distinguish the position of the hands in the early twilight of dawn. An active day of nineteen hours was nothing unusual when he had reached that phase of middle age in which most of us begin to economize on our expenditure of energy. When, in that phase, as secretary of state, he was asked for an appointment—to see an experiment on the distillation of fresh water from salt water—he suggested any time "from five in the morning to twelve at night, all being equal to me." Thus it happened that when he was an old man, free from the burdens of political activity but busy with all his normal varied occupations—to which the organization of his university had been added—he still had free, active days such as others much younger than he would have considered exacting. This, indeed, was the only way in which, in addition to everything else, he could satisfy what he himself, in 1818, called his "canine appetite for reading." This literary appetite had grown over the years, as a French proverb has it, with the habit of eating. There had always been that vigorous curiosity, youthful in origin and never aging, but at an early stage it had been trained and organized to get the most out of the unknown length of mortal life.

He has given an account of a day which he considered normal for a student of law. This account occurs in a letter written to a prospective student, only two years after his own graduation from William and Mary College. It is implied that in these years he had spent his laborious days in the manner recommended. And fifty years later, in 1814, he still considered this standard appropriate for a student of law who hoped to become an efficient lawyer and politician. It is based on an amazing, encyclopedic, eighteenth century breadth of studies which should include reading in mathematics, astronomy, geography, natural science, physics, ethics, religion, natural law, belles-lettres, criticism, rhetoric, oratory. How could anybody combine that with the highly specialized study of law? Well, here it is. It begins, for some hours before eight o'clock in the morning, with reading books on agriculture, chemistry, anatomy, zoology, botany, ethics and "natural religion" (including Latin reading of Cicero's and Seneca's philosophical treatises), religion, natural law. Then the four hours until noon are given to reading law. There follows, from twelve to one, an hour of study of books on politics and economics. By this time the student would have spent at least seven solid hours on reading. It would seem to approximate a full working day. But, in the afternoon (one may assume for at least two hours) the student should read "the Greek and Latin originals" in ancient history, and books on ancient, and later—particularly English and American—history. But that is not yet the end. From dark to bedtime, he is supposed to read "Belles-Lettres," poetry (for instance, Shakespeare) and prose, and oratory such as that of Demosthenes and Cicero. Even then, at the end of a day of strenuous intellectual activity, the student is expected to read critically, and his brain is assumed to be energetic enough to analyze and examine the correctness of the disposition, language, figures of speech, statements about legal cases, arguments, and so forth. All in all, it amounts to at least eleven hours of study and reading. It is hard for us to imagine that it could be done day after day for several years. And one may doubt whether the law students so advised lived up to such standards of exertion. But that Thomas Jefferson did it, at least for some time, is unquestionable.

In this strenuous routine Jefferson may have followed a scholastic pattern of his time. But what matters is the fact that throughout his later life he continued to organize his long and active days after such a pattern.

CHAPTER 2

Books and Monuments

D RIVEN ON by the search for knowledge and ready to
exert himself in long hours of labor, day after day,
Jefferson made a continuous and progressive study of the
ancient Greeks and Romans, of their writings and their
world. This was one of his major objectives along with, and
at times above, all of his other activities. It is no overstatement to say that, at the end of his life, the "Sage of Monticello" had read more of ancient literature, both poetry and
prose, than any other man of his time, apart from a group of
professional classicists. And a study of his writings, letters,
and records reveals that in range and scope, in the variety
of the authors he read and the aspects of antiquity he
studied, if not in the intensity of detailed penetration, as
time went on he even surpassed the standard of the average professional classicist of his day. Today, one might find
but a few great scholars of classical antiquity scattered over
the world who could measure up to his breadth of experience and knowledge in ancient literature while, to be sure,
there is a host of specialists who know the tiniest fragment
and shred of evidence in the area which they have chosen
as their specialty, in addition to having a "reading knowledge" of outstanding works.

As soon as he had mastered the languages well enough,
that is, from the time of his college days, Jefferson's reading
was pre-eminently of Greek and Latin originals, not of translations, and from his twenty-third year on he seems to have

had the firmly established principle of never reading a translation if he could read the original. This he was able to do from that time on in French, Italian, Spanish and Anglo-Saxon, along with Greek and Latin.

His efforts to acquire the books he needed to satisfy his ever expanding thirst for knowledge in general are well known. They resulted in his assembling libraries, one after another, in spite of the misfortunes which he encountered. There had been but a few books—and hardly an ancient author—in his father's home. As a student he had already assembled a first small library, but it was destroyed by a fire in his home at Shadwell. Then he began to build up the amazing library which was his pride until he sold it to Congress in 1815. It was a collection in which classical literature and writings on the ancient world formed a major part. By and large, it can be said that for that age the range and quality of his library of classical poetry and prose constituted a nearly complete laboratory of research. It included obscure authors whose names and works were then, and are today, only vaguely familiar to a professional classicist. He retained but a small part for himself when he sold this library (primarily, as he explicitly stated, classical and mathematical books). This collection of volumes withheld from the sale formed the nucleus of his third library, which grew fast during the last decade of his life, to be sold at auction and dispersed after his death. When he died, in 1826, that library included a somewhat unequal though also amazingly rich collection of classical authors. It reflects his tastes, and distastes, too, and the range and limitation, the interests of his late years. In its character it shows certain trends which had been visible in his former great library. When selling the latter he had eliminated most of the books on ancient history, travel and the like, and retained only authors, dictionaries and reference books which he considered to be necessary tools of research. In building up his new library he acquired again some of the texts and reference books which he had previously sold to Congress.

Already in his earlier library, he had duplicated texts of Greek or Latin authors, often buying three or four different editions, sometimes even more. This trend becomes increasingly prominent in the library of his old age. His correspondence with George Ticknor, who purchased books, primarily classical authors, for Jefferson while in Europe, not only reveals the old man's zeal for possession of the best modern, critical editions of his beloved Greek and Latin authors, it also shows that at this late stage Jefferson aimed at assembling various editions in order to be able to consult the often differing opinions of scholars about the conjectural reconstruction of mutilated and the adequate interpretation of ambiguous passages. In other words, he had taught himself to search for exact meaning and form by the critical means which the professional philologist uses.

He had arrived at a stage where he could appreciate progress in the technique of philological criticism as reflected in a new type of edition of an ancient author, for instance, when he received Heyne's *Iliad*—still a milestone in philological development: "It exceeds anything I had ever conceived in editorial merit. . . . This style of editing . . . urges us to read again the authors we have formerly read, to obtain a new and different understanding of them." He was always primarily interested in understanding the exact meaning of texts. He evidently cared little about "various readings" and "verbal criticism," so far as they did not affect intrinsic meaning. But if one possessed various editions, the notes of modern scholars gave different possible explanations and one could arrive at one's own opinion.

His searching mind returned in old age to valuing the work of the translator, too. While from his youth he had abandoned reading translations of classical authors, he now began to collect them. Indeed, they were as good as explanatory notes. In the wording he chooses, the translator is an interpreter of the original, and one should avail oneself of his learned opinion better to understand that original. Thus when requesting translations of Cicero's works he says: "You know in how defective and deformed a state his philosophical writings especially have come down to us. In every page his annotations are challenging the text with '*glossema interpretum*,' '*emblema librariorum*,' '*a sciolis intrusa*,' '*ab homine stolido barbaroque profectum*,' etc. and in truth the corruptions of the text render the sentiments oft indecypherable. Translations aid us with the conjectures of those who have made it a particular business to study the subject and its text." In this context, the preserved antique annotations, the "scholia," were valuable possessions, too, and he studied them so carefully that on occasion he quoted a passage from "some of the scholiasts, without recollecting where."

The use of the Greek scholia, later antique and Byzantine annotations, dull reading though they are, fascinated him in a very personal way. "I am attracted to the Scholia of the Greek classics because they give us the language of another age"; that is to say, if you read Homer along with scholia ranging from Greek of the time after Alexander the Great through medieval Byzantine, you can trace the linguistic development of words and the varieties of poetical or vernacular language. Ideas are words and words are ideas, according to Locke, one of Jefferson's intellectual sources, and the change of language reflected the change of ideas. Dictionaries, too, therefore, reflect changing ideas and should not be looked upon as giving a static, correct, and permanent rule. They "are but the depositories of words already legitimated by usage. Society is the workshop in which new ones are elaborated." With Jefferson, then, dictionaries, too, became more and more cherished possessions. Along with the major Byzantine dictionaries (such as Pollux, Suidas and the *Etymologicum Magnum*), his great library included such expensive works as Stephanus's *Thesaurus Linguae Graecae* and Du Cange's *Glossary* of medieval Latin, even today rare and cherished books in the private libraries of only a few philologists. After the sale of his library Jefferson felt it necessary to acquire once more these two expensive works. He was a keen critic of the quality of dictionaries, and used them systematically for research. When George Ticknor visited Jefferson in 1824 he "saw his Greek Lexicon printed in 1817; it was much worn with use, and contained many curious notes."

What mattered, evidently, in studying the classics, was to be aware constantly of changing developments. Jefferson attempted to unearth the original and exact truth beneath the accumulated strata of later transformations and reflections. Originally this endeavor had been in the nature of a direct and more naïve approach, of reading masses of the original authors in whatever editions he could find. But as he penetrated farther and farther, it became a complicated interwoven study of all the aspects, ideas and forms involved. In his youth, for example, he had read many general books on ancient history. Later they became mere reference books, because ever increasing knowledge made their statements and synthesis appear to be of dubious value. Thus the *Ancient Universal History* was to be put on the shelves of the library in the University of Virginia as a mere "book of general reference," while the real study of ancient history should be based on ancient authors. Even a classic of historiography like Gibbon's *Decline and Fall of the Roman Empire* was the work of a mere "compiler." Reluctantly, old Jefferson included it in his reading requirements for students of ancient history, because of the absence of coherent ancient sources for the late Roman Empire. When he was young, it had been an important source of knowledge for him, leaving its mark on his ideas about that age throughout his life; and during his second presidential term, not having his own library at hand in Washington, he had found it necessary to borrow a copy for some time.

Even in his own big library he had such "reference" books containing quotations of rare authors. He had to quote some of the Church Fathers, for instance, from an abridgment of Brucker's *History of Philosophy,* although he owned many of them along with the Byzantine church historians. He wished he could own that work of Brucker's itself, "as a book of reference or special research only, for who could read six volumes quarto, of one thousand pages each, closely printed, of modern Latin?" (A phrase, incidentally, full of subtle irony, referring to a letter by John Adams in which the latter had tried to impress and outdo Jefferson by his extensive reading of Latin Humanists.)

In addition to dictionaries and reference books, Jefferson possessed certain authors ønly for individual reference, hardly ever reading a major part of them: Aristotle, for example, and most of Plato. But he had to have them, and the time might come when he would have to take them up. In spite of his deep aversion to Plato, he got through the "task work" of reading the *Republic* from the first page to the last, to satisfy his conscience about his instinctive and negative judgment. And even later his studies led him to take up and read Plato's *Timaeus.*

His library was there to satisfy his steady and growing demand for knowledge. And one could not quite predict the direction in which that demand would move next. There were practical and technical problems in which he might become involved, such, for instance, as the means of getting water from a well. And, in that case, a travel book reporting primitive devices surviving in Egypt, and editions of Diodorus and Vitruvius, who describe the "screw of Archimedes," might be consulted. It was good, too, to own a full edition of Pliny's *Natural History,* though this was the dullest and most unreadable compilation ever written. But in 1812 he had to give a legal opinion on property rights on the river bank in the "Batture" of New Orleans, in the great new territory he, as President, had added to the United States. It was customary, of course, to refer to Roman law and to look up the Digests. They used the term *ager* and via dictionaries he was led to Pliny, who asserted that Latin *ager* was derived from Greek ἀγρός. Thus he had to find out the meaning of ἀγρός in Greek law, and here his big dictionary of Stephanus was handy. This and other terminological problems entailed more and more research in Greek, Latin, Anglo-Saxon, French, German and Spanish. The modern reader of this legal opinion may wonder how the court reacted to this seminar in linguistics. This was the wonderful fascination and the toilsome compulsion of all those books. One thing led to another, and they contained an immense storage of wisdom, facts and points of view.

There were not only practical problems like wells and legal decisions. Things happened all the time which startled his curiosity and drove him to the bookshelves. For example, in early years there came a foreign visitor, the Marquis de Chastellux. It was a delightful evening and, among other things, the discussion touched on English verse and prosody. That was around 1780. Later, Jefferson and Chastellux met again in Paris and discussed the matter further. In the meantime Jefferson had made observations on accent and prosody, English, Latin and Greek, and all this resulted in an essay on English prosody, which he sent to Chastellux before the Frenchman's death in 1788. It is full of quotations of ancient authors collected from his precious books.

Then, again, there were new publications, books and pamphlets. Among those which set the wheels of the searching mind in motion and drove him to his books, the copies received from authors or friends occupied the first place. They requested an acknowledgement and he had to make up his own mind about their subjects. Sometimes, a pamphlet was like a spark igniting the fire of a long smoldering interest and stirred him to reading and research. In 1803, for instance, there was the Unitarian Priestley's treatise on *Socrates and Jesus.*

The relationship between the ethics of antique philosophers and Christianity, their merits and differences, had been on Jefferson's mind since his youth. But Priestley did not go far enough. What was needed was a synopsis of the ethical principles of all the major ancient philosophical schools and those of Jesus. He began to read ancient philosophers again, tried to get Priestley to make such a synopsis, continued to search after Priestley's death, to read and assemble data.

In Paris in the eighties Jefferson had met some Greeks, and from them he acquired knowledge of the modern pronunciation of Greek. How different it was from what he had learned in school! It was tantalizing not to know the real sound of ancient Greek poetry. Had modern Greek preserved survivals? Could it help to restore the authentic sound of the language of Homer and Demosthenes which already then, forty years ahead of his time, he hoped would revive with a liberated Greek nation? Thirty years later, Adams sent him a copy of a recent pamphlet on the pronunciation of ancient Greek. Thus started again a line of research, reading, looking up passages, trying to clarify the issue of how much of ancient Greek phonetics survived in the modern language.

Curiosity was forever startled by the expansion of knowledge, the opening up of new vistas. Jefferson was keenly aware of the deplorable incompleteness of the ancient authors preserved. So much had been lost before the invention of the art of printing, which alone could guarantee the more or less complete survival of records and sources of knowledge, whatever disasters might cause material destruction. Livy, for example, one of the greatest historians of all times, whom he read time and again from his earliest to his last days, was incomplete. Early Roman history was largely unknown. If only the lost books of Livy could be found! The specter of these lost books, like the lost tribes of Israel, has haunted the minds of Humanists since the Renaissance. In the twenties of the present century, columns of newspapers were filled with stories about their rediscovery in a monastery in southern Italy. People were credulous or skeptical. It turned out to be the sensational blunder of an impostor. Nearly a hundred and fifty years earlier, when Jefferson was ambassador in Paris, he wrote to Madison: "Having seen announced in a gazette, that some person had found in a library of Sicily, an Arabic translation of Livy, which was thought to be complete, I got the chargé des affaires of Naples here, to write to Naples to inquire into the fact." The answer was affirmative. "There are persons, however, who doubt the truth of this discovery, founding their doubts on some personal circumstances relating to the person who says he has this translation. I find, nevertheless, that the chargé des affaires believes in the discovery, which makes me hope it may be true." It was a bluff at that time, too. But it is interesting to see Jefferson's curiosity using all means to find out about this rumor. What were diplomatic channels good for? They, too, might be exploited to satisfy one's demand for knowledge.

More than thirty years later another rumor reached Jefferson in his retirement in Monticello. "I have been informed that there has been lately discovered at Athens, in a subterranean vault, a collection of 2,000 volumes, or rolls of papyrus of Grecian authors, in a great state of perfection, with several statues of the highest order of sculpture, which it was probable was sunk by an earthquake, or was buried to save it from the barbarous hands of Mussulmans . . . am sorry it stands on the indefinite ground of 'I have been informed.' If true, we may recover what had been lost of Diodorus

Siculus, Polybius, and Dion Cassius. I would rather, however, it should have been of Livy, Tacitus and Cicero." The letter is addressed to the American consul at Leghorn, who, Jefferson hoped, would be able to get more definite information. This strange rumor—antedating the modern discovery of lost authors on papyrus rolls in Egypt by several generations—was, of course, a fake, as the alleged Arabic translation of Livy had been. It might have been the result of a mix-up with discoveries made in Herculaneum, or the transport of papyrus rolls from Egypt to Athens, and the clever salesmanship of local antique dealers. But anything seemed possible after the discovery of Herculaneum and Pompeii and with the rapidly broadening horizon of hitherto unknown ancient lands.

At the beginning of the century, Napoleon's expedition to Egypt had opened up the Nile Valley, and what Jefferson had read in Herodotus and Diodorus suddenly became reality. It would be fascinating, indeed, to learn more about Egypt. As early as 1802, he acknowledged receipt of a model of the Pyramid of Cheops sent to him from France by Volney. "It has corrected the idea I had preconceived of the form of those masses which I had not supposed to appear so flat. Whenever any good work comes out, giving a general view of Egypt, its inhabitants and antiquities . . . I will thank you to indicate it to me." He put the model in the hall at Monticello, not far from a marble copy of the reclining Ariadne, a Greek sculpture in the Vatican which, in his time, was believed to be a representation of the dying Cleopatra, the last queen of Egypt. And in his late years he used to call the attention of his visitors to the shape of a Blue Ridge mountain and its similarity to the shape of the Pyramid of Cheops.

Monuments offered a great visual approach to that ancient world, along with the texts of ancient authors. In Thomas

Jefferson's rich personality, there was a natural strain and instinct for archaeological research. It found its most curious expression in his invention of a method of "stratigraphical" observation in the course of excavating an Indian mound on his property. Indeed, he established the fundamental principle of modern scientific excavation about a century before its discovery by modern archaeologists. On the other hand, his lifelong concern with architecture led him to studies of ancient monuments all the time. Professor Kimball's research on Jefferson's architectural activities has traced his interest in ancient monuments as it is reflected in his purchase of books which illustrate and discuss them. The number of these books is rather limited in comparison with his great collection of authors. This may be due primarily to the great financial expense involved in purchasing archaeological books. But within this limitation, the collection shows a careful selection of the best. He had early purchased the French seventeenth century travel work of Spon, as well as the etcher Perrier's remarkable collection of engravings of ancient statuary, along with the best books of art criticism of the early eighteenth century, those of Jonathan Richardson; all three are classics in their own right. He later added such milestones of the study of monuments as Stuart and Revett's *Antiquities of Athens,* the *Antiquities of Herculaneum,* Desgodets's *Buildings of Rome,* Wood's work on Palmyra and Baalbek and, in criticism of art, Winckelmann's *History of Art,* the fountainhead of modern archaeology.

Jefferson's combination of literary and artistic interests, though not unusual in the eighteenth century, strongly contrasts with the attitude of those of his contemporaries and of the younger generation in America with whom he could exchange views about the Greeks and Romans. John Adams, his greatest correspondent on the classics, was completely uninterested in art. And George Ticknor, bookish as he was, reveals his remoteness from monumental experience in describing the library of the University of Virginia as fashioned after the Parthenon in Athens instead of the Pantheon in Rome. The sound is somewhat similar, indeed.

But, however keen Jefferson's own eyes were, and however ready he was to absorb visual impressions of the ancient world, together with its literary works, there were limitations to his visual approach. In part they lay within his own personality, in part they were due to external circumstances. It must be admitted that his immense vitality did not include more than the common interest of a cultured eighteenth century man in sculpture and painting. True, in his early years, he drew up a list of ancient sculptures, casts or copies of which he wanted to own; it was based on his looking at Perrier's engravings and his reading of Jonathan Richardson. Only the "Cleopatra" of this list did he actually acquire in later years. And the paintings he bought while in Paris, most of them at one sale, seem to have been more or less third-class works. They included copies of Renaissance and Baroque masterpieces. But the selection seems to reflect interest in subject matter—the life of Christ, ancient philosophy, portraits of great men, Homeric mythology—rather than in artistic quality.

In sculpture and painting, indeed, though not so much in ancient sculpture and painting, he had the chance to see great things in Europe, in Paris and on his travels. He voiced occasional interest in and promoted any artistic activity which crossed his way in America as part of a general development of culture. But sculpture and painting were never one of his cherished concerns.

Naturally, the foremost American architect of his age was throughout his life an ardent student of ancient architecture. And here his own creative genius could retranslate the diagrams, drawings and etchings of books into vital and splendid reality. In his earlier life, as Kimball has shown, it was rather indirect study of antique monuments via the work of the great Italian, Palladio, that made him visualize antique buildings and adapt their features in his own creations. Later, he made increasing and direct use of accurate portrayals and details of antique monuments which he found in the source books he had acquired. Thus elements of the interior decoration of Monticello—the stucco friezes of the hall and the drawing room, respectively from the temples of Faustina and Vespasian in Rome—are copied from engravings in Desgodets' *Edifices antiques de Rome*. The same work was probably used as the source for details of the Pantheon in its "copy," the library of the University of Virginia. He evidently took most of the details of the orders and decorations of the pavilions surrounding the campus from Fréart's *Parallel of the Antient Architecture with the Modern*, an excellent seventeenth century work which he owned. But books did not contain the original monuments of the ancient world as they contained the original words of the ancient writers. And here one meets the limitation of circumstances; a limitation more painful to Jefferson than it would have been to most men of his time. He was always longing for direct contact with reality, for the immediate facing of the thing itself. But throughout his life he lacked this direct contact with ancient monuments save for the brief interlude of his travel to southern France. There he could, indeed, see original monuments of the Roman Empire. There he was, for short days, "immersed in antiquities from morning to night" and "nourished with the remains of Roman grandeur."

It is curious that in spite of these emphatic statements, modern critics have expressed disappointment at Jefferson's lack of interest in art, because his travel notes do not refer very much to the ancient monuments which he saw. But these travel notes were made primarily, if not exclusively, as an account of the official business, chiefly the study of agriculture, for the sake of which the American ambassador traveled. Thus, the incidental remarks on ancient monuments found in them refer only to points which he felt needed exact recording. Among them are two remarkable passages. One is an accurate professional description of a Roman structure in Vienne, containing all the basic measurements as far as he could take them. Obviously, he traveled with the equipment of a professional student of ancient architecture. And he himself indicated the reason why he recorded this monument as exactly as he did, and studied and measured it, by stating at the end: "This monument is inedited." In other words, Jefferson prepared himself for his journey by studies of the then available publications of ancient monuments of the region, equipped himself to record whatever new evidence he might find, and felt himself bound to make such records—all in the manner of a modern archaeologist. Again, when he visited Bordeaux on his return, he took exact measurements of Roman brickwork—of the big variety having a length of two Roman feet—and compared its excellent quality with that of the brickwork then used in southern France. He consulted his notes when secretary of state and suggested the use of such models to the commissioners in charge of building the Capitol in Washington: "The remains of antiquity in Europe prove brick more durable than stone. The Roman brick appears in these remains to have been 22 inches long, 11 inches wide and 2 inches or 2½ inches thick. The grain is as fine as that of our best earthenware."

One might think that this excitement about Roman buildings was merely the enthusiasm of a creative architect of the neoclassic school. But it is evident that it was also the excitement of one who could finally have the immediate and direct experience of visual relics of the ancient world. "For me, the city of Rome is actually existing in all the splendour of its empire," he wrote. And his preparation for the journey as well as his experience on it were not merely concerned with buildings. He aimed at visualization, concrete reconstruction of historical drama, as well.

From southern France he crossed the Alps to northern Italy. "I took with me some of the writings, in which endeavors have been made to investigate the passage of Annibal over the Alps, and was just able to satisfy myself, from a view of the country, that the descriptions given of his march are not sufficiently particular to enable us, at this day, even to guess at his track across the Alps." It seems, then, that he traveled with a small collection of books, the statements of which he could verify or reject by his own visual experience. The following year when he journeyed through the Rhineland, again to assemble data on agricultural facts, he crossed the Rhine from Holland into Westphalia and visited Duisburg, then a small village. "I had understood that near that were remains of the encampment of Varus, in which he and his legions fell by the arms of Arminius (in the time of Tiberius I think it was), but there was not a person to be found in Duysberg, who could understand either English, French, Italian or Latin. So I could make no inquiry." He did not remember the exact date of the fateful battle of the Teutoburger Wald—it took place during the reign of Augustus, not of Tiberius. But from his reading he remembered fairly accurately the region in which the battle took place that stopped the expansion of the Roman Empire into Germany: a decision establishing that cultural frontier between western civilization and Germany which has affected the course of history to our own day. Hannibal's route through the Alps seems to be established now. The site of the Westphalian battlefield is still an enigma, though today Jefferson would find in any village of that region, if not a person speaking Latin, French or Italian, an elementary-school teacher who has located that site in his vicinity.

Clearly, travel through classical lands offered him an opportunity of visualizing ancient civilization and verifying facts of ancient history. Not only were the accounts of ancient sources ambiguous, so that investigation on the spot was needed; there also was a good deal of legendary or half-legendary tradition which he would have liked to test. For instance, there was the alleged tomb of Virgil in the suburbs of Naples, for many centuries called by that name. And the local guides would show visitors making a pilgrimage to the sacred site the laurel of the *poeta laureatus* growing from the tomb; they would give them a few leaves from it as a precious relic—and get a generous tip in return.

Jefferson had read about this in editions of Virgil or in travel books. While he, himself, was not able to test the truth, William Short, his secretary and friend, went to Naples in 1788, and Jefferson wrote to him from Paris where he continued to carry on the business of the ministry: "The dispute about Virgil's tomb and the laurel seems to be at length settled by the testimony of two travellers, given separately, and without a communication with each other. These both say, that attempting to pluck off a branch of the Laurel, it followed their hand, being in fact nothing more than a plant or bough, recently cut and stuck in the ground for the occasion. The Cicerone acknowledged the roguery, and said they practiced it with almost every traveller, to get money. You will of course tug well at the laurel which shall be shewn you, to see if this be the true solution."

What a rich harvest of knowledge visually acquired, of facts tested and verified, Jefferson could have gathered if he had been able to travel to Italy and Greece! How different from Goethe's, for example, would have been his experience of Pompeii! Goethe was unable to grasp the enchanting fullness and vitality of antique life as it was resurrected there, and only carried away on his tongue the evil taste of death and destruction which he tried to wash down by a hearty drink of wine. Jefferson would have eagerly seized upon all the details of that comprehensive life, related them to the many, many things he knew from his voracious reading, rounded out the picture he already had to fuller size and vitality. But he "scarcely got into classical ground." Short was lucky to be "amidst the classical enjoyments of Rome." Jefferson felt himself "kindle at the reflection to make that journey." When he left Paris in 1789, he hoped to return soon from a temporary leave and to continue his life as minister to France. Then circumstances might allow him to make the journey he now had to "postpone." About thirty years later, he nostalgically wrote: ". . . were I twenty years younger, instead of writing, I should meet him [George Ticknor] there [in Paris] and take with him his classical voyage to Rome, Naples and Athens."

CHAPTER 3

Youthful Studies

F ATE DENIED Jefferson what it allowed many minor men of his age. And so he carried on his unique conversation with the ancients, far from their physical world, for nearly forty long and rich years, reading and studying with unfaltering enthusiasm. Though the direction of that enthusiasm and the means of satisfying it were entirely his own, in itself it was typical of the last great century of a continuous tradition of classicism which had come down from the early days of the Renaissance in Italy.

Jefferson himself was fully aware of this tradition. By the time of his youth, it had grown in extensiveness, if not in intensity, until it penetrated every corner of civilized life. Classical phraseology, allusions and formulas had become an embroidery of life in its totality, in its daily surrounding. Even in distant Virginia this was so. At the age of nine when he entered the household of his teacher, the Reverend Mr. Maury, he would find himself surrounded by servants with the high-sounding names of Cato, Ajax, Memnon and the Muse Clio. Later his own faithful slave had the name Caesar. He, like everybody else, would call his horses not Dolly or Speed, but Tarquin (the superb), Diomede (the courageous), Castor (the horseman-Dioscure's name), Celer (the speedy), and Arcturus (the star that watches the bear), for a hunting horse. The columnists of the day would call themselves Aristides, Leonidas, Decius, Brutus, Crassus, or Catullus. When men met in the inn at Williamsburg to discuss the situation and plans for the Revolution, it would be in the "Apollo" room of the Raleigh Tavern, where a Latin inscription over the mantelpiece referred to the more normal use of the room for the enjoyment of "gaiety the offspring of wisdom and a virtuous life." And when he planned to sail to France, the ship he originally chose was called *Romulus,* while later it turned out to be *Ceres.* He called one of his farms "Pantops," a Jeffersonian contribution to ancient Greek meaning "place with a view all around." Sticking to this kind of eighteenth century embroidery, he proposed high-sounding classical names in 1784 for new western territories: Cherronesus (the peninsula), Metropotamia (the land measured by the rivers), Polypotamia (the land rich in streams). This endeavor has been ridiculed as exaggerated. But then there had been Philadelphia, the city of brotherly love, followed in the eighteenth century by many a Greek or Roman town name in America. He would, of course, approve of Latin rather than English inscriptions to explain the actions of the Revolutionary War on the reliefs of a proposed monument for Washington by Houdon, the great French sculptor whose portraits of several leaders of the young American republic bear the facial expression of Roman republicans of old. And when Governor Lee of Virginia proposed to make the rattlesnake the emblem of the state of Virginia, he would remark that "there is in man as well as in beasts an antipathy to the snake, which renders it a disgusting object wherever it is represented." And he would suggest alternatives, among others "the Roman staves and axe," a cherished Humanistic symbol of the republican dignity of elected magistrates before Mussolini and his rowdies reversed that original meaning. All this was part of eighteenth century life in general. Antique or pseudoantique forms filled the air. One inhaled them continually. There was no escape from them.

Thomas Jefferson, curious, searching, eager to learn as he was by natural endowment, would have formed ideas about the ancient world in any case. If he had not received a classical training in early life, he would have taken up translations and modern books on the Greeks and Romans and thus satisfied his natural curiosity. But given his sense of concreteness, his awareness of the difference between original and secondhand experience, that classical world would never have become the great leaven of his understanding of humanity that it did become.

Chance, or rather, providence, providence on the part of his father, above all, had early opened to him the outer gate of that immense storehouse of human experience. Throughout his life he was aware that the early, elementary training which he had received in Latin and Greek had handed him a tool for the understanding of humanity which was of fundamental value. "I thank on my knees him who directed my early education, for having put into my possession this rich source of delight; and I would not exchange it for anything which I could then have acquired and have not since acquired," he wrote in the stormy campaign year of 1800. And again: "I think myself more indebted to my father for this than for all the other luxuries his cares and affections have placed within my reach; and more now than when younger, and more susceptible of delights from other sources" (1818). His grandchildren remembered repeated assertions of that kind from his late days: "If he had to decide between the pleasure derived from the classical education which his father had given him, and the estate left him, he would decide in favor of the former." These emphatic statements, made by a man who was unusually reticent and reserved in revealing his most personal experiences, show how deeply Jefferson appreciated the fact that he had learned the classical languages at an early age, how well he was aware that without that privilege his life would have been basically different and—as he saw it—deficient.

Many boys in America from families more wealthy and

Above: MANTELPIECE IN MONTICELLO.

Below: FRIEZE FROM THE TEMPLE OF VESPASIAN, ROME.

Above: UNIVERSITY OF VIRGINIA, PAVILION I. DETAIL.

Below: DETAIL FROM THE BATHS OF DIOCLETIAN, ROME. FROM FRÉART.

"ARIADNE" ("DYING CLEOPATRA"). ROME, VATICAN MUSEUM. SEE PP. 24 ff.

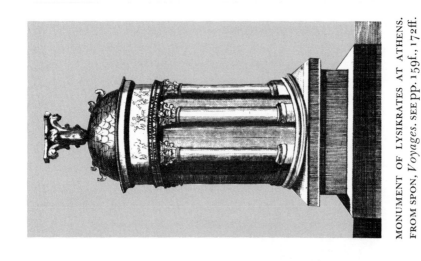

MONUMENT OF LYSIKRATES AT ATHENS.
FROM SPON, *Voyages.* SEE PP. 159f., 172ff.

OBELISK-MONUMENT AT VIENNE.
SEE p. 28.

more prominent than his did not receive the "classical education" he had, and it is well enough known that without it
they could go far in the world and become great historical
figures. On the other hand, by the middle of the eighteenth
century an American boy could get what was then considered
in Europe to be a good standard "grammar school" education anywhere in the colonies—grammar school corresponding to the high school of today. Thomas Jefferson got such
an education for about six years, first with Mr. Douglas, "a
clergyman from Scotland" who taught him "the rudiments"
of the Latin and Greek languages and French, and then with
the Reverend "Mr. Maury, a correct classical scholar." All
in all, it amounted to about six years of a training that,
apart from some mathematics, rudiments of geography and
religious instruction, was pre-eminently in Latin and Greek
grammar, more and more grammar, memorizing, translating
from English into the old languages and back into English,
exercises and reading of ancient authors; reading in the
meticulous, dull, painful, purely linguistic manner which
kills the author and in nine out of ten students kills any
further interest in the classics after they have escaped that
mill; the kind of reading which a man who was merely a
"correct classical scholar" would know as the only approach
to the classics, and indeed, the only safe method devised so
far for learning the ancient languages solidly and thoroughly. Some of us have still experienced a certain amount
of it, though not in the quantitative overdoses which eighteenth century boys were fed in good schoolrooms.

Thomas Jefferson, at least in later years, regarded this
kind of training, as it was offered in the "grammar" schools,
as adequate. About six years of Latin and Greek from the
tenth to the sixteenth year was what he required in his bill
for public education in Virginia when he himself was in
the thirties. At that time, "six years" of Latin and Greek
meant much more than it would in the record of a modern

American schoolboy. The emphasis was pre-eminently on these fields, and two periods daily of Latin, one period of Greek, plus a considerable amount of "homework" throughout these six years would seem to be a minimum rather than the average for that age. Thomas Jefferson has left a record of what he achieved by this training in a letter in which he states the range of reading knowledge in Greek and Latin that a boy leaving school would normally have. Apart from Greek and Latin historians (such as Xenophon, Herodotus, possibly Thucydides, Plutarch's *Lives,* Caesar, Livy and Tacitus) and some of Cicero's orations, he evidently had read Homer and Virgil, plays of Euripides, Sophocles, and Terence, Anacreon's poems, Theocritus, Horace and, probably, Ovid. He had studied some works of these authors of ancient epic and lyric poetry, of tragedy and comedy, history, biography and oratory when he was fifteen years old. But above all, he had acquired a very thorough command of the ancient languages themselves, the linguistic foundation which enabled him to carry on his direct conversation with the ancients throughout his life.

It is not unfair to modern students to state that in a competition the boy of fifteen might surpass in linguistic and reading knowledge the average student majoring in classics in any modern college. That was merely a result of the different standards and patterns of the eighteenth century. As it was, the American education which Thomas Jefferson got in his childhood was as good as one could get anywhere. To be sure, a "classical" education of some kind was not a necessary prerequisite for a public career in the colonies as it may have been in Europe and England. George Washington and Patrick Henry illustrate that fact. But whoever received such an education received one as substantial as that of the schools overseas and often better. America, in its infancy, was backward in the "sciences and arts" as far as tradition and creative men were concerned. Contributions to scholarship were still lacking in the classical field. The best teachers were newcomers from England and Scotland who had received their college and university training at home. And when, at the end of his life, Thomas Jefferson organized his university, he insisted against parochial reaction that men of first quality had to be procured from abroad for most fields, including the classics. But on the background of his own experience and his observations in Europe he insisted that in America the basic schooling was as good as if not better than overseas. The result of it was visible in Thomas Jefferson himself. A listing of his various explicit statements in this regard would be tiresome. But there is a delectable episode which illustrates his views as they were formed by personal experience.

Benjamin Franklin was familiar with the New Jersey farmers' practice of making the circumference of a wheel of one single piece by "bending it while green and juicy" and leaving it to dry until it was seasoned. While in London, he experimented with a craftsman and worked out a process by which, instead of fresh saplings, more seasoned wood could be plied for the purpose of making a wheel. The man got a patent for his process, manufactured wheels that way, and soon they were exported from England. In 1787 an article appeared in a Paris newspaper alleging that the invention had originally been made by a farmer in England and, for that matter, inspired by a passage in Homer in which a similar process of wheelmaking is described. The successor of Franklin as American minister in Paris was indignant. In a letter to Monsieur de Crèvecoeur he stated the facts as they were known to him, and he added: "The writer in the paper, supposes the English workman got his idea from Homer. But it is more likely the Jersey farmer got his idea from thence, because ours are the only farmers who can read Homer." Then he went on to explain that the practice of the New Jersey farmers corresponded exactly to the Homeric description, while the English process differed from it to some extent.

The merit of the case may remain unsettled. But there is no reason whatsoever to doubt Jefferson's sincerity regarding the American farmers who read Homer and to accuse him of having manufactured a sentimental propagandistic lie, as a modern critic has done; of depicting the blessings of American democracy by inventing an imaginary farmer who read Homer in an innocent bucolic world. Indeed, all indications are that Jefferson was right and that America was the only country in which you could find farmers who read Homer. For one thing, it was a country of farmers and not of noblemen, yeomen and peasants. But it also was a country where one found boys who had gone through the exertion of five or six years of studying Latin and Greek only to return to their farms. Jefferson himself was a farmer and so were Madison, Monroe and others who read Homer. And had not his beloved teacher of law, George Wythe, earlier in the century learned Greek from his mother far in the backwoods on the frontier of civilization? Indeed, when Locke (who knew Greek) wrote his *Thoughts Concerning Reading and Study for a Gentleman,* he could not request that any Greek authors be read in the original. And what did Jefferson observe in France, the cradle of science and art? In 1785 he had come there with exalted expectations, and in many respects they were fulfilled. But what did he find, as far as reading the classics was concerned? "Greek and Roman authors are dearer here than I believe anywhere in the world. Nobody here reads them, wherefore they are not reprinted." And "the languages are badly taught here. If you propose he should learn the Latin, perhaps you will prefer the having him taught it in America."

Jefferson was not alone in this comparison of European and American knowledge in the classics. French travelers in America noted the widespread knowledge of Latin. They could sometimes use it to make themselves understood, and the degree of literacy in general in America is reported to have been higher at least than that of Continental Europe.

Thus young Thomas Jefferson, according to the standards of his or any time, was well equipped to become a student of the ancient world when in 1760 he enrolled for three years at William and Mary College. But there is no indication that his interest in the classics during those years was strong enough to induce him to deeper and more extensive studies. He later judged that "Classical knowledge," too, could be acquired as well at William and Mary as anywhere in Europe. There was a professor of Greek and Latin on the faculty, but his teaching, like that of many a college professor today, seems to have been exclusively in the nature of elementary language courses in "grammar school." Jefferson had had a sufficient amount of that, and there is no indication that he profited from college instruction in the classics. The scarcity of preserved early letters makes it impossible to decide whether and to what extent he indulged in extracurricular study of the classics. During these years and afterward he continued to play with Greek letters for cryptograms, as many a schoolboy has done, and to use phrases of "hog Latin" in correspondence with his friend Page. But it is well known that his real intellectual experience during those years was based on the teaching of and personal contact with the professor of mathematics and sciences, Small. He was a fine and remarkable specimen of the culture of his century and a fascinating teacher, the first whom a boy of the extraordinary abilities of young Jefferson could admire.

The spirit of the "scientific" eighteenth century, of rationalism and mathematical logic, seized Jefferson via Small. But, happily, it was a variety in which human interests and Humanistic traditions were blended with the scientific approach. Small, indeed, taught "Belles Lettres," too, and that, in this age, included a continuous weighing of the aesthetic values of classical writings. If anywhere, the balance between humanistic and naturalistic interests which defined Jefferson's later life had its source or at least its leaven in this experience. It is well known how Small introduced the boy as a fourth member in the little intellectual circle that used to gather at the governor's mansion. Governor Fauquier, a sparkling *esprit* of the age, Small, the refined "philosopher," and George Wythe, the Humanistic lawyer, must have been fully aware of the genius growing in young Jefferson to allow him to join those worldly and literary dinner parties which he, in later years, characterized as "truly Attic societies." Small represented the unity of the searching mind. He was a scientist of Humanistic taste. George Wythe was the incarnation of Humanism, always directed by classical ideas in practical action, in law and in politics. Jefferson later characterized him as "the best Latin and Greek scholar in the State." It is told that the scribes who had to copy his legal opinions were harassed by the array of Greek quotations in them.

The lawyer-Humanist became Jefferson's master and teacher in the legal profession, and this connection, which was to last for years, was evidently the decisive factor in fermenting the ceaseless interest in the ancient world which continued and grew through his later life. The tools of solid elementary classical education he had acquired in childhood. But was it worth while to go on with his reading, or rather to resume it, to spend long hours on it, to struggle again with the dictionary and sometimes with the grammar— which Jefferson hated as any normal schoolboy who has been through that mill did and does? It may be safely assumed that sooner or later, on the basis of his good linguistic training, he would have returned to some classical reading; that he, with his zeal for original search, could not for long have avoided opening Greek and Latin authors to inquire about facts and opinions. Yet the enthusiasm with which during the sixties he took up classical reading for its own sake in the aura of George Wythe, was something different.

From now on a continuous reading of ancient writers developed and increased over the years within the possible limits of a turbulent life in a stormy age. And it was the continuity of Jefferson's conversation with the ancients which made him the outstanding Humanist he was in later years. John Adams, on the other hand, whose early education in the classics had been at least as thorough as Jefferson's, failed to carry on. This is his own spiritual confession to Jefferson, one septuagenarian addressing the other: "Lord! Lord! What can I do with so much Greek? When I was of your age, young man, i.e., seven or eight or nine years ago, I felt a kind of pang of affection for one of the flames of my youth and again paid my addresses to Isocrates, and Dionysius of Halicarnassus, etc. etc. I collected all my Lexicons, and Grammars, and sat down to περὶ συνθήσεως ὀνομάτων, etc. In this way I amused myself for some time; but I found that if I looked up a word today, in less than a week I had to look it again. It was to little better purpose than writing letters on a pail of water." When he had reached that age, Jefferson easily quoted things he had read somewhere in scholia, scribbled learned linguistic observations on the torn pages of his Greek dictionary, engaged in professional discussions of a philological kind and, above all, read, read Greek and Latin poetry and prose even more voraciously to combat the *"taedium vitae"* of old age by pleasant experience of sounds and ideas.

He developed his method of studying the classics while reading law with George Wythe and in the succeeding decade, when the stormy clouds of the American Revolution filled the skies. First, it was largely reading the classics for the sake of general human experience and, as such, it was focused on philosophy and poetry. For "the true province of poetry" was "knowledge of the human heart." Homer and Virgil, Horace, the Greek plays—above all, those of the passionate Euripides—were the cherished poets he read during these years—authors whom he already knew to some extent from school.

We have to take his word that in reading classical and English poetry he searched for confirmation that man was noble and good. The actor John Bernard reports that Jefferson told him: "I was bred to the law; that gave me a view of the dark side of humanity. Then, I read poetry to qualify it with a gaze upon its bright side; and between the two extremes I have continued through life to draw the due medium." This, evidently, means that great emotion, passion controlled by dignity, tender sentiment, courage, noble pride, which were the constant themes of most of the ancient poets he read, contrasted with the pettiness, the small selfishness, the materialism, which are matters of daily experience to the lawyer. In Cicero's dialogues, especially, he found the reasoning mind joining the reflections of poets to form a conscious pattern of the behavior of wise and virtuous men. It was a composite canon of guidance rather than a philosophical system based, as Cicero's philosophy was, on an eclectic combination of elements which he borrowed from various schools. It is obvious that in the twenties of his life Jefferson yearned for such a comprehensive guidance toward goodness and wisdom, and that he was fascinated by the aspects of noble behavior which poetical pictures of the human heart presented.

Only a pale reflection of this experience is preserved in what somewhat misleadingly has been called his *Literary Bible*. This is a scrapbook in which he began to note down passages from his reading while he was studying law with George Wythe, and which by and large belongs to the sixties of the century with but a few later additions. The title *Literary Bible,* under which Professor Chinard published it, would imply that it was a reflection of what Jefferson had selected as the most beautiful and valuable from Greek, Latin and French writers. And, indeed, conclusions that are hardly justified have been drawn from this collection as to his purely moralizing and in no way poetical interest. All this seems to be wrong and in contradiction to Jefferson's own explicit statements concerning his devotion to reading. The collection of notes starts with some passages from Herodotus regarding circumcision in Egypt (with a cross reference to Genesis) and Egyptian and Thracian ideas of immortality. Toward the middle it includes excerpts from Pope's *Essay on Man* and, among others, a long passage from Bolingbroke on historical probability. To be sure, the bulk of the selections is composed of quotations from Greek, Latin and English poetry. Nearly all of them are sententious lines which condense in lapidary form thoughts and ideas about man and society, fate, happiness, misery, friendship, death and the uncertainty of an after life, the power of speech and the evil of demagogy, the wisdom of resignation and the blessings of country life, the relationship of master and slave, criticism of wealth and power, praise of patriotic unselfishness, the natural goodness of human instinct and its depravation by education and convention, natural religion. Extensive excerpts from Cicero's *Tusculan Dialogues* are of similar character. It contains many points of view which already were or were to become basic for Jefferson's philosophy; for example, these:

> . . . Equality
> which knitteth friends to friends,
> Cities to cities, allies to allies.
> Nature gave men the law of equal rights.
> —EURIPIDES, *Phoenissæ*

> Mortals hold their possessions not their own.
> We are but stewards of the gifts of God.
> —*Ibid.*

These are some of the sentences to which he wished to have easy access in later years. Quotations from this notebook occur here and there in his later writings, and his use of it for that purpose is evident from some later additions. And this was evidently the main purpose which Jefferson had in mind when he copied these passages from some of the books he read. Here were sentences which, happily, condensed his own ideas about many things and which expressed these ideas better than he himself might be able to do—with the added authority of hallowed tradition. These were records, too, of facts and opinions which he liked to keep. The collection thus was "useful" for both literary expression and later research. For example, thère was a passage from Euripides' *Hecuba* stressing man's natural aversion to crime. About ten years later, when he read and excerpted Lord Kames' discussion on criminal law, in another commonplace book, he looked up that earlier little booklet again and added the excerpt from Euripides to Kames' own similar statement.

By and large, this so-called *Literary Bible* was but another useful tool of the incipient organization of Jefferson's intellectual life, limited in its scope to collecting sentences and facts to be referred to when the occasion should present itself. But it is obviously incorrect to draw the conclusion that Jefferson's taste and literary experience were confined to what he excerpted on these sheets, and that the greatness of Homeric language and similes, for instance, did not mean anything to him. At least some of these excerpts contradict such assertions; for instance, a grandiose description of a clash of arms which is compared with the thunderous mixture of torrential mountain streams, from the fourth book of the *Iliad*. It is followed by an excerpt from the thirteenth book which reverberates with the sound of clashing armor—and to these, in turn, are added, for the stylistic comparison of poetical expressions, two later imitations of the passage from Virgil and Statius. And here is what Jefferson, himself, has to say about the fascination which Homeric language already had for him during these years. When—still a student of law—he listened to Patrick Henry's historic speech on the Stamp Act in 1765, "He appeared to me to speak as Homer wrote." Patrick Henry's oratory he later characterized as being endowed with "poetical fancy . . . sublime imagination," and "lofty and overwhelming diction." That statement gives us only a glimpse at the variety of great experiences which his reading of the classics included. They were emotional as well as reasonable, experiences of sound as well as of ideas; but, generally, the latter category alone was retained in excerpts to be used for later reference.

All this explains, too, why these excerpts do not reveal the "bright side" of human life except by the indirect implications of Homeric epos, Greek tragedy, and ancient philosophy, all of which assert that man can be greater than his fate. The works of the ancients were drenched with that deep pessimism which is so typically Greek and which Jefferson encountered throughout his classical reading. The frailty and misery of human life and the struggle of men to overcome them by courage and virtue, entanglement in guilt and suffering, physical pain and mental mortification—these were the fate of man in his short earthly journey. Beyond, there was the unknown realm of hope or fear or nothing. This pessimistic outlook was voiced everywhere by those great ancients, and it is visible in the majority of the sententious excerpts which young Jefferson made from his reading. Was he, as has been concluded, in a preromantic "Wertherian" mood during his twenties, and did he feel that mood or try to cure it by his reading, by a premature philosophy of stoicism? We may doubt the correctness of such an interpretation in view of his life and activities. It rather seems that Thomas Jefferson's affinity to the Greeks, not only then but throughout his life, included a mixture of reflective pessimism and emotional optimism widespread in his century. Such a mixture was typical of them from the beginning. The Greek attitude, from Homer on, is reflected in one of the passages from Euripides' *Hippolytus* which Jefferson copied at that time:

> For if it swell with every generation
> And the new age reaches heights of villainy
> Above the old, God . . . must create a new world.

And yet Greek men were continually busy improving the extant, miserable world driven by a spontaneous, deep-rooted emotional belief in the perfectibility of man, such a belief as Jefferson had within himself.

Most of the contents of the so-called *Literary Bible* reflect Jefferson's reading in belles-lettres. But the young lawyer also began to take up that reading of ancient historians and orators which he recommended in a letter already referred to, as indispensable to any student of law. In the sixties he read orations of Cicero and Demosthenes and most of the outstanding historians of antiquity in the original, along with more of Cicero's and Seneca's philosophical writings. Gibbon's monumental work, *The Decline and Fall of the Roman Empire,* was the most important of various books on ancient history, but Jefferson also included antiquarian works such as *The Husbandry of the Ancients.*

All this was in the nature of self-education carried on beyond student days to create an ever broadening range of knowledge and experience of humanity and human affairs. But in that age a lawyer had more direct and unavoidable ties to antiquity. Roman law and the Latin legal texts of the medieval and postmedieval world still represented the great sources of legal knowledge, though a forensic lawyer and politician like Patrick Henry might do without them. Legal Latin was still a living language, however depraved and cumbersome. And besides, many scientific books, classics not only in law but in all fields of human knowledge, were written in Latin.

CHAPTER 4

Mature Exploration

IN THE EARLY Revolutionary days of 1769, Jefferson was elected to the legislature of his state and entered upon his political career. From now on, for forty years, with only short interruptions, service to his country was paramount. By this time his habit of conversing with the ancients had been firmly established. The unique spectacle which results from this constellation of time, chance, education and inclination can be traced in his writings. There were, to be sure, painful intervals during which stormy events prohibited reading, studying, reflection. There were, too, quiet spells even in the seventies, in France in the eighties and, again, in the years of his vice-presidency, when he could give more time than usual to the ancients. There was the possibility of ever-deepening search, and it was exploited with unfaltering energy. It is fascinating to see him branch out and take up new realms and issues, to witness how the problems of the day led him to investigate this or that side of the old world. So far, his study and reading of the ancients had been primarily, if not exclusively, in the nature of the general classicism of his century: a search for emotional satisfaction in poetry; for the hallowed wisdom of the first spokesmen of Western civilization; an experience of great form and style in prose and oratory; a study of ancient historians as the basis of political education.

Now when he himself entered the grand stage of political history, when he had to take part in the council and decision of a smoldering revolution, when he was called upon to draft laws and declarations, he might have abandoned his studies of the ancient world. Instead, he expanded them in a new direction, trying to explore what ancient man had thought and done in regard to the basic issues involved. There was a good deal of normal eighteenth century thought behind this endeavor: the pragmatic doctrine that historical examples can be used as guidance toward good and away from evil; the search for natural law, religion, morality in early records of humanity; the comparative approach to customs and mores of various peoples in order to form a reasonable judgment about human behavior in general. In Jefferson these tendencies, which were in the air that surrounded him and emanated from the books he read, were coupled with the lawyer's search for precedent. This combination resulted in his interest in and enthusiasm for the customs and society of early ancestors, the Anglo-Saxons, which anticipate the romanticisms of the later historical school of law. Here and there such interest and enthusiasm led to the development of a truly historical method. When the synthesis of his new energetic study of specific historical issues with his humanistic zeal for understanding the classics and his faculties and wishes for study of original sources had been achieved, Jefferson had developed what one might call his personal method. That development took place during the seventies, when he had matured to full manhood. His first and only book, the *Notes on Virginia,* an excellent scholarly treatise on past and present, pervaded by his Humanistic ideals, was the mature product of that preceding phase.

Fortunately, in his *Commonplace Book* we possess a revealing document of his progressive integration of historical study and actuality. Most of the excerpts of this collection were gathered in the years before the Declaration of Independence, as Professor Chinard has shown. As he read various books on history, law and government, he copied out passages which seemed to him to be important, and often he commented critically upon them. It is obvious that most of them had a direct connection with problems of the day and that the main purpose of this "commonplacing," as he called it, was to assemble research notes for legislative and political action. Yet, as he took up one book after another, he unexpectedly found many other things that interested him and of which he kept records for future research. Thus, while his objective was to assemble historical precedents and facts regarding acute issues, the study of such issues opened up new historical vistas. The original law and government of Great Britain, for example, played a very important part in the argument of the rights of America as he saw them. One had not only to study the Anglo-Saxon legal precedent. Research about the government and customs of the original Celtic inhabitants of the British Isles would lead back even further. There was a book, published in France about twenty years earlier, by Simon Pelloutier, on the history of the Celts and Gauls. One had to read it to see what evidence there was. And so he did read it and he "commonplaced" in the original French wording passages related to his subject, the constitutions and government of the Celtic peoples. But as he read, a fascinating new world of history and of approach to history by comprehensive search in all kinds of ancient authors and by use of linguistic arguments and comparisons appeared. Thus Jefferson made extensive excerpts—in English—regarding the much broader problem of the spreading of the Celts over Europe and of their historical importance.

It was a learned book, full of quotations from ancient sources, impressing the reader with typically French erudition. And Jefferson, here as elsewhere, followed the scholarly method of condensing the author's own argument while including all his references to sources, so that at any time if, indeed, time would allow, he might go back to the sources himself, and make up his mind directly from them. Because, if this was a learned book it was also, as Jefferson with his innate critical judgment clearly saw, a crazy book. It is, indeed, an early example of that abominable chauvinistic historiography in which an imposing amount of "scientific" facts but thinly conceals their unscientific opinionated use. The author sees the Celts everywhere. Greeks and Romans, Spanish aborigines and Germanic tribes, all are Celtic, and the Celtic language becomes the race and root of all languages today called Indo-European. As Jefferson went on reading and excerpting, he added more and more remarks and comments. They show an amazing degree of criticism. He is not satisfied with the author's interpretation of Greek and Latin authors. He has a sound aversion to the rash use of linguistic comparisons and such—still dangerous—methods as the comparison of place names. Yet there is no doubt that his outlook on historical method, his familiarity with compiling masses of literary sources, and his interest in comparative linguistics were greatly enhanced by the critical study of this odd book. Give a bad book to a good reader and it may become valuable.

The reading of these years was saturated with references to classical authors, many of whom had been unknown to Jefferson before. Greek and Latin examples were quoted everywhere in Lord Kames' works on criminal law or property rights, and in connection with legislative work of his own. Sometimes Jefferson added contributions in the nature of a passage from Euripides or Tacitus to his excerpts from modern writings. Again, there was the great issue— the issue of the *Summary View* and of the Declaration of Independence—about the rights of colonies in relation to the mother country. Stanyan's *Grecian History* gave him much material for that. For constitutions he read Montesquieu, whose work was full of ancient history, and for the problem of religious history—in connection with the bill for religious freedom—Voltaire's *Essai sur les moeurs.* Here as everywhere he was startled by new discoveries which had little or no bearing on the immediate objective. Voltaire, for example, alluded to the Greek mystery religions and to their anticipation of the unity of God, or again to Greek contributions to astronomy. And that line, though hardly related to actual issues of the day, induced a search for the history of the calendar. Reading Newton's *Observations upon the Prophecies of Daniel,* he excerpted a passage on that subject and added a quotation from the original Greek text of the Constitutions of the Apostles. This text he of course read again in connection with the problem of Church and State, and made original excerpts for that purpose. Indeed, that subject and studies in Locke and Shaftesbury made him familiar with the vast realm of early Christian literature in Greek and Latin. But he found time to return to the study of the calendar. He read Dion Cassius's discussion of the calendar in Greek which he had found quoted somewhere, commenting on the respective Egyptian, Jewish, Roman and Nordic customs in notes preparatory of future research which he did not find time to complete.

The *Literary Bible* and the *Commonplace Book* thus reveal the development of Jefferson's approach before 1776. It moved on from the enjoyable reading of the cherished authors of great poetry, of the masters of form and the ancient sages, to the concrete study of individual issues and problems via modern books; these broadened his historical horizon both in range of facts and sources and in methods; it led from one problem to another; and it finally reached a stage in which he felt able to do original research himself.

Research he did in his own way, too, indirect and direct research in ancient life and architecture. It was also an attempt to integrate classical experience in the living present. As is well known, the decade of the seventies was the period during which Thomas Jefferson embarked on his important career as creative architect with the elaboration of his famous mansion at Monticello. It was to be "antique" in style, antique as one could take it from the Renaissance architect Palladio's work. But this endeavor to build an antique house by adapting Palladio's model was to Jefferson, as to his century, not a mere matter of good taste. In curious notes in which he considered plans for a burial ground and a garden, he shows himself a true child of his at once classical and preromantic age: a small Gothic temple, pedestals with urns, a pyramid of rocks, a spring with a Chinese or Grecian temple, and a reclining nymph, all this he considered. As an alternative he thought of a copy of the monument of Lysikrates in Athens—then known to him from one of his books—for the temple of the nymph. At the same time he made a list of the antique sculptures of which he wanted copies for the decoration of Monticello. But, above all, there should be Latin inscriptions, among them Horace's famous epode glorifying rural life, most of which he had written down in his *Literary Bible*. It was evidently to be country life in antique style such as Cicero hinted at in the *Tusculan Dialogues* which he had read and excerpted. There were other writers of antiquity, such as Cato and Varro and especially Pliny the Younger, whom Jefferson owned and read. There is also a book by Castell, on ancient villas, a copy of which he possessed in the eighties. It refers to villas and villa life as described by Latin authors, and has as its motto lines from Horace. We have, to be sure, but scant documentary evidence for Jefferson's reading these books as early as the seventies. Yet it seems highly probable that he extended his research beyond Palladio when he planned his house in the country according to explicitly Latin ideas of rural and yet urban beatitude. Exactly those features not to be found in Palladio, and equally novel in the Virginia of his time, are typical of the

Roman villas described by ancient authors. Monticello, as it emerged in concrete form, was a symptom of the accomplished integration of ideas that resulted from his previous study of the ancient world. It was more than a pure form to be grafted on a life that was and had to be essentially alien to it.

To be sure, the ancient world was very different from his own surroundings, in spite of the many and surprising analogies which he discovered at every step. There was rural slavery, for example, such as it appeared in Cato's book on agriculture, not so unlike the type of agricultural labor and domestic service he himself had inherited. At the very beginning of his political career, Jefferson had made a futile abolitionist move. Now, in 1781, in writing his *Notes on Virginia* he studied the subject again, reading Cato, Plutarch, Suetonius, among others, finding that great intellectuals of antiquity had been slaves in their time. But they had been of a race and color homogeneous with their surrounding. There was analogy and difference, time and again. Studying the ancients, one might clarify one's own mind more and more about the basic issues and about the actual forms in which these issues appeared in the historical world, past as well as present.

Whenever one got down to the essentials, however, to fundamental ideals of life in general, those ancients had thought them through, had given them form and expression in great style. Architecture was one such expression, poetry another. This is the philosophy which is manifest in Jefferson's actions and words during the Revolutionary period, and it remained alive throughout later years. It is natural, then—and anything but affectation—that in the hours of deepest emotional experience he would select a quotation from Homer to express his own ideas. When, in his student days, his beloved sister Jane, companion of his musical interests, had died, young Jefferson had composed a naïve

and quite charming poetical epitaph in Latin. It was a
conventional gesture, and it has the romantic ring of medieval poems. But in 1782 when the death of his wife plunged
Jefferson into a grief that is shrouded as well as revealed
by long silence, he selected lines from Homer and had them
inscribed on the monument in the original Greek wording:

Nay if even in the house of Hades the dead forget
their dead, yet will I even there be mindful of my dear comrade.

His biographers have wondered why, if Jefferson chose
a quotation from Homer, he preferred to have it inscribed
in Greek instead of in an English translation which every
visitor of the tomb could have understood. And the sugges-
tion has been made that Jefferson, reticent as he was to
express his emotions about the most personal experience
of his love and loss, chose a Greek epitaph in order to with-
hold that emotion from public knowledge. A strange idea,
indeed, and one characteristic of an age in which reading
Greek has become cryptic knowledge. It is not Jefferson, who
quotes the words of Achilles, spoken though they originally
were by the surviving man over his dead friend's body. In
the Greek text the beloved companion to be remembered
beyond death is a man, not a woman, while the sex of the
speaker is not defined by the lines once they have been
isolated from the Homeric narrative. As is so often the case
in ancient epitaphs, it is the deceased who speaks to the
survivor from his tomb: asserting against reasonable doubt
about afterlife the emotional wish of two loving souls for
continued relationship. But why is the epitaph in Greek?
We have to remember that by this time Jefferson had lost
his faith in translation, and had long since arrived at a
stage in which the full, undistorted vigor of original thought
did not allow for any tampering. More than anything else
it was its grand vigorous wording which made him prefer
an epitaph from Homer.

The ancients had become living companions of Jefferson's own personal world. Homer stood by him in the days of trial as Horace had been the articulate spokesman of his dream of a happy country life in his "villa."

It was the rude interference of death which threw Jefferson back on the stormy sea of history, and he went as American minister to Paris. The four years there were rich and full of intellectual experiences. We have already seen him come to grips with the reality of ancient monuments in southern France and, in regard to his studies of the ancient world, that experience was undoubtedly the most fruitful which he brought home. Even before that, in the concentrated intellectual and artistic atmosphere of Paris, the physical world of the ancients had come closer and, as it were, a third dimension had been added to its diagrams.

Shortly after his arrival in Paris, he was consulted about plans for the Capitol of Virginia. He advocated the direct adaptation of an antique model, more specifically, the Maison Carrée in Nîmes, known to him from the excellent publication by Clérisseau. It was a new idea, this literal quotation of an antique building, and this "first monument of the classical revival in America," as Professor Kimball has shown, preceded all such efforts made in Europe. At the time it was a typical Jeffersonian idea, "literal" use of the antique formula, like the epitaph for his wife. The elaboration of that scheme brought him in touch with Clérisseau, an eminent architect and teacher of creative architects, who had spent twenty years in Rome and had been a friend of the great archaeologist Winckelmann. The work on this model entailed intimate study of the plan, elevation, proportion, details of a preserved antique building. Shortly after his arrival, there was to be seen in Paris an exhibition of models of ancient buildings which the connoisseur-ambassador, Choiseul-Gouffier, had had made by craftsmen in Greece. Jefferson engaged one of these craftsmen for the model of the Capitol, and he reluctantly yielded to the replacing of "more noble" antique capitals by a more modern variety.

In Paris he was surrounded by a classicistic eighteenth century society of artists and connoisseurs, saturated with antique motives and forms: the sculptor Houdon, with whom he had to discuss a monument for Washington and whom he dispatched to America; the young painter David, whose "pencil" was the only one in which he felt "interest"; the American painter Trumbull, who stayed for some time with Jefferson and was in his judgment "superior to any historical painter of the time except David"; Wedgwood, the inventor of "earthen ware in the antique style," who visited Paris in 1787 and some of whose plaques with Muses from an antique sarcophagus were later to decorate the mantelpiece in Jefferson's dining room in Monticello, though he may not have met him personally. There were classicistic connoisseurs of ancient and contemporary art, like the Baron Grimm, "the oracle of taste," who came to Jefferson's house to see Trumbull's pictures.

There was a host of fascinating intellectuals, men and women to whom one could talk about belles-lettres and art in a more superficial vein. And there were also great scientists, but it seems that Jefferson met few serious students of ancient history and literature. He bought for Madison and himself copies of the *Voyages of Anacharsis* by the learned Abbé Barthélemy, who had painfully worked for thirty years to compile that somewhat stale reconstruction of the daily life of the Greeks—a much read work in the eighteenth century and even throughout the nineteenth. It was a book of "great classical learning," but "useless, indeed, to him who has read the original authors." He had met the author, who used to stay for spells of quiet study at the same Carthusian monastery outside Paris to which Jefferson went occasionally. But there seems to have been no spark between them. It was evidently another of those "correct classical scholars" whom Jefferson had first met in his early school days. We have seen him complain that "nobody read the ancient authors," that classical education in France was poor. And he was shocked to see the complete neglect of the precious Roman ruins in southern France. The temple of Vienne was "defaced by the barbarians who have converted it to its present purpose." That had happened in the Middle Ages. But: "Would you believe, Madam, that in this eighteenth century, in France, under the reign of Louis XVI, they are at this moment pulling down the circular wall of this superb remain [the Arena in Orange] to pave a road?"

As far as his own classical interests were concerned, the acquaintance and friendship of a few Greeks may have been the most fruitful personal contact. He learned modern Greek pronunciation from them as we have seen, and behind that endeavor may have been his hope to go to Greece himself. In any case, it was an invaluable experience for a friend and amateur of music, a man who was an assiduous admirer of Greek literature, and a historian who searched for connections throughout the ages. And while he thought and wrote about the difference between English and Greek meter and accentuation, he tried to recapture the original sound of the "language of Homer."

All in all, if Jefferson had not already been the enthusiastic and scholarly-minded student of the ancient world that he was when he arrived in Paris, Paris would not have stimulated him to become one. He left it hoping to return and to go to Italy and Greece. But he had to stay in America and to carry on his reading, his use of antique models in architecture and interior decoration from the books. He had at least brought back from France a prodigious number of editions of ancient authors and books on ancient monuments.

His correspondence during the twenty years of his leadership of American affairs is naturally mostly concerned with events and issues of the day. But his quotations of ancient authors and references to ancient history show that he carried on his conversation with the ancients as much as he could. He read the historians and his cherished poets, Homer, Horace and Virgil, time and again. During the later nineties an increased interest in the moral and ethical ideas of the various ancient philosophical schools is visible. And during the reaction of the Adams Era behind which, as he saw it, intolerant bigotry raised its ugly head, the problem of what seemed to him to be a complete perversion of Christianity by the established churches became paramount in his mind.

After 1800 we find continuous references to his studies of original Christianity. Soon both issues—the clarification of the morality of ancient philosophers and the documented "original purity and simplicity" of the teachings of Jesus —are merged. Reading of the New Testament in Greek, of ancient philosophers and historians, was carried on during his two presidential terms. At the same time chance, less than his own scholarly mind taking advantage of given opportunities, stimulated his linguistic interest. It had been smoldering under the surface since the days when he had read Pelloutier's book on the Celts. He had always been interested in Indian folklore and the origins of the American Indians. When he was in Paris, one of several wild theories advanced during his lifetime had been brought to his attention. According to this theory, the Creek Indians were Carthaginians carried overseas by chance and the winds. However, being naturally skeptical, Jefferson was glad that the author of this theory meant "to appeal to the similarity of language, which I consider as the strongest kind of proof it is possible to adduce." One may note the careful qualification of the statement which implies that even similarity of language does not furnish absolute proof in such cases, a qualification justified even today after great progress in comparative linguistics. He continues: "I have somewhere read that the language of the ancient Carthaginians is still spoken by their descendants inhabiting the mountainous interior parts of Barbary. . . . If so, a vocabulary of their tongue can still be got, and if your friend will get one of the Creek languages, the comparison will decide." And he ends up by offering his diplomatic services in order to find out about the alleged survivals of Punic in northern Africa. He himself had early started his famous collection of Indian vocabularies. During his presidency, new possibilities of using official channels for linguistic exploration arose connected with the purchase of Louisiana and the famous exploration of Lewis and Clark. Indeed, he envisioned world-wide studies of comparative linguistics. Such interests could not fail to stimulate his thought on linguistic problems of the classics, too.

Finally, in 1809, the long-desired moment drew close, the moment he had waited for: to return to his family, his farm and his books. Among his "first emploiments" after the end of his second presidential term would be the task of giving the Greek version of the Old Testament "an attentive perusal." Finally, he would find time to study, read, search; because this amazing man did not intend to sit back and enjoy the quiet days of leisure, to ruminate and digest, to remember and sift out, to organize and generalize. His was a never-ending process of learning and expanding his own powers. There were, indeed, many things he could think over again, cherished poems and great historical writings he might read again and again as the years went on. He would have time for that. And there were so many books he had hardly opened, ancient writers whose works contained thoughts and discussions relevant to the many problems he was interested in. Approaching the biblical age of seventy, he did not feel that it was too late to start on renewed and new intellectual adventures. Time and opportunity for that had come late, to be sure. But it was never too late. His physical health was not as it had been in earlier years. But, thank God, his mind was vigorous and filled with the old exuberant curiosity. He might now "indulge" his "canine appetite" for classical reading "to beguile the wearisomeness of declining life."

His extensive correspondence, quotations from and references to ancient authors allow us, if not to reconstruct, at least to visualize vaguely the incredible amount of his classical reading during the last sixteen years of his life. The quotations and phrases in Latin—it had to be Latin for the sake of his correspondents, though he, himself, read more Greek—suddenly increase with his retirement from the political stage. More and more frequently it becomes his practice to end a letter with a Latin phrase borrowed from the ancient epistolographers Pliny and Cicero, whom he outdid in the extent of his correspondence. He began to read Cicero again, starting with his philosophical works, but in 1820 he reports that he read all his letters, which fill several volumes. The historians, particularly Thucydides and Tacitus, but also Livy and Sallust, he read again in the first years of his retirement, and they remained his companions through all the following years. He also took up again Dion Cassius, the Greek historian of the later Roman Empire, as well as Polybius, the great writer on the origin of that empire. Among the poets, he reread Horace—the spokesman of his long desired urbane country life—and he conversed with him year after year till his death. Horace's Epicurean philosophy was voiced in terms congenial to Jefferson's own philosophy in the days of his old age. Homer and Virgil he read time and again, Homer, above all, possibly the only epic poet whom one could always read without getting tired of narrative in verse. The Greek lyrical poets Theocritus, Pindar, Sappho and Alcaeus he took up in 1813; Ovid and Terence, known to him from his school days, in the early twenties. Though he hated it, he read the whole of Plato's *Republic* in 1814, not failing to recognize the sublime style of that prose, and during the following years he read Diogenes Laertius' *Lives of the Ancient Philosophers* and what he could find of Epicurean writings. In 1814, a visitor noted copies of the works of Livy and Orosius lying around on a mantelpiece in Monticello, and ten years later, Ticknor reports that he used to read "much Greek" and Anglo-Saxon. During the last year of his life, he read the tragedies of Euripides from some of which he had made excerpts sixty years before, and also those of Sophocles and Aeschylus. And shortly before his death a visitor found him reading Pliny's *Letters*.

This somewhat long and tiresome list of Jefferson's classical reading is based solely on explicit or implicit statements of his and on the testimony of contemporary witnesses. If one turns to his requests for books and editions and to his references to authors who interested him and whom he looked up in order to read a book, a chapter, a passage, the vista extends over the length and breadth of Greek and Latin poetry and prose from the early periods through the Middle Ages. Many an author whom one might miss in what already has been mentioned appears: great poets such as Hesiod and Aristophanes among the Greeks, Juvenal among the Latins; Demosthenes, the orator, and Lucian, the witty satirist; Josephus, the Jewish-Greek historian, and Dionysius of Halicarnassus, the student of Roman origins and customs; the technical writers on ancient agriculture, medicine, strategy, mathematics; philosophical books of Aristotle, Xenophon and Plutarch; treatises of the late mystics, Pythagoreans and Platonists; the Church Fathers, Greek and Latin; Thomas Aquinas and John the Scot.

Classical reading in such prodigious amounts was indeed a strong antidote to the wearisomeness of age. Wherever he went, he had to have some of the ancient authors around him. Like Pliny the Younger who kept a small library in his villa on the seashore, Jefferson had in his farmhouse at Poplar Forest, to which he went from time to time, a "petit format" library. Along with English, Italian and French books it contained a "few favorite Greek and Latin poets, and a large number of prose writers of the same languages." And, in 1816, he allows us a glimpse into the way he, the septuagenarian, moved around with classical books by a reference to Ovid and Nepos whom "I sent to be bound in time for the pocket in my Bedford trip."

During this last phase of his life his conversation with the ancients was vigorous and extensive. It branched out in all directions in time and subject matter. But there were some important problems which largely defined its course. Even now, to be sure, there were incidental impulses which stimulated his research. It was in 1812, for example, that his work on a legal opinion in the affair of the "Batture" of New Orleans led him into a network of studies on Roman law and linguistics. And during the last decade of his life, the building of the University of Virginia and the organization of its curriculum intensified his study of ancient architecture and made him consider the values of classical reading for students.

There were new books, too, eagerly purchased for use as reference books. They might be surprisingly interesting, and he would sit down to read them through and to discover new aspects. In 1817, he wrote to John Adams: "I have been occupied and delighted with reading another work, the title of which did not promise much useful information or amusement, *L'Italia avanti il dominio dei Romani dal Micali*. It has often, you know, been a subject of regret, that Carthage had no writer to give her side of her own history, while her wealth, power and splendor prove she must have had a very distinguished policy and government. Micali has given the counterpart of the Roman history, for the nations over which they extended their dominion. For this he has gleaned up matter from every quarter, and furnished materials for reflection and digestion to those who, thinking as they read, have perceived that there was a great deal of matter behind the curtain, could that be fully withdrawn. He certainly gives new views of a nation whose splendor has masked and palliated their barbarous ambition." Micali's book, an early work of historical romanticism, attempted to trace the remarkable individual civilizations of ancient Italy which were blended or suppressed by Roman conquest. It still is of scholarly value.

But over and above these incidental experiences, the classical interests of the "Sage of Monticello," as he was now called, showed two strangely contrasting leitmotifs. On the one hand, there was his persistent effort to study ancient philosophy. As early as 1813 the Epicurean *summum bonum* appears in his correspondence, and it was the philosophy of Epicurus that he professed more and more between 1815 and 1820. This study of ancient philosophy was intimately related to the long-cherished interest in original Christianity, which at the time of his presidency had resulted in the synopsis of the original teachings of Christ known as the Jefferson Bible. After the death of the Unitarian Priestley, who had published a comparison of the doctrines of Jesus and Socrates and had promised to extend that comparison to the other ancient schools of philosophy, Jefferson resumed these studies himself in 1813, and carried them on for six years.

A the same time his second outstanding interest appeared, prepared as it was by many former experiences, and it remained persistent to the end of his life. It was a purely linguistic interest in word structure and sound, including accent, pronunciation and orthography. The growth of language, the richness of dialects and the formation of new words, the flexibility of "roots" in Greek, Latin and English were from now on repeatedly discussed topics. Did the Greeks have an ablative like the Romans or not? How was Greek to be pronounced? Was the accent of the Greeks emphatic or musically pitched? And, in the last years of his life, we find him making a statement about what he called philosophy of language, that is, comparative linguistics, which is animated by the youthful spirit of never-ending willingness to explore and to learn. This statement was made in acknowledging receipt of a Cherokee grammar, and in connection with his cherished interest in the history of the American Indians. But it leads into the realm of modern world-wide linguistic studies. "Their grammatical devices for the modification of their words by a syllable prefixed to, or inserted in the middle, or added to its end, and by other combinations so different from ours, prove that if man came from one stock, his language did not. . . . I have known some children learn to speak, not by a word at a time, but by whole phrases. . . . A complex idea being a fasciculus of simple ideas bundled together, it is rare that different languages make up their bundles alike, and hence the difficulty of translating from one language to another." The study of primitive languages "will open a wide field for reflection on the grammatical organization of languages, their structure and character." True, such ideas were in the air of that time, but here they are the product of an independent mind that had been carried away by the fascination of linguistic problems. The Greeks and the American Indians, antipodes as they were, had both become concrete realities on the stormy journey of Jefferson's manhood and in the quiet waters of his youth and age. During his last days, everything seemed to spread out in a rich and fascinating landscape with many roads still unexplored and left for future generations.

The classical world had been a great leaven in his life and thought. But was that approach to humanity by means of the classics still to be found around him? In this changing world, was it possibly only a survival of a bygone century that had been his? For moments it might seem as if the scholarly interest in Greek was increasing, as indeed it was: "Our country begins to have a taste for something more than merely as much Greek as will pass a candidate for clerical ordination," he wrote in 1819. But a year later, he who throughout his life had used Latin authors and scientific books as if they were written in English warned the prospective editor of a cultural magazine in Latin that there would be no subscribers in America. Two years earlier, discussing the choice of professors for his university, he had declared that "A critical classic is scarcely to be found in the United States." And about a year before his death, he knew of only three or four good high school teachers of the classics in Virginia and went on to say: "We were obliged the last year to receive shameful Latinists into the classical school of the University, such as we will certainly refuse as soon as we can get from better schools a sufficiency of those properly instructed to form a class. We must get rid of this Connecticut Latin, of this barbarous confusion of long and short syllables, which renders doubtful whether we are listening to a reader of Cherokee, Shawnee, Iroquois, or what."

As he appeared to visitors during his last years to be a figure of another age, he himself felt lonely in his intense classical interests. Winding up a long discussion on Plato's *Republic* which he had just perused, he had already written to John Adams in 1814: "But why am I dosing you with these antediluvian topics? Because I am glad to have some one to whom they are familiar, and who will not receive them as if dropped from the moon." And a year later he said to Charles Thomson, an "ancient" friend from his Revolutionary days: "We remain in existence, the monuments of another age."

The amazing correspondence between John Adams and Thomas Jefferson is a document of the nostalgic overtone which hangs over the last thirteen years of their lives. Resumed after long estrangement, this correspondence blossomed with a singular sentimental note of cultural ties. The two great antagonists in the political arena of the early American republic, two men as different as men can be in taste and temperament, pour out thoughts and ideas to each other as the years go on: Adams spirited, vigorous, cynical and often bragging, Jefferson moderate, penetrating, hopeful and always scholarly. The correspondence starts with a discussion of the customs of American Indians but moves on to topics of classical history and literature. Homer, Theocritus, Virgil are quoted. Soon Jefferson's cherished theme, the comparison of ancient philosophy and Christianity, appears. Ultimately, however, even Adams could not stand so much Greek. And in a somewhat slower trickle, the letters return to America and the Revolutionary days.

Thomas Jefferson, no doubt, even in his earlier days had so far surpassed his own world in the intensity of his interest in the ancients that he had been somewhat lonely in that respect for most of his lifetime. It had not been so with Wythe and Small in his student days in Williamsburg. But later on, even in Paris, it had been so. He read and searched by himself and for himself, and only scattered remnants remain of his thoughts about those great ancients who had such a fascination for him: in letters, a sentence or paragraph here and there, and in allusions throughout his writings. Behind them was the integration of experience into a pattern that was his wisdom. When, on the same day with John Adams and on the fiftieth anniversary of the Declaration of Independence, he closed his eyes, that wisdom seemed to be lost. Yet, a good deal of what he gathered in ideas about the ancient world, of what he admired as valuable in classical civilization, and what he thought about Humanistic education can still be extracted from his writings.

PART II

Fact and Reflection

CHAPTER 5

Experience versus Theory

H E WAS a strange man, indeed, this Thomas Jefferson—
and full of contradictions. So it seemed to many of
his contemporaries and to some of his posthumous critics,
even to those who admired and eulogized him. He seemed
to be fond of the paradox in conversation, too.

On the surface, his intense and perpetual habit of conversing with the ancients might appear to be a great paradox in itself. John Adams remarked that Jefferson was
"the best brusher off of dust" he had ever known. Classical
studies, in his time, were hallowed by an aged tradition,
covered with the schoolroom dust of two thousand and more
years since the days of the Alexandrian and Pergamenian
philologists. Even in the early nineteenth century this subject might seem "antediluvian" to many men. And incidentally, borrowing a phrase from Lord Bolingbroke, he himself might speak about the "learned lumber of Greek and
Latin." But this is what his granddaughter had to say:
"Of history he was very fond and this he studied in all
languages, though always, I think, preferring the ancients."
This is an understatement, as his incredible amount of
classical reading and research reveals.

Though he was well versed in medieval and modern history, too, a survey of his libraries and, above all, his own
allusions to and discussions of history show an overwhelming interest in the world of the Greeks and Romans. This
excessive emphasis on ancient history contrasts with that

of many men of his century, notably such outstanding philosophers of history as Bolingbroke in England, Voltaire in France, Schiller or Herder in Germany. Since the age of Louis XIV, a trend toward universal or general history with equal emphasis on all the ages then known had emerged more and more. And Bolingbroke, whom Jefferson admired very much, strongly advocated didactic concentration on what was, in his age, modern history, that is, the better documented history of Europe since the Renaissance.

Jefferson, too, considered man to be "in all his stages a curious animal." But in practice, together with and even above the study of Anglo-Saxon origins and contemporary history, the Greek and Roman world was the center of his collection of historical facts and his reflection on them. The ancient world was the pole toward which the compass of historical orientation, his searching approach, was directed. "I feel a much greater interest in knowing what has passed two or three thousand years ago, than in what is now passing. I read nothing, therefore, but of the heroes of Troy, of the wars of Lacedaemon and Athens, of Pompey and Caesar, and of Augustus, too, the Bonaparte and parricide scoundrel of that day . . . and review in my dreams the visions of antiquity," he wrote in 1819. And one of the reasons for reading Greek and Latin authors was the store of scientific knowledge contained in them, primarily in the science of history. Mingling studies of ancient history with daily experience as time went on, Jefferson developed his general outlook on the course of human affairs, his philosophy of history.

Jefferson was a child of his—the eighteenth—century, and it goes without saying that his basic concepts were nurtured by the climate of that vigorous intellectual age. Like other men of his time, he saw history within the framework of contemporary mental categories. His philosophy of history was philosophy in the eighteenth century sense of the word and it was in this sense, of philosophy as the comprehensive result of an active search for knowledge and wisdom in general, that others called him a philosopher. It was not philosophy in the sense of a logical system, and for this reason some critics have denied him the title of philosopher. Others have stressed the fact that his ideas form a coherent pattern, in spite of the lack of such a system. All agree, however, that he was an eclectic who combined thoughts from various and often heterogeneous sources. In fact, his broad statements about nature and man in general are largely based on Bacon, Locke, the ancestor of positivistic empiricism, Lord Kames, the Scotch realist, and, as time went on, he included ideas of the French *encyclopédistes, idéologues* and physiocrats. His theory of knowledge as expressed in his methods of approach was also derived from such heterogeneous sources of the past and present. This very eclectic procedure, by no means uncommon in his age, appealed to Jefferson and to his personal needs of flexibility of thought. But it also was more or less the method of Cicero, the ancient philosopher whom he had studied so extensively since his student days. Reduced to and connected by British-American common sense rather than by French *raison,* the heterogeneous elements of such an eclectic assemblage became coherent in the very process of application to history and to problems of the day. They were, so to speak, tools with which to acquire knowledge, to understand facts, to draw conclusions. Surgeon of society that he was, he might use such tools for practical operations as well as for searching in the body of mankind.

History, indeed, presented to Thomas Jefferson "a vast anatomy of fact and reflection," and it offered "to the human mind a wonderful mass for contemplation."

Jefferson was an empiricist of the most radical denomination in so far as knowledge and the procedures which lead to it are concerned. As to religion, morality, taste—that was different. But knowledge, within the bounds of human possibilities, was a matter of experience. The range and direction of experience were fluctuating. Man never stopped having new experiences. What the future would bring was uncertain. The past was an enormous storehouse of facts. History was but extended, personal experience. It does not matter whether this conviction was borrowed from one of his eclectically used sources, from Thucydides, whose work, the first book of critical historiography, is based on this concept, or from Bolingbroke. Experience of the day thus is part of the same process of self-education of which the study of history is another part. "Experience shows" or "History informs us" are recurrent expressions in Jefferson's writings and may be applied equally to past and present. As early as 1779, he made history the principal subject of public education and defined the usefulness of historical studies for all citizens in the preamble of his Bill for the More General Diffusion of Knowledge, as follows: "To give them knowledge of those facts, which history exhibiteth, that, possessed thereby of the experience of other ages and countries, they may be enabled to know ambition under all its shapes." History was equivalent to the concrete experience of one's own time. A few years later he recommends sending potential American monarchists to Europe so that they may return good republicans after having seen what monarchy is like in action.

The classics, with their accumulated mass of written statements about all realms of life, furnished him with experience extended beyond his natural range not only, and not even primarily, in politics. While a law student, the young farmer read a book on ancient husbandry. And he read, at least in his early years, Cato and Varro, outstanding Roman writers on agriculture. When, in 1796, a French gentleman came to visit him in Monticello, he was impressed with Jefferson's attempt to apply knowledge from books to agriculture in actual practice on his farms; in that age of the infancy of modern agricultural science such books were largely historical repositories of past experience. Jefferson consulted Vitruvius in building, and in his libraries the various writers of antiquity are classed as living sources of knowledge and ideas in their respective fields: ancient philosophical books by one author were separated from each other in the various subdivisions of philosophy, natural, moral, and so on; Cicero's orations were on a shelf with those of other ancient and later works of the sort, apart from his philosophical writings and from his epistles, which were in turn included in a section of epistolography; Strabo and Ptolemy, the Greek geographers, were placed with modern geographical works as repositories of present knowledge in that field; Cato and Varro, of course, were classed with modern books on agricultural subjects. And so it goes on, all down the line to the cookbooks—a brand of literature highly appreciated by Jefferson—among which one finds the Latin handbook of Apicius of old.

Jefferson's empiricism made the ancient world of long-past history the object of all-inclusive, extended and ever-expanding concrete experience. It was a process of conjuring the ghosts of the past and making them come alive. The degree to which it was accomplished in each phase of his life depended on the range of material available to him. It is understandable, thus, that his judgment could be misled when and where only a limited experience was his. This is true in the case of monuments of ancient art. His short stay in southern France offered the only physical contact he had with major monuments. The concreteness of that experience was so overwhelming that it erased anything he had learned from books. Hence the ruins of Nîmes, including the Maison Carrée, a fine building, to be sure, of the age of Augustus, but not of the great quality of other ancient buildings about which he had read and which he knew from illustration only, become "the most perfect remains of antiquity which exist on earth."

In early years, he had copied a passage from Euripides' *Hippolytus* in his so-called *Literary Bible*: "We cling to what we see and know without knowledge of the beyond." Propositions "beyond finite comprehension" he abandoned as "a weight which human strength cannot lift," he said more than fifty years after he had made that entry. This statement is found in a letter to John Adams at the end of which he quotes a phrase from Cicero which he had also copied in his youth in the *Literary Bible*. Obviously then, Euripides' words, read in early years, were apt in expressing a basic idea that he retained throughout life. This skepticism about human speculation beyond the realm of the tangible and visible, and a painful awareness of the limitations of concrete experience which was the only safe basis of knowledge, were fundamental to Jefferson. In matters insoluble "ignorance is the softest pillow on which we can lay our heads," he said. This conviction had been strengthened by the powerful influence of Locke, the ancestor of modern positivistic philosophy. And it was no pure coincidence that when Jefferson was old, Comte, the founder of nineteenth century positivism, sent him a treatise. Comte, indeed, being an admirer of Jefferson, seems to have been encouraged if not inspired by the great American's ideas and words. In that essay which Jefferson received only two years before he passed away into the realm of the unknown, Comte advocated the application of exact scientific methods to the social sciences.

But positivistic theory of knowledge and philosophy, from Locke through their modern advocates in experimental psychologism, was always anything but a strict philosophical system. Its nerve was and is flexibility and the subordination of thought to ever-changing experience. And those who have attempted, as Comte did, to give to it the character of a true philosophical system have undertaken the task of Sisyphus of moving a rock up a mountain only to see it roll down again. The true philosophical system builders of modern times, rationalistic logicians, idealists and phenomenologists alike, have therefore condemned positivistic empiricism as nonphilosophical. Jefferson might have agreed. For one thing, his positivism was limited to the sphere of knowledge and balanced by a different set of equally if not more important approaches to human progress and a good life through moral intuition and aesthetic sense.

Jefferson himself would surely have had no objection to being called "unphilosophical." In his empirical theory of science, he went radically to the very end. He abominated and hated all systems and doctrinary theories. This aversion of his was so violent that it must be regarded as deeply rooted in his basic personality. It is unparalleled, if not in direction, in intensity. For one thing, he was not "fond of reading what is merely abstract." Although in his time he was ridiculed by his opponents as a theorist who was under the spell of newfangled French philosophies, to him the philosophers in France who did not prefer ignorance to error seemed to be on a level with the writers of romance.

Systems always needed a complicated terminology and involved language. Again, in a sentence which he early copied, Euripides gave adequate form to his own belief that the expression of truth is simple while the "wise," that is, the philosophers who called themselves sophists, distort simple truth by verbiage. The same was true of legal systems and their invariably complicated lingo. In his early years he had also read in Tacitus that lapidary phrase: "The more corrupt the commonwealth is the more laws you have." He remembered it years later when he read in a modern history praise of the justice, brevity and perspicuity of Danish laws and added it in his *Commonplace Book* beneath that excerpt. On this point he continued to agree with Montesquieu, from whom he copied, at the same time, a passage contrasting the simplicity of language of the early Roman laws, the Twelve Tables, with the diffuse wording of the *Novellae* of the Byzantine emperor Justinian. The simplicity of his own legal opinions, in argument and language—for instance, in the discussion of the rights at the "Batture" in New Orleans—though less elevated is, in principle, not different from the lucid expression of human and natural rights in the *Summary View of the Rights of British America* and in the Declaration of Independence.

His aversion to theories and systems lashed out in all directions: against geological hypotheses as well as against theorems of the economists. Above all, he distrusted medical theories. While his fundamental aversion to systems in general was a basic feature of his character, his skepticism about medical theory, in particular, had been strengthened by personal experience, above all by the inadequate treatment of an injury to his right wrist, in Paris, which to the end of his life made the cherished art of letter writing a physically painful process. It is natural, too, that he shared the not unjustified skepticism of many of his contemporaries about the actual abilities of the practitioners of the day. But he himself gathered practical experience in medicine and is even reported to have been capable of sewing up wounds like a professional surgeon. And he took an active part in the first experiments with the new art of vaccination in America. Among his medical handbooks were Hippocrates and Galen, the Greek ancestors of medical science. He expressed the opinion that the wisdom of Hippocrates should be seriously considered by medical students. He had purchased a book which made a remarkable attempt to trace the changing fashions of medicine in history in connection with the changes of religion and government. In medical education he advocated preference for the study of anatomy and the experience of clinical practice. But above all it was the *vis medicatrix naturae* which he trusted more than human knowledge.

This is the background on which we have to understand his fundamental approach to history. He regarded general and universal histories as mere reference books and compilations. There is no indication that he was interested in the deterministic, pragmatic or idealistic philosophies of history of his age. True, when young he read Voltaire's *Philosophie de l'histoire*, but what he copied from it was not a philosophical generalization but an interesting fact. He abhorred the fashionable allegorical approach to history, which incidentally crossed his way.

Theory of any kind was an obstacle to the progress of historical knowledge. "The moment a person forms a theory his imagination sees in every object only the traits which favor that theory." He stated this axiom in connection with theories regarding the origin of American Indians at a time when he was surrounded by French philosophers in Paris, and he recommended to the American Philosophical Society the collection and publication of "naked" and exact descriptions of Indian monuments.

Within the historical fields which were of particular interest to Jefferson, linguistic studies became, as time went on, a real battlefield on which he fought the theorists. The tradition of grammatical training in the ancient languages was overwhelmingly strong, as very aged traditions are. It had become a practice to consider the rules of "correct" usage of classical Greek or Ciceronian Latin as general categories of language. And the rigid application of the classical rules of grammar was often applied in a manner exceeding the structural analogies of what we now call the Indo-European languages. Beyond that, naïve attempts were abroad to understand languages of entirely different structure by the application of classical norms to them. On an arbitrary basis, such languages were, in turn, derived from Greek and Latin.

At a time when modern linguistic science was just beginning to take its first steps, all this was not surprising. On the other hand, it was natural that Jefferson revolted against the schematism and against the norm of such approaches. To him, grammars were necessary evils, crude first aids to the understanding of languages. Grammatical systems were even worse. They were wrong. Because languages were fluid, dynamic vehicles of the human mind. They changed in time and space. Their historical life—and their beauty, too —were rooted in the richness and variety of linguistic development. Animated by such a concept, Jefferson looked on grammatical rules as at best a measuring tool or ruler to define the changes of linguistic experience. Usage, he stated, gave laws to grammar, and not grammar to usage.

Purism in any form was an attempt to kill life and development. The formation of an American language of individual character was already visible, and the purists thundered that the Americans began to speak English incorrectly. Jefferson, of course, advocated their right to do so, and he recognized in the process a mature and fertile development. In addition, the formation of new words which accompanies all revolutions at a quicker pace than that customary in ordinary times had in France, too, been consciously perceived. Jefferson owned a new dictionary containing the words added to the standard dictionary of the French Academy as "creations of the French People" during the Revolution. It was listed in the catalogue of his library as "Dictionaire néologique Français," though its actual title did not include that qualifying term. It was "neology" which he strongly advocated against purism or, as he jokingly elaborated, neologism, neologist, neologisation, neologous, neological, neologistical, neologize, neologically. This neological instead of the alleged logical approach to linguistics was strengthened in Jefferson by the concrete problems of his own time. But his antipurist position was clarified by, if not originally based on his experience in the ancient languages, particularly in Greek. The wealth and flexibility of the Greek language, above all, the richness of composite words and the great variety of modulations caused by changing termination were to him expressions of a dynamic antipurist attitude. He thought the English language was capable of this Greek flexibility, too. In fact, in the strong influx of Greek and Latin words into English, he recognized not a mere historical fact but a fertilization of ideas and of modes of thought. As interested as he was in Anglo-Saxon, he stated that without neology "we should still be held to the vocabulary of Alfred or of Ulphilas; and held to their state of science also: for I am sure they had no words which could have conveyed the ideas of oxygen, cotyledons, zoophytes, magnetism, electricity, hyaline, and thousands of others expressing ideas not then existing, nor of possible communication in the state of their language. . . . And if, in this process of sound neologisation, our trans-Atlantic brethren shall not choose to accompany us, we may furnish, after the Ionians, a second example of a colonial dialect improving on its primitive."

Grammatical rule as well as purism of vocabulary were artificial barriers made by school teachers. This, too, Jefferson had experienced in reading the classics. "I readily sacrifice the niceties of syntax to euphony and strength. It is by boldly neglecting the rigorisms of grammar, that Tacitus has made himself the strongest writer in the world. The Hyperesthitics call him barbarous; but I should be sorry to exchange his barbarisms for their wise drawn purisms. Some of his sentences are as strong as language can make them. Had he scrupulously filled up the whole of their syntax, they would have been merely common." Characteristically, he applied the experience obtained from reading Tacitus to actual practice, aware of the force of linguistic expression in the arena of political discussion. To President Madison, who had sent him the draft of a document, he wrote: "Where strictness of grammar does not weaken expression, it should be attended to in complaisance to the purists of New England. But where by small grammatical negligence, the energy of an idea is condensed, or a word stand for a sentence, I hold grammatical rigor in contempt." The implication here is that the clergymen-teachers, the school teachers of what he called "Connecticut Latin," who were also, as he saw it, the principal reactionary political opponents of progress, were reactionaries in linguistics, too. They would call the ungrammatical language of Tacitus barbarian, while he attempted to brush the grammarian's dust off the ancient languages, to restore them to their original copiousness and flexibility, to their immediate creativeness.

Grammar, indeed, was as dangerous to progress and to true historical understanding as were all systems. In comparative linguistics, too, he had noted the dangers of systems at the time of his first contact with them, in the seventies. As rich as was the amount of facts he gathered in his notebook from Pelloutier's history of the Celtic tribes, already at that time he criticized "the ardor of the author to establish his system." His later studies in Anglo-Saxon and the Indian languages were directed against schematic subordination of the richness of phenomena to general systems and theories.

This aversion of Jefferson's to theorems and theorists was so strong and spontaneous, so intimately tied up with his basic ideas of knowledge, that it found its violent expression in personal hatred of individual authors of great systems of thought. He tended to see in such personalities destructive powers, and their writings seemed to him to be more harmful than the actions of ravaging armies. The two outstanding examples of this personal antagonism were, not by mere co-incidence, a Greek and a contemporary thinker: Plato and Montesquieu.

When young, he had carefully studied Montesquieu, as did every student of government in his time. And he had made copious excerpts from him in his *Commonplace Book*. He learned a good deal from that study. But in later years one finds repeated and impetuous criticism of Montesquieu in Jefferson's writings. It has been suggested that Montesquieu's statement that democratic government is possible only in small territories, a statement which Jefferson excerpted, was responsible for his violent antipathy toward the commonly revered French philosopher. Indeed, such a viewpoint—largely coinciding with the tenets of his federalist opponents in America—was utterly opposed to Jefferson's political convictions. Yet he himself explicitly admitted that democracy in pure form, implying the direct participation of the people in government, was possible only within the limits of small territories. Only in them could all the citizens gather for legislative action. But he also believed that the petty Greek republics of pure democratic government had failed. The solution was, of course, representative government, which the world had not known before parliamentary systems were introduced. And Jefferson, rightly, did not see the slightest reason why government by the people could not work in a great country via representation. Not to have seen that was a grave error in Montesquieu. But Jefferson admitted that such government was not pure democracy, that it had a purity of the second grade only, while he worked out a scheme of his own. According to this scheme school wards should constitute small cells in local affairs and keep the purely democratic practice alive to serve as a spiritual leaven of representative government. Therefore this issue, in which Jefferson had no objection to a good many of Montesquieu's conclusions, is not sufficient to explain his condemnation of Montesquieu's work. This condemnation is based rather on the schematic character of Montesquieu's book. Like Aristotle, he recognized only a few fundamental forms of government which, with but secondary modifications, recurred in history. They were fixed types in themselves. However, Jefferson's own historical and actual experience led him to believe in the best possible solutions, given the conditions of time and space. A fixed scheme by which each new development would be classifiable as the expression of an ideal prototype was contrary to his dynamic, positivistic concept of history, apart from the fact that it implied a fixation similar in character to purism and grammatical norm in languages.

His invectives against Montesquieu during the later part of his life are mild, however, in comparison with his outright hatred of Plato. In his later years, amid all his classical reading, even Aristotle, the great system-builder, logicist and clarifier in government as well as in ethics, sciences and aesthetics, had no place. This neglect, in spite of his awareness of Aristotle's powerful influence on medieval and modern thought, ranks with his lack of interest in Descartes and Leibnitz, among others. His concept of system-builders and theorists made them uninteresting and negligible but relatively harmless. He did not bother about them. And he concentrated his studies of ancient philosophers on the practical moralists, Cicero, Seneca, Epictetus, Marcus Aurelius. Though he professed to be an Epicurean, he failed to appreciate the only extensive and systematic book on the natural philosophy of that school, Lucretius' poetical work on the nature of the world, *De Rerum Natura*. All that was speculation, theory and system, and he felt he need not bother with it. But the case of Plato was different. Jefferson's violent feelings against ignorance, corruption and reaction which, as he saw it, were entrenched in the clergy of the established churches, made him single out Plato and his system as a target for attack. What he considered to be the fateful and demoralizing distortion of the simple truth of the doctrines of Jesus in the development of Christianity was inspired by Platonism and Neo-Platonism of late antiquity. The metaphysicians had taken the simple gospel of Jesus' own authentic words and concealed it beneath unintelligible systems of speculation. These speculations of a priesthood that associated itself with wealth and power had led to the decay of morality, as well as of reason and intelligence, ever since the end of antiquity.

Jefferson exaggerated the actual historical influence of Platonism on Christianity, however strong it was. But he sharply recognized what is undoubtedly true, that Plato stood at the beginning of the continuous line of systematic speculation which he inaugurated and which, indeed, superseded the simple faith of the early church in the transition from antique to medieval intellectualism. In his opinion, Plato had used the name of Socrates to cover the "whimsies of his own brain" in exactly the same way that the metaphysicists of the Christian Church had used the name of Jesus. He believed with the Unitarian Priestley that Jesus and Socrates, whose true and simple doctrines of practical morality could be found in Xenophon rather than in Plato, had much in common, though Jesus was immensely superior. But Socrates and Jesus were no metaphysical system-builders. "Our savior did not come into the world to save metaphysicians only," he exclaimed in a particularly violent invective against theologians, including Calvin, which seems to be unpublished. The "impious dogmatists" and Platonists had faked the evidence by engrafting their speculative systems on the simple truth of the words of Jesus.

Plato had brought that obnoxious disease into this world. Though Jefferson acknowledged that Plato was a superb writer, he recognized instinctively and correctly, in spite of his limited knowledge of Plato's original work, that he was a reactionary aristocrat. And Plato's doctrine of the supremacy of the state over the individual must, of course, have been utterly antagonistic to him.

In addition, he hated the obscurity of Plato's language and what he called his foggy or misty brain. Voltaire, the pure rationalist, judged mildly ironically about what may be appreciated in Plato's pre-Aristotelian and prelogical reasoning as a half-poetical, half-mythical expression. Jefferson, though poetically imaginative, drew a sharp line between imagination and the realms of knowledge, as Bacon had done. But, above all, there remained the fact that Plato started humanity on the road toward complicated speculation in philosophical systems.

Plato is and always will remain the ancestor of speculative systematic philosophy. He was detested exactly as such by Jefferson, as he has been worshiped for the same reason by most later thinkers and by all conventional classicists. However biased his judgment was, Jefferson's statement that the worship of Plato "with the moderns . . . is rather a matter of fashion and authority" should be a stimulus to thought, even today.

Jefferson's antipathy to Plato was but the most vehement expression of his empirical theory of knowledge and of his positivistic resignation to the realm of fact. This factual empiricism of his excluded systems of defined determinism in history. It entailed important methodical approaches and intuitive directions in his historical studies. These approaches were and are altogether fundamental to positive historical research as it has developed and expanded since the nineteenth century.

CHAPTER 6

Pursuit of the Concrete

HISTORY WAS the realm of facts. Its scope was reflection on them, whether silent or expressed in words. To gather the authentic facts necessitated critical study of the sources. To be critical about their reports required use of reason, common sense and, above all, personal experience of the real world of one's own time. Past and present are connected by a continuous tradition; therefore, survivals in the living organism of society elucidate the past. But the very life of history is as individual as any other form of natural life, and each period and country, each group and cultural phenomenon is singular in spite of the light that analogy and survivals can throw on its basic tracts. These four tools—original sources, use of analogy based on personal experience, study of living remnants of the past, and grasp of the singularity of the specific facts—were instrumental in Jefferson's approach to the world of the ancients.

Criticism of the sources of historical knowledge had been the very nerve of historical understanding. Historians, from the days of Thucydides on, had created a firm tradition on this principle which had been revived and expanded in and after the Renaissance. Locke and Bolingbroke had defined an almost juridical procedure of hearings to which the historical "witnesses" and "testimonies" had to be subjected. Jefferson depended on both of them, and in his *Literary Bible* he had early copied an extensive passage from Bolingbroke referring to this critical method. It involved Jefferson's principle of preference of "original" authorities to "compilers." What is new with Jefferson is that he not only recognizes this fundamental axiom of historical research but postulates the direct study of the earliest and most authentic historical source by any educated individual; every educated man should himself go directly to the fountainhead of factual knowledge and form his own historical judgment, wherever possible. He should not satisfy himself with the judgment of digests and compilations whose authors invariably added their own reflections.

The most explicit statements of Jefferson about this need for going back to the fountainhead of knowledge, and for critically judging historical reports, were made in connection with biblical studies. This is what he recommended to young Peter Carr in 1787: "Read the bible then, as you would read Livy or Tacitus. The facts which are within the ordinary course of nature you will believe on the authority of the writer, as you do those of the same kind in Livy and Tacitus. The testimony of the writer weighs in their favor in one scale, and their not being against the laws of nature does not weigh against them. But those facts in the bible which contradict the laws of nature, must be examined with more care, and under a variety of faces. . . . For example in the book of Joshua we are told the sun stood still several hours. Were we to read that fact in Livy or Tacitus we should class it with their showers of blood, speaking of statues, beasts, etc." He continues to advise the youngster, however, to examine carefully the writer's pretension that he was inspired—which "is entitled to your inquiry, because millions believe it." And later on he continues: "I forgot to observe when speaking of the new testament that you should read all the histories of Christ, as well of those whom a council of ecclesiastics have decided for us to be Pseudo-evangelists, as those they named Evangelists. Because these Pseudo-evangelists pretended to inspiration as much as the others, and you are to judge their pretensions by your own reason, and not by the reason of those ecclesiastics. Most of these are lost. There are some however still extant, collected by Fabricius which I will endeavor to get and send you." In the study of the vital issue of original Christianity, he sharpened his own historical judgment about the character of the sources of history on which all later interpretation depended. The original sources about Jesus, he concluded in later years, were written by "unlettered and ignorant men," and for that matter, solely from memory. Ultimately, in this as in almost any other antique case, the truly original source, the authentic sayings of Jesus, was lost. He had early excerpted a passage from Locke stating that only the words of Jesus were the foundation of Christianity, and that all the extant sources were historically conditioned. Priestley, the Unitarian, and he, himself, attempted to unearth these original sources beneath the secondary reports. And the so-called Jefferson Bible was the result of his effort.

His critical approach to the original sources of Christianity is but the outstanding example of his approach to writings on history in general. His insistence that students should read the original Greek and Latin authors instead of digests and compilations, and his own practice of nearly exclusively doing just that, reveal that the advice given to young Carr in the case of the evangelists is simply a specific application of one of his general principles. His skepticism about the possibility of accurate translation and his awareness of the uniqueness of the linguistic expression of ideas had led him to read the original sources in their original wording wherever he could and particularly in the classical languages. It has been shown how he increasingly learned and applied the critical philological methods of adequate restoration and interpretation of these original texts.

But "original sources" was a relative term. The ancient writers were only to a very limited degree original witnesses of the events they reported. The development of modern epigraphical and archaeological research, which has largely corrected and modified their reports since Jefferson's time, began only at the end of his life. In his late years, his appreciation of the contemporary witnesses of events among the ancient historians is felt more and more. Among the Latins Tacitus, the bitter critic of the early Roman Empire, among the Greeks Thucydides, the eyewitness and recorder of the Peloponnesian War, and Polybius, the one preserved great contemporary of the age after Alexander the Great, became his most cherished historians. But it was preferable to read even the secondary reports of ancient historians who were closer to the original sources and events than later writers, wherever the reports of eyewitnesses were lacking. Jefferson was painfully aware of the incompleteness of the records left from antiquity. The original documents—in his time— seemed to be definitely lost, almost everywhere. And while he himself collected newspapers and laws, he was aware of the documentary value of letters in history. Only very few collections of historically important letters like those of Cicero and, though of minor significance, of the younger Pliny were available. Speaking of the importance of the unpublished archive of Washington for a correct judgment of contemporary history, he emphasized "What a treasure will be found . . . when no longer, like Caesar's notes and memorandums in the hands of Anthony, it shall be open to the high priests of federalism only, and garbled to say so much, and no more, as suits their views!"

As he witnessed what appeared to him to be a growing distortion of the truth about the history of the young American republic, he voiced, as early as 1787, his increasing skepticism about historiography in general. "If contemporary histories are thus false, what will future compilations be? And what are all those of preceding times?" A book against which he sent a protest to a Paris newspaper had compared the leagues of history—those of the Greeks, Swiss and Dutch—with the American confederacy. He said that he had not been a part of any of the former, but knew better than the author, Mayer, what had happened in America. And he wound up his ironical letter with "regrets, and . . . adieux to history, to travels, to Mayer" and to the unhappy editor.

He was aware of the intentional or unintentional bias of historical writers—for instance, of the one-sided Roman reports available about Carthage and other nations conquered by the Romans—and eager to learn the other side of the story. On the other hand, he detested eulogy which he called "panegyric biography." What he wanted was facts, and, as he had remarked to young Carr, even Tacitus and other candid historians of antiquity, such as Livy and Diodorus, often reported incredible miracles which contradicted the laws of nature. . . . "when they tell us of calves speaking, of statues sweating blood, and other things against the course of nature, we reject these as fables not belonging to history." Even the most reliable and cherished ancient historians indulged in the conventional practice of fictional speeches to present the opinions of protagonists, and he regretted the copying of this antique model in modern historiography.

His healthy skepticism against such legendary identifications of monuments as that of the tomb of Virgil near Naples, or of the alleged residence of Caesar in a château at Nimwegen in Holland, is a natural outgrowth of his criticism of historical sources. He drew a sharp line between poetical "fancy" and historical knowledge. However, one might gather that he was interested in the problem of the reflection of history in poetry as a secondary means of historical study. In fact, while President he made a scrapbook of contemporary poems clipped from newspapers. Its character seems to point to a collection of poetical reflections of contemporary history and life in America. But Jefferson's judgment was not at all influenced by poetical references to historical personalities.

He might have conceded his revered Latin poet Horace's candid admiration for Augustus—who, however, as concrete historical personality remained to him a "scoundrel and parricide."

As to art as a source of factual information, the poet himself gave him a catchword: "The painting lately executed by Colo. Trumbull, I have never seen, but as far back as the days of Horace at least we are told that *'pictoribus atque poetis quidlibet audendi semper fuit aequa potestas.'* He has exercised this *licentia pictoris* in like manner in the surrender of York, where he has placed Ld. Cornwallis at the head of the surrender altho' it is well known that he was excused by General Washington from appearing." He tried to find the literary source of the event pictured in David's *Daughters of Brutus,* without being successful. Following a Renaissance tradition, however, he considered the concrete representation of personages as a valuable means of historical experience: provided that the portrait was authentic and, if possible, even in correct life size. Thus he advocated such exact preservation of the physical appearance of leaders of the American Revolution. He collected copies of portraits of early explorers made for him in the portrait gallery of the Uffizi in Florence; he had the pictures of Bacon, Locke and Newton in his dining room while secretary of state; and in Monticello he exhibited all these portraits along with those of contemporary personalities of importance, including characters whom he disliked, such as Hamilton and Napoleon. But there is no hint that he shared the common interest in portraits of personalities of the ancient world. He may have had an intuitive knowledge of the problematic faithfulness of most of the preserved antique portraits of intellectuals whose countenances he might have been eager to know: Socrates, Thucydides, Cicero, and Virgil, not to mention the imaginary portraits of Homer, and the lack of any portraits of such cherished writers as Horace and Tacitus.

Using the sharp weapon of historical criticism of sources, Jefferson limited himself to what, in his age, still seemed to be the only source material, the writings of the ancient historians. But the complement to this approach, as it is consciously or unconsciously with every serious student of history, was the application of present experience to the understanding of the past. Like other men of his age, he interpreted ancient history within the framework of eighteenth century "philosophy." And his judgment was colored throughout by his emotional reactions to the events of his own time. His mind from his school days on had been filled with images of the actions, characters, issues of the ancient world. They intruded on the events of his day. And as their analogy threw light on what happened around him, the concrete experience of his own world, in turn, reflected its sharp light on them.

Patrick Henry seemed to speak like Homer, and Homer's language could not fail to be imbued with a new and concrete vitality after listening to Henry, with that analogy in mind. General Arnold's famous march to Quebec was a parallel to Xenophon s retreat in Asia Minor as narrated in his *Anabasis*. John Adams, like Themistocles in Athens, had been the constant advocate of the "wooden walls" of a navy. And the King of England would welcome American Tory-traitors, as the Persian king had given refuge to the fugitive aristocracy of Greece. Burr was the Catiline of the American republic and Napoleon was a new Alexander or, even worse than that, Caesar. Such parallels were mostly in the nature of direct illustration of the present by the antique past or vice versa. In addition, antique movements and figures as they had been sculptured by ancient historians seemed to be prototypes of events in other historical ages. Cola di Rienzi, the medieval popular revolutionary of Rome, was a "poor counterfeit of the Gracchi" tribunes of old.

Among the first historical studies which Jefferson made in 1774 in connection with the basic issue of the American Revolution, was an examination of the evidence for the relationship between Greek emigrants and colonists to the mother country. From the excerpts in his *Commonplace Book* it is obvious that the establishment of self-government by colonists and emigrants from Greece was considered by him to be analogous to what had happened in the settlement of British America. And though he failed to use this parallelism in the *Summary View of the Rights of British America,* this failure is evidently due to tactical considerations which made it advisable to stick to strictly legal British precedent at a time when there was still a hope of preserving the union with the British Crown. Legal precedent and natural law were common elements of appeal rather than his personal infatuation with the experiences of the ancients.

After the revolution and again during the stormy years from 1810 to 1815, there appears, time and again, the simile of England and Carthage that has often been used by later critics of British policy. The English government and social structure, directed as it appeared to him to be, by moneyed and commercial interests, the actions of this imperialistic sea power, the risks which it took and their possibly impending fate were analogous to Carthage. Carthage, in turn, became an interesting object of study, with a distinguished government and society. It was a republic of moneyed aristocracy, and Jefferson also regarded it as a symbol of the Hamiltonian and reactionary bankers of America. The conflict between Great Britain and America, between a rising, fundamentally agricultural power and an established mercantile empire seemed to him to be, at times, exactly like that between Rome and Carthage. The difference was that the modern system of balance of power and alliances would not allow this conflict to end with the extinction of British might. In addition, he had never ceased to recognize the insoluble cultural bonds between Britain and America which, even in the hours of greatest wrath, made him feel sympathetic with the people of England, if not with their governing class. Here, too, an antique analogy was at hand: "I should myself feel with great strength the ties which bind us together, of origin, language, laws and manners; and I am persuaded the two people would become in future, as it was with the ancient Greeks, among whom it was reproachful for Greek to be found fighting against Greek in a foreign army," he wrote prophetically in 1816.

The use of direct analogy between present and ancient history illuminates the former and revitalizes the latter. Related to that common and genuinely historical approach of Jefferson's is his eagerness to gather living traditions from remote antiquity and to use the concrete experience gained from them for the understanding of their historical root.

Still unaware of the concept of historical evolution and of the just beginning romantic interest in survivals in folklore, Jefferson developed his own, at times, somewhat abstruse method of using survivals for the reconstruction of phenomena of a distant past. While this method was valuable to him in obtaining a more vital experience of history, it entailed odd conclusions; but it also focused on important historical problems and, incidentally, hit on discoveries of considerable value.

The young lawyer had learned to consider the actual survival of Roman law as a practical tool which had been included in the legislative, judicial and interpretative practice of the world to which he belonged. As late as the preamble of his opinion on the litigation about the rights on the "Batture" of New Orleans, he states that the laws of that territory were composed of the Roman, French and Spanish codes and written in the languages quoted in his memorandum. And he added a masterly historical résumé about the way in which Roman law imposed itself on original French, feudal law. One might assume that it was this experience of concrete and practical legal survival which led him on the road toward utilization of the obsolete for the current. The way in which Jefferson used the earlier Anglo-Saxon precedent at the beginning of the American Revolution to prove the right of the settlers of America in his time has been criticized as dubious. It implied, indeed, that original Anglo-Saxon law was as living a legal reality as Roman law—which it was not. He attempted to resurrect it and elevate it to that position. In fact, Anglo-Saxon law had continued to form principles of legal outlook and approach which were still alive. And as he studied it, it became to him a reality surviving in the notion of Britons in America; it received new blood from their spontaneous reactions. Though on the surface conditions and practices might have changed, it seemed that there were vital and inherited forces at work in history and they could flare up. Roman tradition, he thought later, was smoldering somewhere in the very marrow of Italian personalities. Napoleon's dream of an empire, for example, was conditioned by "the bigotry of an Italian to the antient splendour of his country."

Such more or less conscious notions defined his curious approach to linguistic survivals, an approach which was abstruse and at the same time fertile. Here, too, his basic experience was obtained in the classical field, though the later applications of that experience in Anglo-Saxon are better known and were of greater consequence. Characteristically, his reflections about the utilization of concrete and contemporary linguistic survivals, true or alleged, were stimulated by chance and local circumstances. He used his acquaintance with educated Greeks in Paris to learn the pronunciation of modern Greek. And from that time on, he tried to recapture the concrete sound of the ancient language by means of that modern pronunciation. Under the fresh impression of this experience, he wrote in 1785 "The modern Greek is not yet so far departed from its ancient model, but that we might still hope to see the language of Homer and Demosthenes flow

with purity, from the lips of a free and ingenious people."
Mr. Paradise, one of his Greek friends who visited America,
believed that this renascence of ancient Greek could easily
be achieved. Forty years later, after the liberation of Greece,
the actual renascence of the ancient language, the so-called
"pure" language, began in official usage; and a bitter conflict
with the "folk" language has raged in Greece ever since. In
recent times this conflict has been animated with political
associations, the "pure" language being regarded as an ideal
of the conservative, the folk language as a symbol of the progressive elements of society.

Jefferson had, indeed, focused on a remarkable issue of tradition in history. And it is curious that his enthusiasm about
the ancient Greeks would seem in this instance to put him
on the side of the hated reactionary purists. However, that impression is somewhat erroneous, because he had a quite clear
picture of the development of language as a gradual growth.
He tried to use the survivals which might exist within that
later phase for solving debated problems of its original character. In respect to this, he wrote in 1819: "Early in life, the
idea occurred to me that the people now inhabiting the ancient seats of the Greeks and Romans, although their languages in the intermediate ages had suffered great changes,
and especially in the declension of their nouns, and in the
termination of their words generally, yet having preserved
the body of the word radically the same, so they could preserve more of its pronunciation." He went on to state that
for that reason he used the Italian pronunciation of Latin—
which he may have learned from his Italian neighbor Mazzei
—and that, in Paris, he had accepted the modern pronunciation of ancient Greek. He continued by qualifying this use
of modern native pronunciation, admitting that changes
caused by degeneracies of sound as well as of structure must
have occurred, and he discussed the resulting problems for the
pronunciation of Greek vowels and diphthongs. He stated

that if one preferred the "Erasmian" pronunciation, that is, the one based on Byzantine scholarship and the language used at the time of the conquest of Constantinople, one "must go to Italy for it, as we must do for the most probably correct pronunciation of the language of the Romans." This he said in consideration of the influx into Italy of Byzantine scholars who had brought their Greek language to that country and established a scholarly tradition there.

He made his fourteen-year-old daughter read Livy, not in an English but in an Italian translation, the difficult and "ancient" language of which drove her to despair. Evidently, in his characteristic method of killing two birds with one stone, he thought that she could in this fashion learn Italian and, at the same time, read Livy in a language still close to the original. The implication of these views was of far-reaching importance, because this theory, or rather practical experimentation, was a step toward an understanding of the gradual phonetic changes which accompany the linguistic development of the classical languages from earlier strata via their late "vulgar" stages to their modern derivatives. Jefferson early regarded Italian, French and Spanish as "degenerated dialects of the Latin." His use of Italian and modern Greek for recapturing the authentic sounds of the classical languages thus implied a further step: to look for survivals of earlier linguistic strata in the living dialects of a modern language.

In his fight against purism he stressed the richness of dialects in Greek literature as an expression of a particular wealth of ideas and language. There is no question that it was the early experience of the variety of sound in the Greek dialects which caused his enthusiasm for dialects in general. This enthusiasm was quite different from that of the later romanticists. To him, dialectic developments were less an expression of folklore than of the flexibility and creativeness of the human mind. While he prophetically suggested that the day might come when, like the "Ionic" dialects of Greek, American language would add to the richness of English, the other British dialects also became a subject of interest to him. Thus he discovered what has been called the process of "dialectic regeneration" nearly half a century before the professional scholars. He advocated the study of all the English dialects as a subject of both linguistic fertilization and historical enlightenment. These were great and productive ideas prompted by his study of the ancient languages and his desire for vital experience. On the other hand, he exaggerated this approach in his curious views about Anglo-Saxon grammar and spelling. He was "inclined to see in the older language only those features which correspond to characteristics in the language of his own day."

Jefferson's revitalization of the past by experience of the present and of true or alleged survivals was, however, checked by his awareness of the singularity of historical phenomena.

His concept of life as a continuously changing dynamic process and his aversion to systems and generalizations not only balanced but, in general, superseded his tendencies to interpret the past in terms of his time. As it was, the basic experience of his youth had been one of unprecedented action in which he had a considerable part himself. "We can no longer say there is nothing new under the sun. For this whole chapter in the history of man is new." He had, in addition, an innate respect for and notion of individual behavior. And some of his early readings had strengthened the conviction that each age and country had a quite individual character. Like Montesquieu, Jefferson believed in the modification of fundamental types of government by such circumstances as climate and habit. The meteorological observer Jefferson regarded climate as a very important factor. It not only conditioned economic structure and other social phenomena. It affected the mind. "It is our cloudless sky which has eradicated from our constitutions all disposition to hang ourselves, which we might otherwise have inherited from our English ancestors," he wrote. American optimism and the outlook toward a better world seemed to be a plant growing more easily under the American sky than elsewhere. And even: "A poet is as much the creature of climate as an orange or palm tree."

Virtues and vices of men could not be judged by the same standards in different ages and countries. Their historical appearance was conditioned by a composite mass of natural and social influences. And relative social utility under given conditions determined the codes of morality in actual history. "Man living in different countries, under different circumstances, different habits and regimens, may have different utilities." The innate moral sense of man, his yearning for justice, would manifest itself in different shapes in historical society. From an absolute point of view every human essay would have some defect. Historical reality, thus, was always in the nature of a singular compromise between principles and changing circumstances. Human societies were growing organisms, agglomerations of individuals, each of which was conditioned by innumerable factors. Life in its complexity changed continuously. A generation might agree on standards and actions. But it was questionable whether they would be acceptable even to the immediately succeeding generation. His objection to the theory that governmental forms in history were based on a social contract between the individuals concerned grew from his concept that no such contract could prove valid beyond the time of life of the generation which allegedly had agreed to it. His curious idea that no generation should be allowed to burden the next one by assuming public debts which they themselves could not pay off during their lifetime was a by-product of this philosophy. And when he boldly and unconstitutionally increased American territory by the purchase of Louisiana, he justified that action by arguing that one generation might act as a guardian for the next by making provisions which could be accepted or refuted later.

Jefferson's concept of the singularity of conditions in time and space entailed an emphasis on the uniqueness of historical events. And his concept of society as a mere sum of individuals entailed an emphasis on the role of the individual in history. His experience with the Indians was not compatible with the attempts to parallelize and connect their civilization with others. They seemed to him to be different and unique and, for that matter, to include a great number of varieties within themselves.

As a result, Jefferson developed a stress on and understanding of the singular phenomena of the ancient world, which is genuinely historical, and anticipated the nineteenth century development of scientific history.

His awareness of the singularity of concrete forms and events in all realms of historical life is evident in spite of analogy and the application of modern experience. These are rather subservient to the appraisal of the individual character of historical facts.

Language, the most direct historical expression of the human mind and of human culture, was to be grasped and understood in its uniqueness and singularity. Jefferson's aversion to system and grammar was in that, as in other realms, but another expression of his emphasis on singularity. First, and above all, the ancient writings were to him the high school of this individual creativeness. And what he experienced in them he was able to apply, by contrast and not by analogy, to Indian language and Anglo-Saxon. His insistence on the difference of English from Greek and Latin, sometimes exaggerated as it is, shows this approach to individual character by means of antithesis. In this case, his approach led him to underrate both the common inheritance of Indo-European languages and the historical influence of the Roman occupation of Britain. "Although the Romans had been in possession of that country for nearly five centuries from the time of Julius Caesar, yet it was a military possession chiefly, by their soldiery alone, and with dispositions intermutually jealous and unamicable. They seemed to have aimed at no lasting settlements there, and to have had little familiar mixture with the native Britons." In this he was decidedly wrong, as we know today from the remarkable remnants of the Romans in Great Britain unearthed by the patience and exemplary methods of English archaeologists. But Jefferson was aware of his limited knowledge, and he carefully advanced the alternative that Roman cultural influence in England might have been dislodged and repressed by the Anglo-Saxon immigration. The surprising lack of continuity between Roman and later Britain, in comparison with other provinces of the Roman Empire, is even more conspicuous today in view of the extensive penetration of Roman culture revealed by excavations. And its reasons are still a matter of dispute.

Jefferson elaborated Anglo-Saxon prosody, too, in antithesis to classical meter. The contrast between classical quantitative and English accentual meter led him to the important theory that Greek and Latin accents were musically pitched rather than emphatic, and that in these languages emphasis coincided with quantity of syllables. Strangely enough, he had from early days written Greek without the usual accentuation. The contrast between classical and English verse, as he saw it, was by and large true. He did not know, then, that it is not simply a contrast of innate linguistic differences, and that in the classical languages the late "vulgar" poetry shows a transition from quantitative to accentual meter.

Jefferson's appreciation of the singular character of individual languages and personal linguistic expression led him with Locke to the correct conclusion that truthful translation is ultimately impossible. He stated as an axiom that no translation is a fully adequate representation of the original. To translate the style of poetry was to him, as it is in fact, an impossibility, and he judged that Homer had never been translated. His own practice of reading only originals whenever he knew the languages, and his insistence that every student should be equipped to do this, are a result of his consciousness of the uniqueness of linguistic expression. He further concluded, and again correctly, that it was impossible to attain perfection in writing any foreign language. And it is remarkable that a man of his classical learning did not indulge —with the one youthful exception of an epitaph for his sister Jane—in occasional attempts at writing classical poetry, as did almost every other classicist of his age. Instead, he often quoted original sentences borrowed from ancient authors to express his own ideas and emotions.

The singular phase and character of a civilization was implicitly revealed by its language. And within one language of a given age, too, there existed a variety of dialects and the singularity of personal idioms, in addition to professional languages, vehicles of the ideas and objectives of social groups, those of the scientists, the lawyers, the clergymen, for instance. In a very original manner, he argued that it was impossible and inadmissable immediately to convert Indians to Christianity. Their language, as he saw it, had not yet attained the status of a linguistic instrument by which the ideas of Christianity could be adequately conveyed to them.

In all other realms of culture, too, time, place and habit created singular phenomena in history. True, man had a natural moral instinct and, therefore, the moral branches of all religions had a common denominator. But the dogmas differed.

Montesquieu had taught him that laws must be altered in accordance with climate, local conditions and new circumstances. Laws and institutions, as well as language and religion, should go hand in hand with the progress of the human mind. Comparing the Roman with the Chancery law he said:

"All systems of law indeed profess to be founded on the principles of justice. But the superstructures erected are totally distinct. The institutions of Lycurgus, for example, would not have suited Athens, nor those of Solon Lacedaemon." In this case the law had been molded to the citizens, not the citizens to the law, and it should always be so.

Government, based on law, was equally the expression of ever-changing conditions and circumstances. Montesquieu was entirely wrong in his concept of unavoidably recurring types of government. Jefferson, who was accused of being a theorist and doctrinaire, had the most flexible concept of the relationship of idea and reality. Peoples of other regions and times had limitations within the status of their civilizations, however good they might have been in some respect, that prevented them from even approaching good government. In his time, the true principles of such good government were known, yet their application was a different matter and could always be only relative.

As a student he had copied this passage from Euripides' *Medea:* "If you bring new wisdoms to those unskilled you are useless and not wise." This passage aptly expressed his own, eighteenth century concept. He advocated a cautious and gradual development of democratic institutions—patterned rather on the British than on the American model—during the French Revolution, and he thought its ultimate failure was the result of too radical a direction. He judged that France was not ripe for truly democratic government. The constitutions for the new South American states, he agreed, should be different from the constitution of the United States, and to criticize them from an American point of view would be acting "like a critic on Homer by the laws of the Drama," Homeric epos being part of a primitive world compared with the Attic society which created the classical drama. In a letter to Madame de Staël he stressed the necessity of gradual evolution toward political freedom and enlightenment in South America and prophetically anticipated the dangers of "Bonapartism" there.

Critical study of historical sources, reconstruction of past history on the basis of personal experience, vitalization of it by means of grasping its survivals and seizure of the singular character of events, resulted in an exceptionally concrete and realistic view. Jefferson's scientific criterion, which he applied above all to history, was "a fearless pursuit of truth whithersoever it leads."

CHAPTER 7

The Dark Side of Humanity

I N EARLY YEARS Jefferson's admiration for classical literature and thought had caused him to start that intense and continuous study of the ancient world which occupied so prominent a place among his intellectual activities. But in the sphere of social and political history the "fearless pursuit of truth" made him move away from the "traditional worship of everything Greek or Latin" which was the earmark of the Humanistic inheritance. Neither did that pursuit of truth embark on a compromise cherished by the Greek revivalists of his age and connect a worship of the Greeks with a condemnation of the allegedly degenerate and tasteless Romans. While Greeks and Romans were particularly great in the realms of letters and art, in social and political history their world reflected all the faults of human nature which defined the deplorable course of history in general.

History, as well as his former experience as a lawyer, Jefferson said to John Bernard, reminded him continually of the dark side of humanity. And that was true of the great world of the ancients, too. In fact, the course of Greek and Roman events seemed to him to illustrate that dark side of humanity with particular clarity, and his intense study of ancient history furnished material for useful reflection and cautious action. Gibbon's pessimistic characterization of history as a register of crimes seems to have exercised a powerful influence on him. The alleged Utopian Jefferson nurtured, by sober contemplation of actual events, a deep-rooted pessimism and skepticism about human history. This pessimism had been strengthened in early years by the experience of ancient skepticism about life and men as it appeared in Homer, Euripides and Horace. The continued study of Greek and Roman history made it a matter of reasonable reflection. The ancient world increasingly became a world of grim reality. Anticipating by several generations the pessimistic and realistic views of the great Swiss historian Jacob Burckhardt, he visualized the splendid achievements of Greek and Roman culture against the dark background of a cruel social and political life. What distinguishes him from Burckhardt, however, is his faith in the fundamental reasonableness and morality of humanity. As he saw it, the study of history—of ancient history, above all—revealed the dangers which continually assault the fundamental goodness of man.

A full realization of the weaknesses of human nature, as revealed in history, opened the road to a better future. In his age, the Stoic examples of virtue presented in Greek and Roman history tended in the minds of most other men to balance if not outweigh the examples of vices. In Jefferson's writings there is no trace of this self-edification by *exempla virtutis* of ancient history. From his historical studies, there emerges an emphasis on the general forces of evil which undermine the good nature of man. The lure of wealth and power was present among these evil forces. Denunciations of wealth and power he had early copied from Euripides. And, later, he fed his hatred of reactionary wealth and power by reading ancient poets and philosophers. The lust for wealth and power, he judged, had caused the distortion of true Christianity from the early days of the Church on. It was perpetually behind the efforts of priests. "I have contemplated their order from the Magi of the East to the Saints of the West, and I have found no difference of character, but of more or less caution, in proportion to their information or ignorance of those on whom their interested duperies were to be plaid off." The lust for wealth and power prompted the ambition of individuals in history and, at times, caused "a total extinction of national morality." Such a collapse of public morality had occurred in the age of Alexander and his successors in Greece, at the time of Augustus in Rome, and it was happening again in the Napoleonic Era. Wars, prompted by such ambition, were a deep-rooted and possibly ineradicable evil. "In truth I do not recollect in all the animal kingdom a single species but man which is eternally and systematically engaged in the destruction of its own species. What is called civilization seems to have no other effect on him than to teach him to pursue the principle of *bellum omnium in omnia* on a larger scale, and in place of the little contests of tribe against tribe, to engage all the quarters of the earth in the same work of destruction," he wrote to Madison nearly a hundred and twenty years before the First World War. Society was a great machine, slow to be moved and inflected, and he quoted, in this connection, Solon, the wise Athenian statesman, who had recognized this fact nearly two and a half millennia before.

"It is only by a happy concurrence of good characters and good occasions that a step can now and then be taken to advance the well-being of nations." Even in small matters such as a reform of spelling, it is "very difficult to persuade the great body of mankind to give up what they have once learned." And to persuade "those of the benefit of science who possess none is a slow operation."

There was continuous danger of reversals. When he was in southern France, he half-jokingly wrote that along with the other citizens of that old province of the Roman Empire, he feared a return of barbarism which might destroy civilization. The great example of such a reversal was, of course, the decline of civilization at the end of antiquity. But true Christianity, too, had been prevented from spreading by distortion and deprivation. He saw in the Unitarian's efforts to restore it to its original form a hopeful sign, but warned that they, too, might in due time give up "morals for mysteries and Jesus for Plato."

Not only were evil instincts, like those for wealth and power, continually in ambush against the progress of humanity. There seemed to emerge from history fundamental, emotionally conditioned types of men, and strife of parties was a necessary evil. Jefferson's reflection on that issue, based on the analogy between ancient history and his own experience, was truly Humanistic. It did not satisfy itself with the contrast between economic interests of individuals or groups. However loosely or closely associated with such interests, to him reactionaries and progressives, Tories and Whigs, Federalists and Republicans were permanent, emotionally and habitually conditioned types of humanity. Such types had first emerged in history in that Greek world in which the *aristoi* distinguished themselves from the common people. "Men have differed in opinion, and been divided into parties by these opinions, from the first origin of societies, and in all governments where they have been permitted freely to think and to speak. The same political parties which now agitate the United States, have existed through all time. Whether the power of the people or that of the ἄριστοι should prevail, were questions which kept the States of Greece and Rome in eternal convulsions, as they now schismatize every people whose minds and mouths are not shut by the gag of a despot. And in fact, the terms of whig and tory belong to natural as well as to civil history. They denote the temper and constitution of mind of different individuals."

This theory first occurs in a letter to John Adams which initiated a discussion of considerable interest. Adams, classified by Jefferson and acknowledged by himself as such, was an *aristos*. He accepted the permanent existence of the contrast but concluded, against Jefferson, that the science of government could never make any progress—the best possible illustration of Jefferson's characterization of the behavior of his type. But Adams saw in the *aristoi* those who were stronger by nature, and he advanced Greek sources for this view. Jefferson argued that this was not the true root of the phenomenon and that at least since the invention of gunpowder aristocracy had not been based on any natural superiority. The influence of birth was to Adams a natural and inescapable factor in defining ruling classes, whether one liked it or not. He quoted a passage of the early Greek poet Theognis regarding the breeding of an aristocratic race. Jefferson, in turn, was inclined to see in this passage an ethical rather than a political implication, advocating an artificial breeding of morally superior individuals. As to that, he suspected that "the equal rights of men will rise up against this privileged Solomon and his Harem." To him the true natural aristocracy was one of talent, more or less independent of birth. Evidently, then, the reactionary aristocratic type of man is something entirely different, a product of social tradition and behavior, mentally conditioned by them—and, as he saw it, eternally opposed to progress.

Ancient society was engaged in a continuous struggle between these basic human types. In addition, it included remnants of primitive and brutal practices which were detestable. In certain directions some progress had been made. Already in the age of Homer, he acknowledged, the custom of killing prisoners had given way to the relatively more humane practice of enslaving them. But there was the outrageous Greek and Roman custom of exposing nondesirable infants, for example. And the omnipotence of the Roman father in regard to the life, property, instruction and morals of his children was bad. That it could happen in the ancient civilized and learned nations that a father could sell his child into slavery was a crude survival of natural law. Slavery was a bad remnant of such a state everywhere. Certain aspects of antique slavery were better than some features of slavery in his time, as a result of the fact that most slaves were not of different race and color and, therefore, once freed, could become respected and, often, creative members of society. On the other hand, it seemed to him that in general the conditions of slaves in Rome compared unfavorably with those in the America of his day. His familiarity with ancient slavery was virtually limited to Roman agricultural slavery. We know today that this was only a relatively unimportant section of slave labor in comparison with urban slavery, and that the conditions of the latter were much better and even superior to some aspects of modern free labor. But his comparison of ancient and modern agricultural slavery in the *Notes on Virginia* is still worth reading.

In addition, continuous warfare was a great evil in antiquity. "Their arms and mode of warfare" induced them to make severe gymnastic exercises the principal aim of public education, and modern society should not follow them in that respect. He disapproved of standing armies, such as those of the Roman Empire. However, he approved of general military service, provided it was limited to wartime, as was customary in the Greek city-states and in early Rome. ". . . we can have no standing armies for defense, because we have no paupers to furnish the materials. The Greeks and Romans had no standing armies, yet they defended themselves. The Greeks by their laws, and the Romans by the spirit of their people, took care to put into the hands of their rulers no such engine of oppression as a standing army. Their system was to make every man a soldier, and oblige him to repair to the standard of his country whenever that was reared. This made them invincible."

On the whole, he thought the ancient world lacked the high ethical standard which would eventually enable modern man to improve society. In spite of all his admiration for the Greeks and Romans, he professed sternly and fearlessly that their religious practices remained primitive, however refined some of their poetical expressions might be. Since late antiquity, it had become customary for classicists to avoid facing frankly the issue of ancient religion: by regarding it as a lofty poetical creation of aesthetic value, by allegorizing or humanizing the ancient gods, by assuming that they had once been benefactors of the human race, and had been made the objects of worship by the later born. Jefferson did not indulge in such compromises. In early years, he was interested in antique ideas about immortality, as entries in his so-called *Literary Bible* reveal. And among later excerpts is a passage from Voltaire pointing to the germs of monotheism in Greek mystery religions. The doctrine of one God "was among the efficacious doctrines which gave it [Christianity] triumph over the polytheism of the ancients, sickened with the absurdities of their own theology." The enlightened nations of antiquity indulged in vulgar "idolatry and superstition." As early as 1776, he had copied a passage from Shaftesbury which offered a solution to the paradox: "As the Antients tolerated visionaries and enthusiasts of all kinds so they permitted a free scope to philosophy as a balance. As the Pythagoreans and latter Platonists joined with the superstition of their times the Epicureans and Academicks were allowed all the use of wit and raillery against it. . . . Superstition and enthusiasm thus let alone never raged to bloodshed, persecution, etc."

High ethical standards comparable to those of Jesus were to be found only in ancient philosophy. But even this comparison convinced him that, by and large, the ancient philosophies were deficient. They were chiefly concerned with securing individual tranquillity of the mind and lacked true charity and philanthropy. They weighed their actions rather than their conscience. The very titles of their philosophical treatises showed this. With his typical approach to mathematically defined facts, he stated that out of ten tracts of Seneca, seven dealt with the individual government of passion and with tranquillity, only two related to actions concerning others, and one dealt with Providence. And he continued to give the respective figures for Cicero's philosophical writings which are of similar character. Though the ancient philosophers were great within the range of their considerations, they were short and defective in developing our duties to others. "They embraced, indeed, the circles of kindred and friends, and inculcated patriotism, or the love of our country in the aggregate, as a primary obligation: towards our neighbors and countrymen they taught justice, but scarcely viewed them as within the circle of benevolence. Still less have they inculcated peace, charity and love to our fellow men, or embraced with benevolence the whole family of mankind." The speculative branches of ancient philosophy about God, the universe, the human soul, he rejected as futile, along with all other speculations, and he judged that the ancient philosophers had indulged in dreams and fancies. The practical moral precepts given by Epictetus were useful but, apart from them, he labeled the universally revered Stoic philosophy as hypocrisy and grimace.

If ancient philosophy in its moral branch was largely defined by egocentric viewpoints, ancient government was certainly anything but a model. "History, in general," he stated, "only informs us what bad government is." And the main function of historical studies was exactly to become familiar with the rocks and shoals that threaten any course toward a better society. The Greek and Roman forms of government were conditioned in time and space; they were impracticable today. This he stated in 1823, warning a Greek patriot that the renaissance of liberated Greece might lead to such experiments. The governments of Greek city-states were not really governments respecting the rights and liberties of peoples. "The government of Athens, for example, was that of the people of one city making laws for the whole country subjected to them. That of Lacedaemon was the rule of military monks over the laboring class of the people, reduced to abject slavery." The petty city-states of Greece were agitated by continuous and violent strife between aristocrats and democrats. He thought that the smaller the society, the more bitter the dissensions within it. The "vindictive passions" of the Greek republics he hoped would not be found on the broader scene of the great American continent. These small states were continually at war with each other and their confederacies, so carefully studied by the authors of the *Federalist,* are hardly mentioned anywhere in Jefferson's writings, though he was familiar with them from his study of Polybius.

The Greek writings on the theory of government were without much value, for the simple reason that the viewpoint of their authors was conditioned by what they had experienced. Regarding the *Politics* of Aristotle he wrote: "But so different was the style of society then, and with those people, from what it is now and with us, that I think little edification can be obtained from their writings on the subject of government. They had just ideas of the value of personal liberty, but none at all of the structure of government best calculated to preserve it. They knew no medium between a democracy (the only pure republic, but impracticable beyond the limits of a town) and an abandonment of themselves to an aristocracy, or a tyranny independent of the people. It seems not to have occurred that where the citizens cannot meet to transact their business in person, they alone have the right to choose the agents who shall transact it, and that in this way a republican, or popular government, of the second grade of purity, may be exercised over any extent of country."

The situation was the same with the Romans. The entries in the *Commonplace Book* show that Jefferson had early and firmly established the view that the beginnings of representative government in Great Britain had created a completely new foundation. Before that, good government had been impossible. In 1774 he copied a passage from a historical essay on the British constitution which had been published a few years earlier, contrasting the British Parliament with the Roman Senate, which was not a popularly selected body. The Roman Republic, so revered by many men of his century, offered to him a picture even darker than that of the Greek city states. Even in his early book, the *Notes on Virginia,* he characterized the institution of Roman dictatorship as a necessary part of a republic torn by factions and governed by "a heavy-handed unfeeling aristocracy, over a people ferocious, and rendered desperate by poverty and wretchedness." And with Caesar, dictatorship ended finally and unavoidably in monarchy. In later years, after having read all the letters of Cicero, he conveyed his impressions to John Adams in a remarkable letter: ". . . what was that government which the virtues of Cicero were so zealous to restore, and the ambition of Caesar to subvert? And if Caesar had been as virtuous as he was daring and sagacious, what could he, even in the plenitude of his usurped power, have done to lead his fellow citizens into good government? I do not say to *restore it,* because they never had it, from the rape of the Sabines to the ravages of the Caesars. If their people indeed had been, like ourselves, enlightened, peaceable, and really free, the answer would be obvious. 'Restore independence to all your foreign conquests, relieve Italy from the government of the rabble of Rome, consult it as a nation entitled to self-government, and do its will.' But steeped in corruption, vice and venality, as the whole nation was (and nobody had done more than Caesar to corrupt it,) what could even Cicero, Cato, Brutus have done, had it been referred to them to establish a good government for their country? They had no ideas of government themselves, but of their degenerate Senate, nor the people of liberty, but of the factious opposition of their Tribunes. They had afterwards their Tituses, their Trajans and Antoninusses, who had the will to make them happy, and the power to mould their government into a good and permanent form. But it would seem as if they could not see their way clearly to do it." By that time, he concluded, the people of Rome were so demoralized that it would have taken at least a generation or two to educate them, and within that period tyrants like Nero and Commodus would have quashed the whole process. He put himself in the hopeless situation of Cicero, Cato, and Brutus and, bravely facing it, he stated the fact that delightful Italy throughout its history to the present day had never seen a free and rational government. He was impressed with a lack of political courage on the part of individuals during the Roman Empire. And Roman provincial government, with the oppression of its officials and its pre-eminently military character, seemed to him to present an unfavorable picture which contrasted sharply with the grandeur of the monuments it had left in southern France.

Ancient history acquainted its assiduous student very thoroughly with the dark side of humanity. And the fearless pursuit of truth could not stop short of the traditional worship of the so-called great men in history. Like other eighteenth century radicals, Jefferson had a tendency to dethrone heroes.

Plutarch's *Parallel Lives* of "great men" of antiquity was a cherished book of his age and had been so for a long time: a storehouse of the examples of virtue of which the century was so fond. It is notable that Jefferson seems to have had personal reservations about the value of that famous book, and nowhere is its use apparent in his writings beyond mere references to facts. These are biographies of kings, statesmen, generals, of men of action. Those were the "great men" of history in the schoolbooks of his day. Jefferson formed his own judgment—and greatness crumbled away before it. If one looked at it humanly Agamemnon and Menelaus, Odysseus and Diomedes and all the rest of them might be called "puny heroes who boiled their own kettles before the walls of Troy." Alexander the Great was no better than his father, Philip of Macedonia. The British might make the government of Philip, the conqueror of Greece, their model. Alexander was an advocate of brute will and he, Caesar and Augustus were the devilish models of Napoleon. The daring and sagacious Caesar and Augustus were both "parricides." Augustus, the founder of the Roman Empire, was a scoundrel, though Jefferson's cherished poets, Horace and Virgil, praised and exalted him. He would, of course, acknowledge military genius and political skill in these men. But they and most of the other "great" generals and rulers were fundamentally bad like the whole abominable "race of kings." This race decayed further by inbreeding, inertia and faulty education in hereditary monarchies. To be sure, there were exceptions and benevolent individuals. In Jefferson's day the young czar, Alexander of Russia, seemed to be such an exception and to try his best to reform Russia and make her people happy. Among the Roman emperors there had been such men as Titus, Trajan, Antoninus Pius and Marcus Aurelius, the author of a philosophical confession which Jefferson liked to read. But they were not strong enough to be called great.

There had been wise men among the statesmen of old; Solon, cautiously advancing on the road toward progress and popular government, was such a man in his opinion, a statesman, a philosopher, a man of affairs and a poet. Some of the Plutarchian figures had become veritable allegories of virtue; Aristides, the just, and Cato, the idol of stoic republican uprightness. Jefferson generally did not indulge in the quotation of these symbols of historical virtuousness which were cherished by his age. When he did so, it was done with a characteristic qualification based on realistic appraisal of the concrete individual. There was Cato, for instance. Jefferson shared his age's admiration for the republican simplicity, the stern fight for principles, the scrupulous honesty of which Cato was a symbol. But in early years he had read Plutarch's *Life of Cato,* as well as Cato's own book on agriculture. And he had formed the correct opinion that in practical life Cato, like the rest of his class, had been a ruthless exploiter of land and labor. Thus calling his master and fatherly friend George Wythe the "Cato of his country," he would add "without the avarice of the Roman."

Traditional greatness was dependent on mental standards of posterity. Plato was to him. an outstanding example of this. Even the Romans, with their natural common sense, even Cicero had been taken in by the already established reputation of Plato. He, Jefferson, did not hesitate to dethrone what seemed to him false greatness, neither in this case nor in that of powerful political individuals. If one did not admire power for power's sake or, for that matter, mental speculative ability as such, there was no reason to admire those who were strong in one direction or the other. St. Paul became to his violently antispeculative and anticlerical mind "the great Coryphaeus" of "a band of dupes and impostors" who had depraved the true doctrines of Jesus by mere mental agility.

Hence, Jefferson was inclined to smash cherished idols of humanity. That happened wherever basic issues were at stake, and he saw in the admiration of posterity a force opposed to truth, as he perceived it. But even where great individuals of history were congenial to him in basic issues, he brushed the dust of veneration off their images and in these instances the result of his concrete appraisal could be the vital recapturing of a personality. This is the case with Cicero.

Jefferson had looked up to Cicero as to a preceptor, from the days of his boyhood. Temperamentally, a natural bond existed between these two philosophers in action—eclectic critics, humane Humanists, great letter writers that they were. Even in later years, Jefferson would incidentally and conventionally call Cicero "the father of eloquence and philosophy." But in the realm of oratory itself Cicero was not a model to be followed without qualification and his abilities were but limited. Jefferson contrasted his imaginative oratory with the dense logic of Demosthenes, which he preferred. Ciceronian oratory, he thought, might be good enough for the bar, but it was decidedly detrimental if used on the broader stage of political action. The philosopher, Cicero, had been duped by Plato. As Jefferson became converted to the elevated, truly moral doctrines of Epicureanism, he accused Cicero of having indulged in caricatures of that great philosophy. Cicero, moreover, had flaws of dilettantism of which he did not approve. For example, he had written commentaries on his consulship in Greek, which deservedly perished unknown. But he was virtuous and animated by an exalted patriotism; he was "able, learned, laborious, practised in the business of the world, and honest." Yet he was "diffuse, vapid, rhetorical." His candid character associated itself as an accomplice of the hypocritical Stoics in attacking Epicurus. From all these statements it results that Cicero, who through his extensive writings and personal effusions happens to be the best known character of antiquity, was not great. He was a gifted, charming, struggling human being, "enchanting," as Jefferson called him. It is one of the best and fairest realistic appraisals of Cicero ever made. It steers the right middle course between the uncritical worship of the old-fashioned classicists and the hypercritical condemnation of modern historians.

Jefferson's realistic approach to the traditionally great men of history—rooted as it is in his eighteenth century radicalism—again anticipates Jacob Burckhardt's criticism of greatness. Burckhardt, indeed, did away with the popular notion of great men of action, half a century later. To him true greatness became ultimate creativeness in thought and art. The only truly great men were the founders of religion and, in second degree, the thinkers, poets and artists. To Jefferson, too, Jesus emerged as the greatest individual of history. His identification of morality with religion made him the greatest moralist. Socrates and Epicurus were great in the same sense, though not to the same degree. In early days, he had copied a passage from Cicero's *Tusculan Dialogues* stating that glory should follow virtue like a shadow and that it is without value unless it has that connection with morality. The "seeds of genius which nature sows with even hand through every age and country, and which need only soil and season to germinate," had appeared in many an individual of the ancient world. But virtuous men who were struggling along in the right direction like Cicero, Cato, and Brutus, did not find the soil and season. It is also obvious that the scientists, writers and poets, the culturally creative men of antiquity, were truly great to him; especially Hippocrates and Euclid, Homer (in whose individual personality he believed) and Virgil, Euripides and Horace, Thucydides and Tacitus. There is that well-known incident which Jefferson himself reports. At one of the parties which he gave as secretary of state, his great opponent Hamilton noted three portraits on the wall and asked who they were. Jefferson told him they were Bacon, Locke and Newton, three of the greatest men, all three of them thinkers and scientists. Hamilton reflected a moment and then stated his opinion that to him the greatest man was Caesar. In the sphere of political history of antiquity, there were, for Jefferson, no truly great men.

As to the individual in history, the ancient world, too, had revealed the dark rather than the bright side of humanity. The traditionally great personality more often than not wore a cloak which he did not deserve and which fame and superstition embroidered as time went on. Truly great men could not easily find their way to improve the world by action.

The review of facts and the just reflection arising out of them nevertheless was not to lead the student to despair. They should give him hope that as he became wise through experience he might gather increasing strength to go on in the right direction. In addition, as Jefferson saw it in society, as in nature, providence had established the order of things so that most evils were the means of producing some good.

That was only a slight comfort. But man had the original stuff within himself to do away with the evils that history presented. His natural reasoning power could assert itself by preventing him from committing the faults he had witnessed. However frustrated, his innate moral sense had been a compass toward the good throughout history. His instinctive sense of beauty had achieved great things in the arts. All these are fundamental creeds of the age of enlightenment to which Jefferson belonged. And the belief in moral sense and reason prevented him from despairing about progress as old John Adams did. In his early excerpts, he had copied a passage from Euripides expressing faith in God's having "a scope with man." True, he shared this faith in an innate moral instinct with the men of his time. Yet his own source may have been Cicero, from whom he had early copied the statement that "there are seeds of virtue in our minds which should be allowed to mature; instead, under the present conditions of education, this natural instinct *(instinctus naturalis)* is oppressed and depraved." History could serve as a tool to develop that moral sense. With all its setbacks and reversals, it revealed that fact. And it is at this point that Jefferson's road parted from that of many of his contemporaries. Science and the arts, the great creative objectivations of reason and imagination, might at times go hand in hand with bad social conditions. They might withdraw into a sphere of isolated contemplation. But science was progressive by its own nature. In that respect at least, "Your own consciousness must place you as far before our ancestors as in the rear of our posterity," he told Adams. And violence—military, civil or ecclesiastical—can only temporarily repress truth and reason which are eternal. Indeed, he liked "the dreams of the future better than the history of the past."

But that past, the ancient world, above all, was a storehouse not only of experience of the dark side of humanity. It was a unique storehouse, too, of visions of its bright side. In the spheres of thought, of poetry and art, the books and works of the ancients were a source of other adventures, great and more enjoyable than the gathering of historical facts and reflection on them. Here was the field for another ever-expanding experience of the creative powers which were the natural endowment of man nurtured by true civilization: reason, moral instinct and artistic taste.

PART III

Reason and Imagination

CHAPTER 8

Freedom of Thought

A LONG CONVERSATION with the ancients continued for more than seventy years and revealed to Thomas Jefferson a dark picture of the past. It strengthened his deep-rooted skepticism and pessimism, which were so uniquely balanced by an unshakable faith in the ultimate destinies and abilities of man. In fact, although reading the ancients led to grim and realistic reflections, it was, at the same time, a source of strength and delight. Bacon's three faculties of the human mind—memory, reason and imagination—were equally strengthened and enriched by conversing with the Greeks and Romans. He used these three faculties for the classification of his precious books, so many of which were the works of classical historians, poets, philosophers, scientists, technical writers. Memory, the recorder of history, warned humanity of the dangers inherent in social life. Reason and imagination, forcefully expressed in the works of the ancients, books and buildings alike, gave enjoyment and hope.

A few years after his retirement from political life Jefferson wrote: "It is true that I am tired of practical politics, and happier while reading the history of ancient than of modern times . . . and take refuge in the histories of other times, where, if they also furnish their Tarquins, their Catilines and Caligulas, their stories are handed to us under the brand of a Livy, a Sallust and a Tacitus, and we are comforted with the reflection that the condemnation of all succeeding generations has confirmed the censures of the historian, and consigned their memories to everlasting infamy, a solace we cannot have with the Georges and Napoleons but by anticipation."

Even in the realm of social history, the great ancient historians emerged as free moral judges and carried the reader into a sphere of positive values. The true and great fruits of reason and imagination in works of science and art were ever-encouraging sources of strength. John Adams might be "weary of contemplating nations from the lowest and most beastly degradations of human life to the highest refinement of civilization," and of philosophers, theologians, politicians and historians, who were "immense masses of absurdities, vices, and lies." Thomas Jefferson would agree about most of the theologians and politicians, but certainly not about the refinements of civilization, philosophers and historians. In the classics he found not only useful facts but "good principles" as well. Scientific studies were in themselves precious and delightful. To read Greek and Latin authors was a "sublime luxury," and luxury was at least as justifiable in science as in architecture, painting, gardening or the other arts. The study of the ancient world in itself was such a science. But it included, too, the great experience of works of art. Reason and imagination were equally strengthened by conversation with the ancients.

The essential point was that, with all their social faults, the Greek and Roman nations had been "civilized and learned." In his admiration for antique civilization, Jefferson was a true descendant of the Humanistic tradition of the Renaissance, and there is nothing exceptional in it. His outlook on the course of the history of civilization from the antique through his own age of enlightenment was also generally shared by men of that age.

To him as to almost every other Humanist from the Renaissance on, "dark ages . . . intervened between ancient and modern civilization." "Gothic fanaticism," opposed to common sense and the "Gothic idea that we are to look backwards instead of forwards," were heirlooms from those dark medieval times. With the "barbaric" invasions of late antiquity, ignorance had spread illiteracy and put everything into the hands of power and priestcraft. In Greece, the Moslem rule had added the complete extinction of culture which continued even during his lifetime. In the west, the Renaissance had revived science and art, progressing towards the enlightenment of the eighteenth century, although still conditioned and limited by traditional forces of wealth, power and priestcraft. To the Greeks the world was "indebted for the lights which originally led ourselves out of Gothic darkness." That first of civilized nations had at least "presented examples of what man should be." The Greeks had merits that were "still resting, as a heavy debt, on the shoulders of the living and the future races of men."

All this is part of a traditional concept. And when Jefferson advocated the use of an antique building as a model for the Capitol of Virginia and initiated a new type of classicism in architecture, he could point to the approbation of centuries and the universal esteem in which that antique building was held.

The preromantic denunciation of the Middle Ages which Jefferson voiced with most of his contemporaries is to us a phenomenon of the remote past and of a world no longer ours. Even in his young days, it had begun to disintegrate. And the garden Romanticism of English country houses had caught Jefferson's own imagination. A Gothic chapel of "ancient" appearance was among the features of his youthful dream of a garden and family burial ground and, even in later years, he admitted Gothic forms for garden pavilions along with the classical. But that was only part of a play with the picturesque in the sphere of nature rather than in that of civilization and was, as it were, opposed to the dignified monumental expression of civilized man. He detested the romantic historical novel and, not without connection with his aversion to the Middle Ages, Cervantes' *Don Quixote,* that enchanting satire on feudal folly, was one of his most cherished books.

But in spite of its almost archaic character, Jefferson's antithesis between the high antique civilizations and the dark Middle Ages which was unusually strong even in his age, has features of its own which make it at once Jeffersonian and modern. One of these features is his remoteness from a cult of antiquity as such. What he admired and cherished in ancient civilization, he saw and experienced against the background of a dark, cruel, unhappy social history. This, his historical pessimism and realism, prevented him from any stale idealization of antique life in general. And it also kept him from being impressed with the current worship of the Greeks as the people who had brought beauty into the world in contrast with the degenerate and tasteless Romans. He possessed the main work of Winckelmann, the great exponent of that new, aesthetic Hellenism; and there is no doubt that he read it. Clérisseau, the neoclassic architect with whom he worked in Paris on the plans for the Capitol of Virginia, had been one of Winckelmann's intimate friends. And yet there is no touch—least of all in his own architectural creations—of the worship of the Greeks in that sense and in the sense of the British aesthetic Hellenists. On the contrary, in the realm of architecture he remained an unflinching admirer of the Romans in open opposition to the Greek revival that during his later years had been brought from England to the American shores. He gave both the Greeks and the Romans their fair share of misery and greatness as he saw them. And what he saw in both directions is his own, and neither traditional nor conventional.

The second especially Jeffersonian and progressive note

in his contrast between the dark Middle Ages and the high achievements of ancient civilization was his emphasis on freedom. As he saw it, freedom of reason and imagination —however faulty the social structure of antiquity—was allowed to develop fully in the ancient world of creative thought and art In the Middle Ages, that was not so, because then even sciences and arts were subservient to religion, wealth and power. And even in modern times, since the revival of arts and letters in the Renaissance, there had never been complete and unhampered freedom from the shackles of churches and political powers. For the first time since antiquity such freedom seemed to appear in the enlightenment of his, the eighteenth century. Even in the social-political sphere, the Greeks had at least "just ideas of the value of personal liberty," though they did not implement them in government. The "purest times of Greece and Rome" had decidedly shown a "spirit of freedom." His own time had not yet quite achieved that stage. He hoped "that the human mind will some day get back to the freedom it enjoyed two thousand years ago."

Freedom of the human mind meant freedom of imagination but, above all, freedom of science. Social freedom, in fact, was "the first born daughter of science." The Greeks at least had had a complete freedom of science, the main objectives of which were the "freedom and happiness of man." Ancient scientists had produced works in history, ethics, mathematics, astronomy, natural history and many other fields which were still invaluable. They, in themselves, made a thorough study of the classics desirable to the generally educated as well as to the professional man of modern times. Antique medicine, for example, he considered as good a code of the medical "art as has been given us to this day." It offered "a treasure of facts and sound observations." If one added modern observations and discoveries, one might establish a perfectly good modern medicine. He in his day could not anticipate the tremendous scientific development of the nineteenth and twentieth centuries. But under the aspect of his own time, his admiration of Greek science, even in this particular area, was not unjustified. His keen mathematical interest made him a student of the original writings of Euclid as well as of Newton. And in Euclid he saw the realization of a true scientific language never "using a superfluous word."

If freedom was the first-born daughter of science, science contained the seed of freedom, even if it could not grow under given circumstances. In France he witnessed a flourishing state of science and the arts within a society full of political oppression and moral decay. And he became a witness and counselor in the struggle of the French people to make the scientific seeds of freedom germinate in a soil plowed up by revolution.

Science was the realm of reason. And as such it was relatively detached from the conditions of social life. It could carry on to some extent, as it did in France, if reason was allowed to operate. But there were definite limits to that. Jefferson's statements about science and freedom imply that science itself might develop under such conditions only so long as it did not attack the moral foundations of the society in which it found itself. Ancient thinkers, indeed, had gone far in science, but they had also been allowed to speculate on morality. Implementation of those thoughts on morality had been only partial, hesitating, and never sweeping and successful. Yet, by and large, their thoughts and books had been allowed to spread and develop.

Considerations of moral values were found even in the earliest great books of antiquity. "That a change in the relations in which a man is placed should change his ideas of moral right or wrong, is neither new, nor peculiar to the color of the blacks. Homer tells us it was so two thou-

sand six hundred years ago." In his early days, his excerpts
from ancient poets and philosophers in the so-called *Literary
Bible* are fraught with sententious statements regarding
moral rights, duties and crimes. And along with the concrete transmission of facts, the moral reflections of ancient
historians made them preferable to later historiographers.
"Tacitus," he said, "I consider as the first writer in the
world without a single exception. His book is a compound
of history and morality of which we have no other example."

But Tacitus was the unflinching republican critic of the
power of Roman emperors, their suppression of personal
liberty, and their attacks on the freedom of thought and
speech. Again, Jefferson's interest in moral reflections and
their connection with history is a general feature of his
age. Yet, the direction which it took is specifically his.
Liberty was to him the first moral principle and truth,
probity and honor followed. In Tacitus, the evil of tyranny
was drastically exposed as the root of moral disintegration.

This doctrine of liberty as the natural soil of morality
connects Jefferson's interest in the moral thought of the
ancient world with his appraisal of its respect for personal
liberty. But the connection between liberty and morality
is also related to his conviction that man's moral thought
and behavior are the fruit of his natural "moral sense"
which Jefferson added to the physical senses as a providen-
tial companion of and balance to natural instinct for and
right of liberty. Among his early excerpts from Greek reading, one finds a quotation from Euripides: "We know the
morally good, but fail to do it from lethargy or preferring
other pleasures to it." And he also copied a passage from
Cicero referring to an *instinctus naturalis* for virtue which
could be developed or oppressed by education. The ancients, then, had discovered the principle which he adapted
and developed when he studied the Scotch realist Lord

Kames. Justice is "instinct and innate." And the "moral sense is as much a part of our constitution as that of feeling, seeing, or hearing; as a wise creator must have seen to be necessary in an animal destined to live in society; . . . every human mind feels pleasure in doing good to another."

This sixth sense is the true foundation of morality "and not το καλον, truth etc. as fanciful writers have imagined," he stated with one of his polemical inferences against Platonism. This moral sense operates via reason. But unlike science proper, that amount of reason called common sense is sufficient for its development. Under this aspect of practical morality, truth, the sphere of science, is an important branch of morality. "But presented as its foundation, it is as if a tree taken up by the roots, had its stem reversed in the air, and one of its branches planted in the ground."

Religion—that is, love of God—is but another branch of morality. The foundations of life are in "sentiment" and not in science, and the human heart is the seat of morality, while the head develops its reasonable branch, science. For the sake of convenience, Jefferson continued in his library classification to subordinate moral philosophy with the subdivisions of ethics and jurisprudence to reason, as the related faculty of the human mind. But it would have been more logical to replace that Baconian category by his moral sense, which seemed to be the root rather than the offspring of organized reason. On this foundation Jefferson appraised the merits of two major branches of what he recognized as moral philosophy, the jurisprudence and ethics of the ancients.

The sense of justice was to him, as to Lord Kames, not a convention but a natural social instinct that is part of the moral instinct of man. That instinct was the foundation of all legal systems which were conditioned, in their superstructure, by the standards of given historical societies. Reasonable development of that sense by jurisprudence was relative and defined by historical circumstances. In the ancient world, then, it would seem that the high evolution of enlightenment on the part of the lawgivers clashed with two conditions of their times: their imperfect notions of free government and remnants of the brute laws of nature which survived in such features as the institution of slavery, the omnipotence of the father over his children, and so on.

In Greece, he judged, there had been wise lawgivers who cautiously moved in the right direction like Solon, the Athenian of old. He did not and could not know much about the legal systems of the Greek city-states and Hellenistic kingdoms which are better known today, due to the assembling of shreds and fragments preserved in inscriptions and on papyrus. In his day, the primary source of knowledge of Greek law was the forensic orations of Attic lawyers, nearly all of which he possessed, but they gave only glimpses of actual law. It was different with Roman law, the bulk of which was at hand in the systematic collections of the Byzantine Corpus Iuris. The Corpus Iuris was the bible of legal thought to the jurists of his age, and there is nothing unusual in Jefferson's high respect for Roman law. But to most jurists that respect was based on the actual validity of Roman legal norms ever since their reception into and mingling with Germanic and ecclesiastical law, and on the use of the refined logical deductions of Roman law as an exercise in and model of juridical argumentation. The eighteenth century lawyer Thomas Jefferson acknowledged both points of view. But the moralist Jefferson appraised the merits of Roman law, both as a historical ferment of legal development and as the relatively best expression of the innate sense of justice on a higher plane. Roman law was the legal system of a "nation highly civilized." At the same time, it incorporated and represented universal and natural notions of man about justice, so that the law of nature in its positive aspects, as well as the outlines of the laws of nations, international law, could be experienced in its precepts. But, above all, Roman law represented "the system of civil law most conformable with the principles of justice of any which has ever yet been established among men." In Roman law the innate human sense of justice had reasonably operated to the extent that it had covered most of the possible issues of litigation between citizens. Thus, it was understandable that it became a *ratio scripta,* codified reason and "the dictate, in all cases, of that sound reason which should constitute the law of every country."

The sense of justice was but one facet of the shining crystal of man's innate moral sense which would eventually lead humanity into a better social future. It was connected with man's sense of duty toward himself and toward others, with religion and the love of God. The "Aristides and Catos, the Penns and Tillotsons, Presbyterians and Baptists, will find themselves united in all principles which are in concert with the reason of the supreme mind."

Religion was to him only one expression of moral instinct, and he classified writings on religion under moral philosophy. With "the enlightened nations of antiquity," the idolatry and superstitions of their religions were, therefore, a corruption of reason. Religion, it would seem, was entirely a matter of personal experience to Jefferson, as far as faith in and beliefs about God were concerned. It was definitely not a matter of discussion and confession between men. He accepted a natural instinct which acknowledges divine power and which shows itself in the common consent of all peoples of history, regarding the existence of divinity. Cicero had condensed his own deistic viewpoint in that regard in sentences which he copied in early years. But beyond that, it was every man's own and most personal concern to evolve his ideas about God via thought, sentiment and experience. His own personal reticence in giving expression to his religious creed has veiled it behind a cloud not to be lifted, and it seems that he never talked about these things even to those closest to him. His explicit statements about matters of creed show only that he himself acknowledged a Supreme Being directing the world. For the rest, they are negative and opposed to what seemed to him to be incompatible with reason: polytheism, superstition, mystical speculation, the dogma of the Trinity. As to that, he thought that reason unites "all who cannot perceive the Geometrical logic of Euclid in the demonstrations of St. Athanasius, that three are one, and one is three; and yet that the one is not three nor the three one." To him that was not part of pure and original Christianity. Jefferson's continued adherence to and attendance at a Christian church makes it necessary to believe that, to his satisfaction, he was a Christian in his particular notion of the divine power, however much of the accumulated formulas of creed he rejected. But he never stated his ideas about God. From his point of view, one thing could be definitely said in favor of ancient religious life: the Greeks and Romans had no formulas of religious creed to be professed. "I have never permitted myself to meditate a specified creed. These formulas have been the bane and ruin of the Christian church, its own fatal invention. . . . The religions of antiquity had no particular formulas of creed. Those of the modern world none except those of the religionists calling themselves Christians, and even among these the Quakers have none."

Given Jefferson's approach to ever-broadening experience, it may be assumed that he regarded man's love for God as a continuous search rather than as a static conviction. Freedom of inquiry to be granted to the individual was its necessary foundation. And, as the ancients, by and large, did not require professions of religious creed, they also granted to the individual freedom of inquiry about God. With them the operations of the mind were not subject to the coercion of laws. And: "Had not the Roman government permitted free inquiry, Christianity could never have been introduced." It was only at the end of antiquity that the alliance between political power and the Church had stifled that freedom of inquiry.

Within that ancient world of mental freedom Jesus had conceived his sublime moral thoughts, and with Luther and Calvin, the beginning of enlightenment in the Reformation had made a step toward restoring the true and simple principles of his faith in the period of the rebirth of science and letters. What Jefferson allowed himself to discuss with others and eagerly investigated was not Jesus' ideas about God. Rather it was the most important branch of moral philosophy: our duties toward others. In this respect, Jesus was sublime and his moral ideas were fundamental to the progress of humanity. The Greek New Testament was the only —however indirect and imperfect—source of Jesus' original thoughts and words. He possessed and studied numerous editions of that primary Greek source, weighing the authority of the ancient writers and scrutinizing the philological accuracy of the textual tradition. He read the doctrines of Jesus, he frankly stated, as he read "those of other ancient and modern moralists, with a mixture of approbation and dissent." He did not accept the spiritualism of Jesus' faith. But Jesus' spiritualism, which recognized a supreme mind outside of rather than immanent in the world, was a matter of the relationship between a man and his God. In the basic sphere of morality, our relations to others, Jesus was more "pure, correct and sublime" than any other moralist.

All-embracing charity and the love of our fellow men were the great and fundamental moral virtues which Jesus had advocated. He was, therefore, the greatest moralist, and in Jefferson's judgment, the future of humanity depended on the universal acceptance of his doctrines. Man's natural moral instinct, if allowed to operate freely and reasonably, would, he trusted, spread truly Christian morality and mold society by means of it. And this process would automatically result in personal liberty and happiness, the development of good government, science and art.

Before and after Jesus there had been wise men and great moralists in the ancient world. The wisdom of Socrates was indisputable. And he highly esteemed the ethical writings of the ancients. Moralizing sentences from ancient poets and Cicero fill the pages of his early commonplace book, the so-called *Literary Bible*. His library included all the important and many of the obscure Greek and Roman texts on moral philosophy. In 1785, he recommended to young Peter Carr as the only books to study on morality, Epictetus, Xenophon's *Memorabilia*, Plato's *Socratic Dialogues* (at that time not yet condemned), Cicero, Marcus Aurelius and Seneca of old. Later, when he urged Priestley and started himself to compare the moral teachings of Jesus with those of the ancient philosophers, he eliminated the hated Plato but added Pythagoras. The very fact that he advocated this comparison of ancient moralists with Christian morality assigns to them the second place next to Jesus and above that of all later thinkers.

This appraisal was caused by Jefferson's ideas about the branches of morality. Duty toward God was a matter of personal experience, not to be dictated or even promoted by the thoughts and reflections of others. The duty of men toward each other was the most important, the social branch of morality, and Jesus was its great and unique teacher. In that branch the ancient philosophers, thinking and writing in a social world of imperfection, had been deficient. Here and there they had made sound reflections on friendship, clemency, justice and patriotism, for example. But those had been only timid steps in the right direction. None of them had risen to the high plane of all-embracing charity and love for fellow men. But there was a third branch of morality, that of man's duty toward himself, at once the realm of individual virtue and of ultimate individual happiness. And: "In this branch of philosophy they were really great."

The ancient philosophers gave admirable precepts for rendering the individual "impassible, and unassailable by the evils of life, and for preserving his mind in a state of constant serenity." Virtue equal to the government of man's own passions had been the objective of their writings. Practice of virtue in that sense of individual self-government was fully compatible with Christian philanthropy and charity. Combined with it, it would secure the happiness of oneself and of one's fellow men. The ultimate motive of this antique endeavor to secure personal happiness and self-perfection might have been man's egoism. As Euripides expressed it in a sentence which young Jefferson copied: "Everyone is apt to love himself more than his kin." That egoism clashed with man's moral sense, the sense of justice and charity. But, on a higher plane, directed by moral instinct and reason, even the selfish interest of the individual required virtue and self-control, which seemed to Thomas Jefferson the necessary complement to, if not base of, social morality.

In his early life, his innate experimental and eclectic approach had led him to seize the various expressions of ideas about morality found in ancient poets and in Cicero's writings without much thought about the ideological context to which they belonged. Statements of resignation to mortality and fate, about the value of abstaining from lust for material wealth and pleasure, the overcoming of pain and grief by a recognition of their temporary or imaginary character, fill the pages of his *Literary Bible*. It has been

noted that Stoic elements are strongly represented in that
collection. But Jefferson, due to his sensualism and emotional sentiment, could not adhere to a philosophy which
aimed at an aloofness and detachment from the natural
impulses and passions of man. His independent judgment
soon led him to repudiate Platonism, too, which was an
important element in Cicero and was the cherished philosophy of his master and friend George Wythe. His aversion
to Plato as the originator of speculative philosophy and
Christian Platonism was combined with his opposition to
a philosophy which degraded the life of the senses and
human passions to an inferior sphere. Plato's identification
of the good and the beautiful in a realm of abstract ideas was
as alien to his basic concepts as was his social morality, which
subordinated and sacrificed the human individual to the
interest of the organization of society in an all-powerful
state. In later years he took his deliberate and definite stand
against the Stoics, too, though he continued to esteem the
practical moral precepts which were advocated by Epictetus, Seneca and Marcus Aurelius. They were good,
inasmuch as their warnings against excesses of vice, of sensual pleasures, of uncontrolled passions, of devotion to
unstable external values and so on, resulted in benefits to
human morality.

But among the ancient philosophical systems he could
accept only that of Epicurus. He had met it in his early
reading in Cicero's polemical statements about Epicureanism and, positively, in Horace. That Horace, next to Homer,
remained throughout his life his most cherished poet, was
above all caused by his profession of Epicurean ethics.
Indicative of the future pattern of thought which Epicurean
philosophy was to enter into in Thomas Jefferson's mind,
is a passage which he copied from Horace's *Satires* in his
twenties: "Who then is free? The wise man, who is lord
over himself, whom neither poverty, nor death nor bonds

affright, who bravely defies his passions, and scorns ambition, who in himself, is a whole, smoothed and rounded, so that nothing from outside can rest on the polished surface, and against whom Fortune in her onset is ever defeated." About fifty years later, the Sage of Monticello recommended this very passage as a directing motive to a body of young students, together with one of similar meaning from Cicero.

To set man free, that was the ultimate goal. And freedom was not only the first-born daughter of science, in general, it was particularly enhanced by moral philosophy. The lines just quoted from Horace happen to advocate the Stoic suppression of passions and an aloofness with which the poet does not identify his own personal philosophy. Indeed, in general, he adhered to the Epicurean ethical creed, and it is exactly this creed which Jefferson came to share consciously with him in his later years. Epicureanism had been attacked and libeled by ancient philosophers, the Stoics and even Cicero, and a popular notion of this philosophy as advocating pleasure and material self-indulgence, was and still is abroad. It was logical that Hamilton would accuse Thomas Jefferson of being a voluptuous Epicurean, opposed to Stoic virtue. Yes, he was opposed in his later life to the Stoic concept of virtue which denied the positive value of human passion, desire and enjoyment of the things that are good in this world. He himself thought that the Stoics were simply hypocrites; their basic concept was alien to the real world and to the nature of man. On the other hand, to Jefferson, to Horace and to any other serious student of Epicurus, his philosophy was "frugal of vicious indulgence, and fruitful of virtue." It is true, this philosophy aimed not only at achieving serenity and tranquillity of the human mind, as did all the other philosophies of antiquity. It also aimed at bodily ease. As the latter had to be achieved by good and healthy, enjoyable but not extravagant living, tranquillity of the mind, the *summum bonum* of the Epicureáns was only increased by it.

The acknowledgment of the positive values of physical life finds its expression in "materialism," and in this respect contemporary philosophies—especially the ideas of Cabanis—strengthened Jefferson's Epicureanism. The popular notion of that philosophy was wrong. Materialism was not to be misunderstood as a belief in material values as opposed to intellectual, moral and aesthetic values. Philosophical materialism, as accepted by Jefferson, meant a conviction that there was no dualistic contrast between ideas and reality, spirit and flesh, and that man was a biological unit which embraced body and mind in an inseparable whole. He therefore arrived at a denial of the immortality of the human soul independent from the physical vessel of its body. Quoting Aristotle, he held that the mind operated only by stimulus of the senses. Not abstract and transcendental reason but sensual experience was the one certain fact about man. Descarte's axiom, *"cogito ergo sum,"* he adapted to himself in the modified form "I feel, therefore I exist." This materialism did not seem to him to conflict with Christian morality. Jesus, personally, had been a spiritualist in his concept of a transcendental divine being instead of a God immanent in the world. But as to man, he thought, Jesus, too, had acknowledged his physiological-intellectual unity, and materialism in this sense had been the common belief of pagan poets as well as the early Church Fathers.

Above all, Epicurean philosophy, instead of hypocritically denying and suppressing the values of human sentiment and passions, acknowledged them as positive. Passions were not harmful; they constituted the true life of man. Desires and passions were the very life of man's body and man's mind. Epicurean philosophy taught how to govern desires and passions by reason, by a correct appraisal of consequences. It taught how to keep human passions alive in an equilibrium by means of natural checks, and thus how to make them positive tools of the happiness of man and of the richness of life. "And the perfection of the moral character is, not in a stoical apathy, so hypocritically vaunted, and so untruly too, because impossible, but in a just equilibrium of all the passions." It was primarily on this ground that he considered "the genuine (not the imputed) doctrines of Epicurus as containing everything rational in moral philosophy which Greece and Rome have left us."

To understand the context in which the Epicurean doctrine of the equilibrium of human passions is placed in Jefferson's thought, it is necessary to keep in mind that the individual happiness thus secured was to him unavoidably connected with social happiness resulting from the practice of Christian charity. This combination of Epicureanism and Christianity which Jefferson professed has, on the surface, the aspect of a paradox which it was not to him. The tree of morality was a living, growing plant to him, and its branches could move out in different directions from the common root of moral sense which availed itself of the faculty of reason, a natural endowment of the mind.

CHAPTER 9

Forceful Imagination

THE HUMANISTIC CONFLICT between pagan civilization and Christian religion had found a solution above and beyond the many attempts to project Christian ideals into pagan thought through symbolism and allegory, or to impose pagan speculation on Christian faith. Thomas Jefferson's synthesis of Epicureanism and Christianity allowed for full, rich, earthly enjoyment and development of sensual and intellectual life. It freed him from nostalgia for a lost world of thought and beauty. It allowed the fulfillment of personal life within the destiny of mankind which had been ordained by the invisible supreme mind, creative of and directing the world.

But the tree of morality could extend its branches only if it availed itself of memory, for instance, in the recording of facts, in natural and human history, to guide and admonish by experience. It had to use the faculty of reason to reflect and to establish principles. It also had to exploit the driving power of imagination, the third Baconian faculty of the human mind. Reason and imagination, as it were, had to co-operate in another balance of creative forces. Jefferson held with Locke, for instance, that language was the vehicle of ideas. But it was a sensual vehicle and its very life was expanding imagination, by the sole means of which reason as well as memory could become articulate and the moral sense could crystallize principles. His own Declaration of Independence, a document of moral principles, reasonably stated in an enchanting, imaginative language, had been, as he termed it, but "the genuine effusion of the soul of our country at that time." The true teachings of Jesus, pure morality, could be recaptured among the accumulations of other men's thoughts in the New Testament by the criterion of a "stamp of the eloquence and fine imagination" which had been his. The elevated moral principles of Cicero made the reader enthusiastic by virtue of the power of his pen. Tacitus was a great recorder of historical memory, and a reasonable reflector on human events animated by high moral principles. But the imaginative power of his personal style was his medium of recording facts as well as of presenting reflections to his reader. The realm of poetry included didactic verse and his guide toward Epicureanism, Horace, was classed under that category in his library.

Nevertheless, the human faculty of imagination was in itself something different from both reason and memory, though both of them had to avail themselves of its powers, as did the moral sense, in order to become articulate. Imagination was, as it were, prompted by a second sense —the aesthetic sense—taste. Taste, too, was a natural endowment of man; it was definitely not to be confounded with morality, as Plato and some eighteenth century men did. "We have indeed an innate sense of what we call beautiful, but that is exercised chiefly on subjects addressed to the fancy, whether through the eye in visible forms, as landscape, animal figure, dress, drapery, architecture, the composition of colors, etc., or to the imagination directly, as imagery, style, or measure in prose or poetry, or whatever else constitutes the domain of criticism or taste, a faculty entirely distinct from the moral one." It thus was an "innocent enjoyment" to read ancient poetry; it secured a richness of "delight" not obtainable elsewhere. And within the framework of his Epicurean philosophy, enjoyment and delight, if not harmful, were positive things, part of the birthright of man who is endowed with an innate sense of beauty.

It is clear, then, that unlike the idealistic philosophers of old and of his time, Jefferson did not believe that the primary function of the arts was to make man virtuous. Like Goethe, he saw in them not a quasi-medical institution to purge men from vices, but a positive contribution to the unfolding of personality by the experience of beauty. But in the organism of the human microcosm, works of imagination might well be used as another and especially powerful leaven toward moral experience. While it was by no means confined to that function, some amount of imagination was not only needed for making moral reflections articulate, but pure works of art could incidentally convey more powerful experiences of good and evil in concrete form than actual happenings or records of history.

In his early years, he had copied many sentences of moral philosophy from ancient poems. Behind them, one may gather, was the experience of the superhuman stature of passions in virtue and vice, particularly in his reading of the most passionate of the ancient dramatists, Euripides. At that time, he was still conditioned by a common pragmatism which aimed to abstract moral rules from Romance, Tragedy, Comedy, and Epistolography via the "sympathetic emotion of virtue." Later, he judged that the free power of imagination was in some respects able to promote morality by plastical experience of great passions, good and evil. Works "of imagination . . . have this advantage over history that the incidents of the former may be dressed in the most interesting form, while those of the latter must be confined to fact. They cannot therefore present virtue in the best and vice in the worst forms possible, as the former may." This he wrote in 1800, and it may not be pure coincidence that during the last twenty-five years of his life, one no longer finds a single statement advocating the function of works of imagination in a purely moral context. In early years, following a more general pattern of his time, he had, indeed, considered fiction to be useful to promote the principles and practices of virtue. In his old age he admitted only that a poetical dress of wisdom might be "more acceptable to the fancy of the juvenile" character than a statement in scientific prose. Yet he said this at a time when he continued enthusiastically to read Greek and Latin poetry. Poetry, then, was the realm of pure beauty. It offered a natural experience to man, who was endowed with an innate sense of beauty. Contact with works of imagination was a necessity like breathing the clear air on his mountaintop, smelling the fragrance of his cherished flowers—yes, and eating a good meal. Was it art for art's sake? Hardly so, because it was a natural and ultimately necessary part of human experience. In Jefferson's opinion the enjoyment of beauty was interwoven with and inseparable from the exercise of all the faculties of the body and mind, within the microcosm of individual human life.

Experience was the word for it, as it was the key word for the concern of human memory with the records of history. That experience extended from the depths of human emotions to the glamour of physical shape, sound and color.

Knowledge of the human heart was the true province of that great branch of the tree of imagination, poetry. In the last years of his life Homer, the Greek dramatists and Virgil, along with his Epicurean Horace, with Dante, Corneille, Shakespeare and Milton, were his continuous companions. The Bible and the three great Greek tragedians were his last reading when the shadows closed down upon him. In his youth the tangible and concrete characterizations of the Roman Terence had particularly appealed to him, so that such characters as the bragging soldier Thrason remained fixed human types in his mind. Later, the enlarged stature of the figures of Greek tragedy and of Shakespeare with their sweeping passions appealed more to him.

The epic enlargement of Homer, Virgil, Dante and Milton, that continuous line derived from the Greek ancestor, was equally fraught with the sweeping emotion and gesture of passionate men. Aboriginal Homeric concepts of human behavior had early become real and concrete to him in the simple dignity of American Indians. The greatness of Homeric similes in which man's relationship to nature was cast in forms of analogy had also captured his imagination at the same time. Man's bewilderment before the multitude of things was illustrated to the Greek poet, Theocritus, by Homer's simile of the woodcutter on Mount Ida who found himself among so many great trees that it was hard to choose the right one. Jefferson used that simile to express his own bewilderment in the face of contrasting opinions. As time went on, Homer and his monumental rendering of human nature became to him the essence of poetical imagination. "When young any composition pleases which unites a little sense, some imagination, and some rhythm, in doses however small. But as we advance in life these things fall off one by one, and I suspect, we are left at last with only Homer and Virgil, perhaps with Homer alone. He like 'Hope travels on, nor quits us when we die.'" This was said in connection with Homeric verse and its great rhythmical power. "Poetical fancy," "sublime imagination," a "lofty and overwhelming diction," those were the earmarks of Homeric poetry which, as Jefferson stated in his autobiography, had reminded him of Homer when he listened in his youth to Patrick Henry's famous oration. Emphasis, not on classical or alleged classical restraint, but on vitality and overwhelming strength of imagination in Greek poetry is evident. And that, at a time when most classicists were looking for sober measure and dignified grace, for quiet beauty and static imitable norm. Jefferson, on the contrary, greatly admired "the hyperbolic flights of the Psalmist" in contemplation of God, and gave the palm to the psalmist "over all the hymnists of every language and of every time." His own sober restraint in speculation about God—his entirely antimystical credo—was one thing. To follow a poet into the realm of great emotional experience was another.

Power of vision, fancy, as he called it, and overwhelming strength of forceful expression in sound were to Jefferson the decisive criteria for greatness in poetry. It is natural that language, itself the instrument of poetry, had to be judged by the same dynamic standards of beauty. And it is in this realm that Thomas Jefferson, devoted as he was to Latin reading, was definitely a Hellenist. There is not one word to be found in all his writings in praise of the Latin language as such, and it is implied that he considered it a mediocre instrument, however greatly it had been handled by poets and prose writers of old. In what might seem on the surface to be a strange contradiction to his anti-Hellenic preference for Roman architecture, it was definitely Greek, not Latin, which he admired more than any other language. The traditional scholastic praise of Latin as the vehicle of logical thinking could not mean much to Jefferson. Logical reasoning was to be found in pure mathematics, not in language. Language was a compound of reason and imagination. With Locke and to some extent with the *idéologues* of his day, he looked on language as the vital expression of imaginative thought. Everchanging and haunting imagination crystallized new ideas in words, modified them in the varieties of diction, composition, sound. Language thus reflected the mental richness and creativeness of any given people and age. Therefore "a language cannot be too rich." Reason, morality, taste were all elaborated by the richness of language. From a purely utilitarian point of view, Jefferson admitted that to study Greek was less useful than to learn Latin, French and Spanish. But Greek was to him "the finest of human languages," because it was the "most beautiful of all." The beauty of Greek was not in the nature of a codified, static ideal. It lay in its imaginative richness and expanding elasticity. Homer was "the first of poets, as he must ever remain, until a language equally ductile and copious shall again be spoken." Madison's style was pure but at the same time "classical and copious."

The richness of Greek was not only and primarily one of words. Above everything else, it was the mass of modifications which its structure allowed that made for its ductility and copiousness. "Every language has a set of terminations, which make a part of its peculiar idiom. Every root among the Greeks was permitted to vary its termination, so as to express its radical idea in the form of any one of the parts of speech . . . as a noun, an adjective, a verb, participle, or adverb; . . . each . . . by . . . varying the termination, could vary the shade of idea existing in the mind. . . It was not, then, the number of Grecian roots (for some other languages may have as many) which made it the most copious of ancient languages; but the infinite diversification which each of these admitted." In addition, this Greek verbal copiousness was increased by a wealth of prepositions and composite words. He illustrated the result in figuring out the number of mathematically possible mutations in Greek words by means of terminations, prepositions and compositions. It was to him a spectacle of supreme vitality in which each root (representing a radical idea) became "prolific." The richness of verbal modes in Greek was but another expression of that same vitality. He could not bring himself to believe that such a rich and flexible language lacked the ablative case, as most grammarians asserted. He judged other languages by the standard of this Greek richness and flexibility. English was potentially, but not actually, as rich as Greek. (German he did not know.) But from this point of view modern post-Revolutionary French was superior. It was the "most copious and elegant" language in the living world, because, like Greek, it seemed to be "modifiable *ad infinitum*."

The copiousness and ductility of Greek was the very defiance of grammatical schemes and rules and of purism, against which his empiricism as well as his vital concept of man and his culture revolted. Greek language was in a constant process of "neology" to which life and men of letters as well as a wealth of dialects contributed. The Greeks themselves were anything but obedient to grammatical rules. They had their dual, for instance, to express in noun and verb the number two instead of a plurality. But they used it or did without it as they pleased, and one could even find such combinations as a dual case of a noun with a plural form of a verb. The whole Greek language, it would seem, was animated by poetical license which varied it infinitely in conjunction with the readiness of the Greek public to accept the dialectic forms of Herodotus, Pindar, Theocritus, Sappho, Alcaeus and Homer. Thence its verve and beauty. And in great Latin writers one found the same freedom from rule and grammar to express "rich sentiments." The usage of elimination (ellipsis) and compression (syllepsis) in writers such as Tacitus, Sallust, Livy and others, assured elegance and force, though by implication their native language was less copious and rich.

Jefferson was keenly aware of the differences a slight modulation could make in linguistic expression. There were always differences of life, idea and sound within the intricate pattern of linguistic expression. The insertion of one single letter, one Greek iota or its omission had been capable of dividing mankind into two violently opposed camps: in the fateful debate of the early church concerning the identity of Jesus with or his kinship to God,· *homoousia* or *homoiousia.*

In the realm of sounds, too, Greek was to him superior to any other language. Richness of sound, that is, euphony, and richness of rhythm in prose or metric verse, were the acoustic expressions of that same Greek vitality reflected in copiousness and ductility. Indeed, the musical perfection of a short passage of Homer still would "immortalize its author were every other syllable of his compositions lost." Greek as a whole was remarkable "for the euphony of its sounds." And again "euphony and strength" were preferable to "the niceties of syntax."

It was a great and basic experience, this continuous listening to the verve and beauty of Greek language. In view of Jefferson's intense preoccupation with Greek writers during the years preceding the writing of the Declaration of Independence, it is natural to assume that that experience was instrumental in preducing the vigorous, rich and beautiful style which makes that political document one of the great works of world literature. The direct influence of Greek oratory and tragedy on Jefferson's style has, indeed, been suggested. But it was at best an unconscious influence, prompted by his general ideas about copiousness and euphony which, to be sure, were inspired by the Greeks. His awareness of the singularity of languages included the conviction that direct imitation of another idiom was not the way to form one's own style. "To form your style in your own language" read Milton, Shakespeare, Ossian, Pope, Swift, he recommended to young Peter Carr in 1785. But copiousness and euphony were general principles, principles of vital and forceful progressive formation and expression of ideas. By using these principles in one's own language, ideas as well as beauty could advance. The explicit statement just quoted seems, however, to contradict his repeated recommendation of Greek and Latin oratory as a model for American public speech. This seeming contradiction was based on his awareness of the importance of oratory as a powerful political instrument in the young republic. He went through a lot of experiences as a listener. He himself, by nature, was not gifted for oratorical performances. In his youth he had witnessed the explosive power of Patrick Henry's native and spontaneous eloquence. He had sat through endless hours listening to speeches in the legislature, the Revolutionary conventions; he had heard the debates of the French Revolution; and he had presided for four not very cheerful years over the meetings of the Senate. He was convinced that something, some training, was necessary more to eliminate the empty phrase of cheap demagogy, the muddy disguise of facts by verbiage, than to contribute to the refinement and perfection of the individual. One may assume that he would have recommended English models if there had been any in oratory comparable to the style of Shakespeare and Milton, Pope and Swift— and to the style of ancient orators. But, in his opinion, such a model could be found only in the forensic oratory of Lord Bolingbroke. His "lofty, rhythmical, full-flowing eloquence" was equal to that of Cicero. And both Bolingbroke and Cicero were good models for the pleading lawyer at the bar. Cicero had imagination and combined it with a sublime command of "mere style" that was more important for the purpose than logic and sweeping force. In the courtroom a merely elevated style of oratory was appropriate for the lawyer pleading his case. It seems that he himself, in the last section of his legal opinion concerning the rights on the "Batture" in New Orleans, was definitely inspired by the model of Cicero.

Political life in a democracy depended largely on political oratory. For that neither Cicero nor any English writer he knew of furnished a great model. And one had to pick up the thread where the ancients had left it. The ancient

Greeks had developed a "rational and chaste style of . . . composition" in contrast with the "inflated style of our northern ancestors, or the hyperbolical and vague one of the east." In oratory, in particular, "antiquity has left us the finest models for imitation; and he who studies and imitates them most nearly, will nearest approach the perfection of the art." The speeches found in Livy, Sallust and Tacitus were "pre-eminent specimens of logic, taste, and that sententious brevity which, using not a word to spare, leaves not a moment for inattention to the hearer. Amplification is the vice of modern oratory." On great occasions political oratory in a democracy should count on "an audience of sages, on whom froth and fancy would be but in air." And it was this highest level of at once reasonable, nearly scientific and at the same time forceful speech which he thought of as an ideal. Contrary to poetical imagination and copiousness, it was the "pith and brevity" of these models that impressed him—and characteristically, in this case not the copious and ductile Greek but the more lapidary Latin language offered the greatest values. "But," he continues, "in ordinary cases, and with us particularly, more development is necessary. For senatorial eloquence Demosthenes is the finest model; for the bar, Cicero. The former had more logic, the latter more imagination." Thus, with Demosthenes, he returns to the Greeks, in this sphere, too. His "dense logic," worded in a powerful and flexible language which is the expression of a violent temperament, this unique combination appealed to Jefferson to an unusual degree. Repeatedly he classed Demosthenes as representative of Greek prose, with Homer the greatest of poets. It is significant that no praise of the polished and smooth orator Isocrates of the generation preceding Demosthenes is found in Jefferson's writing, in spite of the popularity of that refined stylist in his time. Demosthenes, whom he admired, was not only a symbol of the Greek sense of liberty; he was not only a powerful stylist—he was one of the most vital and temperamental characters of ancient Greece.

Among the ancient prose writers, the greatest to him was Tacitus, not only because of his realistic and pessimistic approach, his antityrannical and republican convictions, the moral reflections he implied, and the pith and brevity of his speeches; Tacitus was to him, too, a great example of an original, forceful, at times ungrammatical stylist who handled language boldly and unconventionally to produce violent reactions, to expose his own and other men's passions, to highlight sharply vital energies.

But, on the whole, Jefferson was a decided Hellenist in his admiration for language and in his literary tastes. His particular brand of Hellenism was his own, the result of his continuous intercourse with the ancients. It was not the fruit of a search for a static ideal of beauty, for an academic formula of "simplicity and quiet grandeur" which defined the Hellenic classicism of Winckelmann and most of his contemporaries in Europe. It was, rather, in the sense of the Renaissance—and possibly of the future—a search for enrichment by experience, for vital increase and strengthening of imaginative power. The vigor of passion, the awe-inspiring grandeur of epos and tragedy, the copiousness of the richest language, its ductility and ever-increasing volume, forceful expression, breath-taking spell of diction and haunting beauty of euphonious sound—these were the fruits he gathered from the tree of Greek imagination.

Ancient science was primarily Greek science, too, whether it was to be found directly in the Greek books of Euclid, the mathematician; of Hippocrates and Galen, the physicians; of Ptolemy and Strabo, the geographers and astronomers, or, indirectly, in Latin compilers such as the naturalist Pliny. And among the ancient philosophers it was not the eclectic and rather conventional Cicero—aiming at Greek beauty and a quiet ideal like the eighteenth century classicists—but the Greek Epicurus who ultimately became his guide. His vital philosophy, acknowledging the force of positive life and human passion, regulating them in a tense system of powers that checked each other, was to Jefferson the supreme achievement of Greek reflection—in contrast to the static idealism of Plato, the cool grammar of the academics, the reasonable self-denial of the stoics and cynics, and the spiritual escape of the mystics.

Jefferson's dynamic Hellenism was his personal achievement, and one far in advance of his age. It is as refreshing in the frigid preromantic sphere of his generation as is his realistic appraisal of ancient history. But Hellenism it was, nevertheless, in spite of his admiration of individual Roman creators, such as Horace and Tacitus, Livy and Virgil.

CHAPTER 10

Creative Architecture

THE GREAT SPHERE of visual imagination in which the classicist Jefferson made his own important and creative contributions was architecture. The architect Jefferson's ideas, plans and actual works are better known to us than almost any other aspect of his life, thanks to penetrating studies on the part of Fiske Kimball. His sketches and fine drawings, his notes and his preserved works, above all his house, Monticello, the Capitol and the University of Virginia, reveal his basic principles. They allow us to trace the development of this great amateur—a *dilettante* in the Renaissance sense—who conquered a name in the honor roll of architectural history by virtue of the beauty of his works as well as of the influence of his ideas.

Jefferson's architecture is classicistic from beginning to end. Antique concepts, orders, proportions, plans and elevations are its inspiration throughout. In its early stages, this decided and sweeping classicism was even more radical than the classicism of Europe. From about 1770 on for more than half a century, it accompanies continuous preoccupation with the ancient world, its history, languages, thought and literature. It was the most articulate expression of his admiration for antique civilization, for the freedom of thought and imagination which, he hoped, would finally be revived, after a lapse of two thousand years. And in architecture he made his own great and fateful contribution to that revival.

In granting to Thomas Jefferson a prominent place among classicistic architects, one should not forget that his position was different from that of the average professional artist. The latter could and, at that time, generally did look upon classical forms as pure and detached creations of beauty without bothering about the context of life behind them. He might be and often was naïvely inclined to invest with beauty that life which had produced ancient art, and thus idealize and elevate it. But Thomas Jefferson was not merely an aesthetic classicist. He was a student of the classics in every sense; of the dark sides of ancient history, of their good and bad philosophies, of all that vast realm of science and literature. His own classicism in architecture unfolded itself hand in hand with his ever-deepening penetration of the antique world in all its aspects. Therefore, it is necessary to relate his architectural classicism to that process. Without doing this, we should fail fully to understand its function for his time and country as he saw them, and we should overlook particular features of his own architectural creations, of his style.

It is, of course, true that Thomas Jefferson's classicism in architecture is a result of the general Humanistic tradition that emerged in the Renaissance and continued from Palladio through Inigo Jones and Lord Burlington in England to the Adam brothers and the Greek revival. It is true, too, that his classicism, like that of England and, during his later lifetime, of Continental Europe, was strengthened by a reaction against "modern" art. The art of the Baroque Age and its contemporary aftermath seemed to the rationalists and idealists, as well as to the empiricist Jefferson, to be exuberant and decadent. The style of architecture current in France when he arrived there, the Rococo and Louis XVI style, was "far from chaste" in his opinion. The fact that the great works of European architecture almost invariably glorified and enhanced the prestige of ecclesiastical and monarchical power may have been an additional element in making him turn his back on immediate tradition and join the revivalists of ancient architecture. Antique architecture, as form and as the product of man's creative mind, even though it was a part of a social-political world of which he disapproved in many respects, might have seemed to him, like ancient philosophy, science and poetry, a relatively more spontaneous and unhampered fruit of imagination than the pre-Revolutionary architecture of France.

Jefferson's architectural classicism was prompted by a desire to educate the taste of America. To turn from European models of the immediate past and present toward the remote sphere of the ancients was only natural in oratory—where perfect models also seemed to be lacking in the modern world—and he advocated the same direct use of classical forms for the formation of an American style. This analogy is not without significance for a correct understanding of the neoclassic architect Jefferson. Though he had had his own dreams of a beautiful house in Monticello and had begun to realize them, his real career as a creative revivalist began in connection with buildings representative of the sovereignty of the American people's own chosen government. At about the time of the Declaration of Independence, his revolutionary idea of using antique temples as models for public buildings found expression in a plan for a governor's palace in Williamsburg. This design anticipates by several years Jefferson's actual use of the Maison Carrée in Nîmes as a model for the Capitol of Virginia. It seemed to him that the approbation of long centuries entitled that Roman temple to symbolize dignity and power of government by the people. In his *Notes on Virginia,* he denounced the lack of taste and the unseemly appearance of colonial architecture in his native state. This criticism, which today seems so unjustified, was rooted in Jefferson's longing for a monumental architectural expression of the American genius to raise America to the level of other countries, if not above them.

His bias as an enthusiastic and creative architect by natural endowment certainly played a part in his emphasis on the importance of taste in American buildings. However that may be, the fact remains that he saw in the direct continuation of architectural creativeness, from the point where the ancients had left it, a mission of the young republic which was not unrelated to its revival of the liberty of man, his thought and imagination, that had been inaugurated by the American Revolution. In early years, he had shown an interest in acquiring copies of ancient sculptures and had made a list of those which attracted him most in illustrations and descriptions. But with one exception, he did not proceed to acquire them. To be sure, he continued to promote the erection of more or less neoclassic plastic glorifications of the Revolutionary War and of Washington, the symbol of the American republic. He himself played with plans for a garden monument, using the idea of Trajan's famous column, and approved of the project of such a column, with a relief frieze, by the Italian sculptor Ceracchi, long before Napoleon glorified his own wars on the bronze column of the Place Vendôme in Paris. But such a column, like the obelisks and temples in memory of great Americans that followed in the wake of this idea in the nineteenth and twentieth centuries, was basically a work of architecture rather than of sculpture. And he advised Washington to select the round building of Lysikrates in Athens as the model for a Revolutionary monument. It had attracted his imagination in early years in Spon's *Voyages,* and at that time he had the idea of a garden pavilion of that type for Monticello—such as was actually made in England. When old, he suggested its adaptation for a monument on the battlefield of Bunker Hill. Jefferson's changing interest in the monument of Lysikrates reflects his development from a purely formal admiration of antique architecture as an expression of his personal taste toward his use of it as a dignified symbol of American democracy. His conviction that America needed a great monumental architecture to express her dignity caused him to advise American travelers in Europe to study architecture carefully, along with agriculture and other things useful to the young republic. Sculpture and painting, he judged, might be a source of enjoyment to the traveler, but their study, unlike that of architecture, would be a waste of energy. The time had not yet come, he thought, for America to take a really creative part in the plastic arts. Unlike John Adams, who denounced the fine arts and trusted that they would not become a part of the American scene, Jefferson's implied hope was that in a somewhat distant future this might be the case. Young America, however, as he repeatedly stated, had to concentrate on the immediate necessities of a society in the making. Architecture, which has often been characterized as the mother of the other visual arts, was to him such a necessity. The building of the University of Virginia was the most mature profession of the classicist architect Thomas Jefferson. It aimed at establishing a new and higher standard of American culture, and it expressed the desire of that young culture in the plastical terms of buildings. Its models of classical architecture were to surround future generations of Americans during the impressionable and imaginative years of youth and to be a ferment in the formation of taste. Finally, these models of classical style were to be used directly as a means of professional education for young American architects; studying these incarnations of classical taste very closely, they would be enabled to form their own style, as the student of politics would form his by an intense study of the oratory of ancient writers.

Jefferson distinguished between a strict classicism in monumental public buildings and a blend of classical forms with modern ideas in domestic structures. That distinction is visible in his use of entire classical temples for public buildings in contrast to his looser adaptation of classical orders and porches in domestic architecture. To the former category belong his early plan for the governor's palace, his Capitol of Virginia and the Pantheon-Library of the University at Charlottesville; to the latter all the phases of Monticello and the other country houses which he designed. The comprehensive appearance of the pavilions of the University which were at once public-school buildings and residences for the professors and their families, is not quite as strictly based on classical models as the porticos and library, yet the façades and simple rectangular plans are more severe and temple-like than those of his purely residential mansions. In these pavilions and in private mansions, including Monticello in its last phase, Jefferson admitted the orders of Palladio on equal footing with genuine antique models. On the other hand, the library of the University uses and directly imitates the order of a preserved antique structure, the Corinthian order of the Pantheon. In public buildings a pure and exclusive use of true ancient models, having the ring of eternity in forms approved by many centuries, was to express the grandeur and dignity of American society. Good taste in private buildings would follow the same principles in more elastic and freely imaginative adaptations. In accordance with this distinction, Jefferson advocated for the Capitol in Washington, too, a truly classical building. On the other hand, his particular idea of the democratic character of the presidency as an office held by a private citizen who, personally, had no more title to grandeur and splendor than anybody else, was opposed to the attempts to gild the life of the American President with pompous court ceremonials which he witnessed in the days of Washington's administration. It led him to recommend for the White House the style of private French residences of the time. Such residences, of course, included forms, orders and decorative elements of classical origin, like the dome which he himself built in Monticello under the inspiration of the recent Hôtel de Salm in Paris. But this classicism of the second degree of purity, as it were, was different from that of public buildings. As to the Capitol in Washington, he condensed his view on the function of a sweeping classicism in American architecture in a letter to Latrobe: "I shall live in the hope that the day will come when an opportunity will be given you of finishing the middle building in a style worthy of the two wings, and worthy of the first temple dedicated to the sovereignty of the people, embellishing with Athenian taste the course of a nation looking far beyond the range of Athenian destinies."

In harmony with Jefferson's concept of the function of classical architecture in America is his attempt to imitate definite classical models directly and faithfully. But this "literal" classicism of his is also in accordance with his basic approach to everything as a positivist and empiricist, and with his awareness of the singular character of individual creations. It was natural that in the sphere of architectural concepts, too, he would attempt to "brush off" the dust that had accumulated on the true life of antiquity as he did in history, language and literature. It was natural that he would move away from Palladio, the theorist of antique ideas and orders, and go back to face the original buildings preserved from antiquity, to study them and to use them directly as models. He had to rely on books for that purpose, on the work of Palladio himself, on Le Roy's *Ruins of Athens,* Clérisseau's *Monuments antiques de Nîmes,* Fréart's *Parallel of the Ancient Architecture with the Modern,* Desgodets' *Edifices antiques de Rome.* All of them contained measurements, plans, elevations, details. He would use these books as he used the best obtainable editions of ancient writers. His study of the most minute measurements and details of preserved antique architecture corresponds to his own principle of reading original sources of history instead of digests, and of reading the original texts

Above: "MAISON CARRÉE" AT NÎMES.

Below: MODEL OF THE CAPITOL OF VIRGINIA, STATE LIBRARY, RICHMOND, VIRGINIA.

PANTHEON, ROME.

LIBRARY, UNIVERSITY OF VIRGINIA.

UNDERGROUND PASSAGE IN HADRIAN'S VILLA
AT TIVOLI. FROM GUSMAN. SEE p. 184.

UNDERGROUND PASSAGE, MONTICELLO.

instead of translations in so far as he could. His empiricism and positivism, his strong aversion to theories and systems, contributed to the literal classicism of his architecture, and as time went on, led him away from the theorist Palladio and his source Vitruvius.

It is interesting to note that Jefferson, who knew Vitruvius very well, was definitely never under his spell as Palladio had been, in spite of his great architectural genius which unconsciously transformed the dry schemes and rules of the Latin theorist and filled them with an alien vitality. In spite of Jefferson's intense study of ancient authors, including Vitruvius, the latter's book had relatively little place in his thought or work in the sphere of creative architecture. Unlike the theorists of the Renaissance, he did not care for the doctrines of that ancient doctrinary of the laws of architectural types, orders and proportions, and he abstained from playing with graphic or plastical reconstructions of the schemes advocated by Vitruvius. Such reconstructions had been common from the days of Palladio and Serlio, of Scamozzi and Inigo Jones, and were still popular in his own age.

A remark on one of Jefferson's sheets of architectural notes is typical of his own study of Vitruvius. In this note he states that a Vitruvian formula for the Doric order did not correspond to the actual use of that order in Greek antiquity. This formula proposes a solution of what has been called the "angular conflict" of Doric architecture. The mathematical rhythm of triglyphs and metopes, the alternation of narrow fluted and square undecorated fields in the Doric frieze, was connected with the regular position of every second triglyph exactly over the center of a column. Inasmuch as the triglyphs are always considerably narrower than the diameters of the columns below them, in historical times and in preserved ancient buildings, this entailed the necessity of interrupting the regular rhythm of equally repeated forms at the outer corners of temples. The Greeks experimented with various solutions for that angular conflict. They either contracted the intervals of the columns or enlarged the metopes toward the corner; or else they combined both methods to allow the frieze to end at the corner with the solid vertical element of the triglyph which, unlike its companions, was no longer set mathematically over the center of a column. These solutions were elastic, vital and somewhat ungrammatical. Vitruvius, however, the sober theorist, the not very brilliant architect of an academic age, requested the rigid preservation of equal distances in columns as well as frieze. He proposed to add an empty and meaningless half metope at the corners. This Vitruvian scheme, which is not found in any preserved antique building, was an academic studio recipe. Palladio took the precept of the undeservedly worshiped Vitruvius as the norm and popularized it. Jefferson himself used it in Monticello before he discovered that Vitruvius did not say that the half metope was actually used in Greek buildings—and it was too late then to go back to the authentic form.

He was an eclectic in architecture as he was in philosophy. And he was convinced of the right of individual creations to individuality of character. Vitruvius, who admitted only a number of static schemes and equal prototypes in architecture as Montesquieu did in government, was decidedly not his man.

It was a different matter with the actual reality of preserved ancient buildings. One had the choice of using them or not. If one used them it was dangerous to tamper with them and, at the beginning, at least, his literal classicism was rather strict and pedantic. During the work with Clérisseau in Paris on the model for the Capitol of Virginia, a conflict arose between Jefferson's insistence on literal reproduction and the experienced French architect's willingness to modify the scheme of the Maison Carrée, as Professor Kimball has shown. Against Clérisseau, Jefferson insisted that the depth of three columns in the porch of the original Roman building should be preserved and not reduced. "What is good, is often spoilt by trying to make it better," he remarked on that occasion. He rigidly preserved the relative proportions of the Roman temple, though the absolute dimensions had to be enlarged in order to house the legislature. Jefferson did not plan the pilasters on the outer walls which modify the aspect of the less rich prototype in the Capitol of Virginia. In the case of the University of Virginia, he made a careful selection of antique orders from specific buildings and confronted them, under the influence of Fréart, with the equally specific modern-classical orders of Palladio. And though the general idea of building a rotunda at one end of the campus was suggested by Latrobe, the choice of a specific antique model, the Pantheon in Rome, and its reproduction in exactly half size, was his own.

Thomas Jefferson, it has been said, went beyond the artistic radicals of his time in believing that the way of salvation lay in the direct imitation of ancient buildings. In this direct and correct revivalism of monumental public buildings, he looked for beauty in a "chaste and good style" and described its qualities as grandeur, nobility and, at the same time, simplicity. He tried to restore chastity and classical taste in the buildings of the University of Virginia. In these buildings he tried to exhibit "chaste models of the orders of architecture taken from the finest remains of antiquity, and of specimens of the choicest samples of each order." In the more abstract realm of architecture, all this aimed at what he praised as the "ineffable majesty of expression in ancient sculpture." Antique capitals were more "noble" than those of the Renaissance architect Scamozzi.

Nobility, grandeur and simplicity, the cleansing of the antique from Baroque and post-Baroque exuberance, its restoration to chastity and purity—these were ideas which Jefferson shared with the classicists of his age, theorists and artists alike. The terms "nobility," "grandeur," "chastity," "simplicity" belong to the neoclassic dictionary of his age. Winckelmann, or for that matter the Greek revivalists in England, also used them. And for this reason we associate them with an academic taste which sought for a quiet, remote, static appearance of form and interpreted the antique in that sense. The man Jefferson, and particularly the architect Jefferson, was opposed to these static, academic, doctrinary ideals. Yet, as a classicist he was also opposed to the exuberance, the antirational and hyperbolic furor of Baroque style and to the equally irrational subtlety, the irrepressible playfulness of the Rococo. And this reaction, which he shared with all the classicists of his age, motivated his use of the dictionary of a party he had joined, although he did not subscribe to the interpretation of its platform by official spokesmen. The literal imitation of classical buildings, though first initiated by him on a large scale, was not without parallel in the Greek garden temples erected during his lifetime, and his example was soon to be followed in public buildings in France.

In Jefferson's mind and work, these common notions were part of a more general and penetrating attitude which was the result of his character and of his Humanistic exploration of the ancient world. Professor Kimball has pointed out that an original kinship existed between Thomas Jefferson and Andrea Palladio, who served as his guide toward the antique in his early years. The lawfulness and reasonableness of the antique orders, understandable in functional contrasts of vertical supports and horizontal weights, in mathematically defined proportions, were to both men the expression of a law of nature in architectural terms. To Jefferson they must have appeared clear and at the same time refined crystallizations of the innate taste of humanity in general in which he believed. The natural sense of beauty had found its first refined and yet pure expression in antique architecture—the common approbation of its creations by all enlightened men of later ages testified to that fact. As Euclid was the aboriginal source of purest science, of mathematical thought, ancient architecture was the purest art of axiomatic character. This mathematical analogy, indeed, lodged in Jefferson's mind throughout his life. His approach to classicism, not only via an adaptation of ancient orders and their proportions but also by means of a "literal copying of ancient buildings" in order to achieve a completely antique form, distinguishes him from his forerunners and contemporaries. This endeavor was based on his search for complete authenticity as such, and aimed at a full use of ancient models for the new American architecture. But its conscious practice also implies his belief that ancient architecture furnished a definition of beauty in mathematical stereometric forms.

He distinguished between "cubic" and "spherical" architecture as the two basic types of mass rendering which define the variety of extant buildings. Cubic architecture had been crystallized in the type of the antique temple, and the Maison Carrée in Nîmes was its outstanding preserved example, along with the buildings of Athens and Baalbek. The simple rotunda on a circular plan represented "spherical" architecture, and the Pantheon in Rome was its most perfect example; even in its elevation it was logically developed in curves, inasmuch as it contained "a sphere within a cylinder." In addition, he played with another fundamental mathematical form by building on his farm in Poplar Forest the first octagonal structure in America which has no exact prototype either in Europe or in antiquity. This cubism of the neoclassic architect Jefferson, his explicit stress on the three-dimensional simplicity of axiomatic bodies, elaborates a basic and true aspect of ancient architecture. But it also has a strangely modern ring to it.

However, both his literal copying of ancient buildings and his concern with natural and basic forms of mass are only on the surface doctrinary and static. To him, life in all spheres was dynamic, growing, vital. Whoever has visited Monticello and Charlottesville has certainly not experienced the chill and aloofness which are typical of so many neoclassic buildings of his time. His later architectural creations are colorful, varied, full of contrasts and in reality anything but a mechanical reproduction of models. How is the seeming paradox between his literal imitation of the antique (or of Palladio, for that matter) and the vitality of its result to be explained?

First of all, his eclecticism, which in architecture as in philosophy allowed for the combination of ideas from different sources, balanced and actually surpassed his tendency to literal imitation. On the campus of his university it resulted in the unique grouping of buildings, each of which was inspired by a different model. The character of such a comprehensive work of art is something different from that of any of its individual parts. Jefferson himself has stated the issue: "The plan has the two advantages of exhibiting a specimen of every fine model of every order of architecture, purely correct, and yet presenting a whole entirely new and unique." His original plan had provided for a simple shape: a courtyard surrounded on three sides by porticos and pavilions. In the final plan these porticos were limited to the long sides and subordinated to the dominating mass of the rotunda in the background. In this way, his "cubic" and "spherical" styles of architecture were combined and contrasted within a dynamic whole which is dramatic and unique. In a similar way, he had already introduced the "spherical" dome of a French prototype into the Palladian, cubic structure of his house in Monticello. Evidently he himself told an interviewer that this had been a deliberate action aiming at co-ordination of contrasts: "The internal of the house contains specimens of all the different orders except the composite which is not introduced. The Hall is in the Ionic, the dining room is in the Doric, the parlor is in the Corinthian, and dome in the Attic. . . . In the other rooms are introduced several different forms of those orders, all in the truest proportions according to Palladio." The richness and variety of ancient orders derived from different models, their contrast and their subordination to the dome, consciously achieved, result here and there in a symphonic ensemble full of conflicting and yet resolved themes.

Jefferson's literal imitation was satisfied by correct reproduction of the line and proportion of individual units taken from authentic models. His sense of purity and dignity directed him to adhere to the original orders and to eliminate the hybrid Roman combination of Ionic and Corinthian in "composite" capitals which the Renaissance theorists had accepted as equally canonic. The Tuscan column which he used, he recognized as what it historically is—a mere side line of the Greek Doric—and he called it thus. To grasp fully the elasticity and the deliberate variety of Jefferson's eclecticism, it is not sufficient to realize the planned contrast of the basic antique orders and of cubic and spherical elements. In the former respect, he followed an antique idea which first appears in the use of contrasting orders in the propylaea of the Periclean Acropolis and other contemporary Greek buildings. It had been elaborated by the Romans in their superimposition of different orders and accepted by Renaissance and Baroque architects. But the deliberate distribution through the various porticos and interiors of Monticello, the related multiplication, and the extensive use of contrasting orders on the campus of Charlottesville are Jeffersonian. Here in the façades of the pavilions, varieties of the Doric order from three different antique buildings, of the Ionic from two, and of the Corinthian, including the rotunda, again from three ancient models, are contrasted with each other and with specimens from Palladio. Furthermore, the distribution enhances the contrast by a deliberate arrangement, according to which none of the facades of the pavilions shows the same basic order as either of its neighbors. Even across the campus, Doric buildings face Ionic or Corinthian counterparts with the one exception of the central pavilions V and VI, which exhibit two Ionic varieties to provide a minor cross axis.

A further elaboration of Jefferson's eclecticism for the sake of variety is preserved in plans for garden pavilions which he made halfway between his remodeling of Monticello in the last decade of the eighteenth and his building of the University in the second decade of the nineteenth century. Here, too, he planned to contrast the spherical types of the Pantheon and of the monument of Lysikrates with the cubic scheme of the Maison Carrée, and to add in this most private and less austere sphere a Gothic and a Chinese pavilion.

It is hard for us of the twentieth century who live in a healthy reaction against the Victorian and post-Victorian use of historic styles to appreciate Thomas Jefferson's eclecticism fairly. Its root was not lack of originality or imagination. He emerged from an age of traditional colonial simplicity on the one hand, and of equally traditional Baroque on the other. He went back to the fountainhead of natural, grand and yet refined expressions of man's innate sense of beauty. And in doing so he tried to recapture the multiplicity and variety of its expressions, rather than to find a guiding rule. Antique architecture as it appeared on the campus of the University of Virginia was, as it were, a cornucopia full of various, colorful and fragrant fruits, the manifold seeds of which could some day grow in the American soil.

Jefferson's eclectic combination of models from various antique sources, and their use within the new context of a building or a group of buildings, checked his tendency toward literal classicism and prevented it from degenerating into unimaginative copying. In addition, his ideas about the singularity of beauty in linguistic expression and the impossibility of strict translation were not compatible with any real belief that the transfer of the ancient models into media of other building materials and under a different sky could be a mechanical process. With him, it had to be a creative transformation in which his own imagination availed itself of new conditions as well as of a new content. Though his idea of imitating the comprehensive appearance of ancient edifices in modern buildings for practical use was new, it is only in the first actual experiment which he made on this line that he, somewhat timidly, tried to preserve pedantically whatever features of his classical model could be preserved: in the case of the Capitol at Richmond. Even here, he admitted the substitution of Ionic for Corinthian capitals. Later, in the imitation of the Pantheon in Charlottesville, he did anything but schematically copy a model. Though in general he reduced the proportions of the building to one half of the original without modification, though he preserved the Corinthian order and other details of decoration, his changes are far-reaching and very imaginative. In the Pantheon, the porch is somewhat deeper than the height of the columns. In the rotunda, the rate of reduction has been changed so that the depth of the porch corresponds exactly to its height. Moreover, the columns—only six instead of the eight of the prototype—are taller in proportion to the width of the porch than they are in the Pantheon. These changes make Jefferson's building appear less earthbound and heavy, and more balanced, than its prototype. Above all, he refused to accept the strange and rather crude contrast between the temple-like articulated porch of the Pantheon and the unarticulated mass of its round body which, in addition, are only loosely hitched to each other. By extending the entablature of the porch around the body of his rotunda, Jefferson clasped them together in a strong setting and made the building a unified organism. Its interior, again, is but loosely inspired by the prototype. With its unbroken colonnade and the extensively admitted light, it is a free invention made for the function of a library, and only the general dimensions of plan and elevation are preserved from the original. Naturally, in the reduction to half size, the bulky power of the Roman mass and the overwhelming grandeur of the interior of the Pantheon could not be duplicated. In the transformation resulting from the reduction and from the adaptation to the different function of a library, Jefferson has created a work of his own which will bear comparison with the Roman Pantheon, and in its animated and articulate vitality is something entirely different. In that sense, it is more beautiful.

Thomas Jefferson's eclectic and imaginative use of ancient architectural models and inspirations was, with but few exceptions, limited to Roman buildings. True, the Athenian monument of Lysikrates early captured his imagination. It is not impossible that the eight-column temple which he planned in the seventies for the governor's palace was inspired by pictures of the Parthenon in Athens, a building having that rather unusual number of columns. And it is also possible that the adaptation of an octagonal plan for his mansion at Poplar Forest was suggested by the Tower of the Winds in Athens. But by and large, as Professor Kimball has stated, Jefferson was the "most Roman of the Romanists" among the neoclassic architects of his age. Roman models, first from Palladio, then from other sources, were the exclusive models of his major structures and their decoration. The Maison Carrée in Nîmes, the Pantheon, the temples of "Fortuna Virilis," of Vespasian, of Faustina, the Theater of Marcellus, the Thermae of Diocletian, all in Rome, are the models actually used in Richmond, Monticello and Charlottesville, along with Roman types from Palladio. And to the end of his life Jefferson adhered to this nearly exclusive use of Roman architecture, even after he had purchased Stuart and Revett's *Antiquities of Athens* which became the pattern book for the Greek revivalism of the late eighteenth and early nineteenth centuries. Stubbornly, it would seem, he insisted on architectural Romanism in direct opposition to a progressive Neo-Hellenic movement.

In Jefferson's correspondence with Latrobe, the outstanding exponent of that early Greek revival in America, the opposition between the Romanist and the Hellenist became articulate. Latrobe, adhering to the English school which advocated the use of Greek types and forms, shared with this school and with the broad background of idealistic Hellenism of the preceding age of Winckelmann and Stuart, the condemnation of Roman art as derivative and decadent. They admitted preservation of a relatively good, if secondary, level of taste down to the time of the Emperor Hadrian, in the early second century A.D., and thus they could accept the Pantheon of that age as a worthy building. But the period of Hadrian had been a notably neoclassic and philhellenic age, in a sense the last such phase of antiquity. After that there followed a complete decay of good taste, in the opinion of the philhellenists. From this point of view, the orders of the Thermae of Diocletian, including its relief decoration of the bust of the rising Sol, which Jefferson exhibited as one of his models in pavilion I of the University, was not at all a good model.

Jefferson's decided Romanism in architecture is not only at odds with the philhellenic trend of his age. It contrasts curiously with his own equally decided linguistic and poetical philhellenism. Given his vital and penetrating approach and his elastic readiness to change his mind and accept new ideas, it is of small importance that certain phases of his personal experience in architecture were Latin rather than Greek. In his youth, indeed, Palladio had been his guide toward the antique, and due to the circumstances of his age, Palladio was entirely dependent on Roman models. Only indirectly, through Vitruvius, did he have a notion of Greek buildings. In France, Jefferson was associated with Clérisseau, an architect who had lived in Rome for twenty years and was a student of Roman monuments in southern France. These monuments were the only antique buildings Jefferson himself had an opportunity to see, and he greatly admired them.

His desire for concrete contact with antique buildings made this experience one of sweeping excitement. He sat for hours gazing at the Maison Carrée in Nîmes as if it were a beautiful woman with whom he had fallen in love. It seemed to be one of the few most beautiful remains preserved from antiquity. The "Praetorian Palace" in Vienne, a Roman temple of about the same period, was distinguished by fine proportions; the Roman aqueduct, known as the Pont du Gard, and the Arch of Orange, a rather cumbersome provincial work of the early empire, were "sublime," and the Arena of Orange was "superb." Surely this experience contributed strongly to his Romanism in architecture. The fact that French revivalism during and after the Revolution was Roman, too, rather than Greek, as a result of the fundamentally Latin character of that nation, may or may not have been an additional factor in Jefferson's own attitude. But all these facts do not explain the stubborn adherence of the philhellene Jefferson to Roman tradition in architecture. At best, they reveal the pastures on which he fed his innate taste for Roman buildings. Ultimately that architectural taste was directed toward the same qualities which made him a decided philhellenist in linguistics and poetry. Greek architecture is in fact more static and, at the same time, more limited than Roman. It never abandoned the foundations laid in early periods in its structural types and forms. It contributed to Western architecture the natural language of the orders, the dynamic interplay of verticals and horizontals, and the classical triangle of the pediment. It crystallized what Jefferson called cubic architecture. It had its own great historical life, a sensitive growth which includes subtle, musical changes and varieties of constant themes, as well as an unfolding of forms and ideas in changing phases. But in Jefferson's time only a small number of original Greek buildings, primarily those of Athens and a few from Asia Minor, Paestum and Sicily were known and could be studied in books. Even today, after a great variety of Greek buildings and a considerable historical development of Greek architecture is known, it appears less rich and less drastically varied in its adaptation to various functions and in its stylistic changes than Roman architecture.

It is typical of Jefferson's interest in elasticity and variety that, among Greek buildings, he gave preference to the monument of Lysikrates, a rather unorthodox building combining a square dado with a round "temple" and a curved roof. The relatively rich and varied development of Greek architecture in the age of Alexander the Great, to which the monument of Lysikrates belongs, begins to emerge from modern excavations, though it is by no means appreciated even today by professional archaeologists. In Jefferson's day, the few known Greek buildings could be used as the incarnation of a static ideal of Greek beauty for which the philhellenic architects and archaeologists longed. But it definitely could not serve as the source of a rich experience, of a vital and varied application.

Roman architecture, on the other hand, exhibited many different types of buildings, temples, thermae, villas, engineering works, tombs. And even then, so much was preserved and known of it, extending over more than four centuries and across the length and breadth of the Mediterranean world, that its totality was an immense source of creative ideas. Above all, by admitting the arch, the vault and the dome—all of which Jefferson used—and by combining the Greek orders with them, Roman architecture had created an infinite possibility of differentiation and application. It had added the "spherical" element to the cubic, a second natural dialect of taste, and that element was to crown Jefferson's own major works.

"Roman taste, genius, and magnificence, excite ideas," he wrote under the fresh impression of Roman monuments in southern France. It was exactly this richness of ideas which made him the natural opponent of a Philhellenic movement in architecture that aimed at the ideal rather than at a wealth of ideas. It was the same opposition which defined his anti-purism in language, his anti-idealism in philosophy and his aversion to systems in science. And thus it was only a seeming paradox that Jefferson immensely preferred Greek to Latin language and poetry, while in architecture he gave the palm to the Romans. The same longing for copiousness and ductility in imagination directed the Hellenist Jefferson as a reader and the Romanist Jefferson as an architect. In science, oratory and history he gave to the Greeks and the Romans what was theirs, acknowledging merit and quality, rudely denouncing vice and deficiency. His creative imagination was not to be hampered and limited by a Greek ideal which was not his own and, as he saw it, could not be the ideal of an age and a country whose destinies would reach far beyond those of Athens.

CHAPTER 11

The Art of Living

THERE WAS another art which Thomas Jefferson practiced more consciously than most men do. It was the art
of living. It needed reason and imagination as did architecture, the creations of which contributed to this other art's
realization. His continuous conversation with the ancients,
his study of their history to become more experienced in
human nature, his preoccupation with Greek and Roman
thought and works of imagination were in themselves an important part of his art of living. Reflection, wisdom and enjoyment of arts and letters were to be found, above all, in
that receptive and yet creative intercourse with the world of
the ancients.

In its fascinating richness that world offered a variety of
styles in the art of living: the dangerous action and passionate
self-assertion of great individuals in the heroic world reflected
in Homer and in Greek tragedy; the style of the concentrated,
cultured society of that tense microcosm, the Greek city-state;
the rustic simplicity and sturdy thrift of early Rome, and the
reveling congestion of the later city. Among these styles of
living, each of which was reflected in thought, literature and
art, there was one which had a natural attraction for the Vir-
ginian student of the classics because of the striking similarity of traditions and events. It was the style cherished by the
cultured men of the late Roman Republic and early Empire,
the art of living as it was practiced by Cicero, Varro, Horace,
and the younger Pliny, whose writings were filled with its
ideals.

These men, like Thomas Jefferson, had their roots and traditions in the country and on farms. But cultural life of this time, a descendant of Greek urbanism, was the life of the city, in which it thrived, coalesced, developed. And it was so in Thomas Jefferson's own time when Paris, London, Rome and Vienna set the standards and in America, Boston, New York and Philadelphia. Even Williamsburg, the first city in which he lived as a student, though a village rather than a city according to our standards, represented a different mode of living from that traditional to the farmer. But in Virginia more than in Pennsylvania and New England, city life, such as it was, was definitely the result of a more or less temporary concentration of men who had their roots in the country on their farms. There was their real life. In Rome, too, the deeply rooted rustic tradition of upper society was, as it were, in a magnetic tension with urban life. The city exercised its attractive cultural power—and yet city life was repulsed by tradition and instinct.

This tension was enhanced by the political atmosphere and events of both ages. Here and there, men whose heart was in the country had to live their active life in the city or far away from their beloved farms. Varro, the farmer and scholar by inclination, lived in Rome as much as on his estates. Cicero, who owned a number of "villas" in central and southern Italy as Jefferson did in Virginia, had to be in Rome most of the time, or far away in Greece and Asia Minor. Horace, the poor peasant boy from southern Italy who made good in the cultural hothouse of Rome, was happy to own a little farm in the Sabine Hills, thanks to the munificence of his friend Maecenas; but, since he owned it, he was torn between the demands of the imperial court to have its poet live in town and his desire to be on his farm. Pliny the Younger, a farmer's scion from the Alpine region of Italy, who cherished the traditions of the age and person of Cicero, had his rural properties spread out from the Alps to Rome. But even he,

a man of no great political importance, had his career in
Rome and was forced to spend the last years of his life far
away in Asia. Monroe, Madison, Washington, all lived under
the same tension; and so did Jefferson. Williamsburg, Philadelphia, Paris, New York, Washington were in a sense sta-
tions of a calvary on his "road to glory." But what would
Cicero, Varro, Horace and Pliny have been without Rome,
Greece, Asia in their experience? And what would Thomas
Jefferson have been, in spite of all the books he might read
on his farm, without those experiences of urban life?

The curious hybrid product of modern traffic, the sub-
urbanite, and the art of living which goes with him, did not
really exist in ancient Rome, even less so in America, and
least of all in Virginia. In both Rome and Virginia the art
of living which resulted from the conflict between urban concentration of active life and culture on the one hand, and
traditional interest in and ideals of the farmer's life on the
other, was strikingly analogous. The result, here and there,
was the urbanization of life on the farm, the attempt to
carry the positive values of urban life to the country: in
buildings and books, in intellectual and artistic activities, in
social life emulating "Attic society." It was the ideal crystallized in the Roman villa of old, in the villas of Varro, Cicero,
Horace and Pliny and in the mansions of Monroe, Madison
and, above all, of Thomas Jefferson.

A reader of the letters of Pliny the Younger, in which he
describes his own daily life in his villas and that of other
men of his circle, cannot fail to recognize a striking similarity
between the art of living practiced by those Romans and by
the Virginia gentlemen of the Revolutionary and post-Revolutionary Age. "My mornings are devoted to correspondence.
From breakfast to dinner, I am in my shops, my garden, or
on horseback among my farms; from dinner to dark, I give
to society and recreation with my neighbors and friends; and
from candle light to early bed-time, I read.—My health is

perfect, and my strength considerably reinforced by the activity of the course I pursue. . . . I talk of ploughs and harrows, of seeding and harvesting, with my neighbors, and of politics, too . . . and feel, at length, the blessing of being free to say and do what I please, without being responsible for it to any mortal. A part of my occupation, and by no means the least pleasing, is the direction of the studies of such young men as ask it. . . . I endeavor to keep their attention fixed on the main objects of all science, the freedom and happiness of man." This was the essence of what Jefferson called "the enjoyment of my estate." He wrote the sentences just quoted in 1810, shortly after his retirement from the presidency. Already an earlier visitor, such as La Rochefoucauld-Liancourt, had pictured Jefferson's life in Monticello in terms strikingly similar to the ideals of the good Roman *paterfamilias* who supervised his farms from his luxurious mansions and enjoyed the pleasures of physical exercise and intellectual life on their grounds. Reading the descriptions Daniel Webster gave in later years of his visit to Monticello or, for that matter, the report of a visit to the Madisons at Montpelier by Ticknor, one meets with a routine of life strikingly similar to the ideals of Roman villa life as exhibited in detail by Pliny. A careful balance of physical and mental activities, of solitude and intellectual society, of rustic and urban life is the very essence of that ideal. And Jefferson's own statement quoted above reads like a condensed version of the more extensive descriptions of Pliny.

Thomas Jefferson had encountered this Roman ideal of a perfect life in the half-urban, half-rustic microcosm of a villa in his early years. Cicero and Horace were two of the most cherished ancient writers who accompanied him from that time on to the end of his days. And the younger Pliny's letters were among the few books which he read even at the very end of his life. The mediocre intelligence and the rather involved style of that author cannot have had much attrac-

tion for him. Evidently he appreciated Pliny as the advocate
of an art of living he himself had developed. The earliest ancient book in prose from which he made excerpts was Cicero's
Tusculan Disputations, those philosophical dialogues taking
place in the framework of a Roman villa, urbane, Attic discussions among friends and amateur philosophers in a country house within a beautiful landscape setting and a classical
architectural surrounding. And it was in these early days of
his life, even before he articulated his first plans for Monticello, that he copied from Horace that nostalgic picture of
country life by an intellectual of the highest urbanity.

> Happy is he who far from business,
> like the first race of man,
> can till inherited lands with his teams,
> free from all payment of interest.
>
> He who avoids the market and
> the proud thresholds of mighty citizens . . .
>
> He may recline now under an old tree
> and again on the soft meadow,
> while the waters fall down from the steep banks,
> birds lament in the woods,
> and the springs with murmuring veins,
> suggest soft sleep.

He continued to copy the entire poem, leaving out, as Professor Chinard has observed, only such lines as did not allow
for possible application to a Virginia farm. Shortly afterward,
in his plans for a garden and a family burial ground, he proposed to have the poem inscribed near a temple with the
statue of a reclining nymph. Like those Romans of old, he
thought that cities were the centers of the "elegant arts"; but
the useful arts, together with health, virtue and freedom,
could be practiced fully in the country alone. When, happily,
John Adams and not Jefferson was to be president, he hoped

for a while that being vice-president would secure for him for some years a pleasant combination of philosophical evenings in town during the winter and rural days in the summer. But the actual experience was disappointing. And what he longed for from that time on was to go back to his family, his farm and his books. The combination of farm and books —healthily rustic and intellectually urbane life—was the ideal of Cicero, Horace and Pliny. It was the objective of Thomas Jefferson's art of living.

The Roman villa, its buildings, gardens and decoration, had been the plastic incarnation of that art of living. And sufficient evidence seems to exist that Jefferson quite consciously aimed at reviving that very framework of ancient life by adapting comprehensive ideas and details to his own needs.

The position of his house in Monticello on a height overlooking his estates and with a wide view of the mountainous landscape was an innovation in the Virginia of his time. The source of this concept has been a puzzle to Jefferson's biographers and students. It has been characterized as a sign of his "essential aloofness" and of his wish to live "in sunshine above the clouds." But such an attitude was alien to Jefferson's most sociable personality. On the other hand, the villa on a hill in a commanding situation with a view of the wide landscape is a typical feature of the Roman ideal of life. Such a position is recommended by Cato and Varro; it is typical of the villas of Tivoli, Tusculum and their vicinity in the Alban Hills near Rome, alluded to by Roman writers. It is particularly characteristic of the most extensively described Roman villa, the Tuscan villa of Pliny, which was situated on a foothill of the Apennines with a vast view of valley and mountains. The panoramic view is stressed in Jefferson's Greek name for his farm, Pantops, and one may recall that the use of Greek names for features of Roman villas is commonly met with in Varro, Cicero, Pliny and the sources on

Hadrian's famous villa near Tivoli. Under the circumstances, the debated source of the name Monticello, an Italianizing word for a small mountain, becomes understandable. It refers to the situation of his Roman villa and is a Jeffersonian creation. Pantops, too, was not to be found in any Greek dictionary. An Italian form might easily express Jefferson's desire to revive the idea of the ancient villa, particularly in view of the fact that the Italian language was to him but a living dialect of Latin.

More detailed features in Jefferson's planning for his house on the mountaintop connect it with the Roman villa. In a very early sketch, even before 1770, he planned a long narrow terrace with rounded ends, which was not executed in this fashion. Shortly afterward, his house was to be an elongated building with two projecting one-room wings on the ends. Both the garden in the form of a hippodrome or antique circus and the mansion with two projecting one-room wings are outstanding features of the Tuscan villa of Pliny. Furthermore, he planned outbuildings away from the great house; "retired quarters for study, laboratory office and bedroom." The two office buildings now preserved are only cells of that plan. Again such apartments dedicated to solitude, quiet work and study away from the main mansion are a typical feature of the Roman villa. They are called *diaetae* by Pliny, who describes such outbuildings in detail in both his Tuscan and Laurentine villas. They invariably contain bedroom and study, so that the owner of the house could settle down in them in complete remoteness for quiet work and rest. In addition, Jefferson planned to connect the main house and such *diaetae* by porticoes, again following a scheme described by Pliny in both his villas.

But in 1772 he adopted a plan from Palladio which had none of these elements—possibly because of the considerable expense involved in the execution of a truly Roman villa. In the nineties, however, when he remodeled Monticello after his stay in Europe, he tore down the two-storied Palladian porch, supplanted it by a more authentically antique façade and added the dome. He also returned to the ideas of the Roman villa. His introduction of a lower-grade arrangement for the service quarters, an innovation for which no source has been named, so far, the opening of these units into porticoes along the slope, and the connection of the main building with the outbuildings by underground passages are typical features of Roman villa architecture. These underground or half-underground passages built in terraces are amply described by Pliny in both his villas and are called cryptoporticus. The particular scheme in which the tunnels between the main house and the lateral wings in Monticello are lighted by small windows in the upper wall is described by Pliny in the cryptoporticus of his Laurentine villa. That scheme is preserved in many Roman villas and might have been known to Jefferson, even visually, from etchings.

There are, or were planned, other features typical of the Roman villa: an oval, brick-lined fishpool corresponding to the Roman *piscina;* an aviary planned in close connection with the living quarters; a pigeonhouse in the form of a tower-like structure with openings for the birds under the roof—in the basic idea undoubtedly derived from Varro's description of such structures, though using the classical model of an antique mausoleum; underground cisterns to provide for water as suggested by Cato and Varro and, incidentally, lined with "Roman cement"; the installation of a weathervane on the roof of the porch connected with a hand on the ceiling showing the direction of the wind to persons inside, and in conjunction with a clock enabling him to make meteorological observations, devices certainly suggested by Varro's curious description of a similar weathervane and time-telling mechanism in his villa.

A profound inspiration from the Roman villa as the physical setting for an art of living common to both Jefferson and the Romans is evident in Monticello. It is not in the nature of comprehensive imitation nor has it the stale taste of archaeological reconstruction. Rather, it is a vital elaboration of eclectically used "ideas" which in this realm, too, the Romans had "excited."

In his university inspiration from that same source of urban-rustic ideals was active, though mingled with the solemn dignity of public edifices. In the final stage, this latter element is represented in the Pantheon rotunda which towers over the colonnade and pavilions in the background of the lawn. When he first conceived of that combination, he made a sketch which was not executed, suggesting a hippodrome plan for the entire campus with the curved end encircling the rotunda. It is but another reflection of Pliny's hippodrome garden.

The very concept of what he called an "academic village" which defined the plans of the University in general, and has exercised so great an influence on the formal appearance and on the very ideals of American colleges, is related to the Roman villa rather than to any other type of architecture. This concept of an academic village was already in his mind shortly after he had given the final form to his own villa, Monticello. It occurs as early as 1802, during his first presidential term. During these years, when the realization of the plan still seemed far off, he thought that eventually his great library of Monticello would become the library of the academic village. In 1811, we have seen him taking up, from Monticello and his villa library, the direction of the studies of young men who settled in the extant village of Charlottesville. And some years later, he began to build his academic village there, after having secured its location in the country against the ambitions of Williamsburg and Richmond.

The ideal of the academic village was prompted by the same aversion to city life which animated the old Romans and led Jefferson, with them, to transfer his urban intellectual life to the country. It was enhanced by his suspicion of the moral dangers threatening young boys in urban centers. The physical form in which the ideal of the academic village expressed itself contrasted with both the agglomeration of monastic buildings in European universities and the big lumbering schoolhouses that prevailed in America. It was not only to be classical, beautiful and dignified instead of medieval, baroque or nondescript; it was to be an aggregation of individual buildings on a hill, spread out in the open country and connected by porticoes. In the original plan, the pavilions were to surround the lawn on three sides and to be connected by porticoes onto which the dormitory rooms opened. The latter scheme which provided for the monumental accent of the rotunda in the background and caused the breaking up of pavilions and porticoes into two rows facing each other, with isolated hostelry buildings parallel to them on the periphery, is simply a modification of that scheme.

Professor Kimball has suggested that the original plan was inspired by the idea of ancient fora or palaestrae. The latter alternative probably comes close to the truth. The palaestrae and gymnasia of the ancients, though originally public training places for merely physical exercise, had been the buildings in which ancient intellectual life had found its social and educational crystallization. The gymnasia of the Academy, of the Lyceum in Athens, had been the seats of great philosophical schools. "Academy," "lyceum," "gymnasium" were already accepted terms for educational institutions. Jefferson, the Epicurean, might also have thought of the garden of Epicurus, his private estate on which he taught and which he bequeathed to his pupils, as the seat of his school. However that may be, the appearance of the University of Virginia is inspired rather by the loose connection of porticoes and buildings in the Roman villa than by any other type of ancient or later architecture. The pavilions are true *diaetae,* each of them including rooms for study and living quarters within a small unit, like the *diaetae* described by Pliny and once planned by Jefferson for Monticello. The rows of living rooms opening upon porticoes are equally typical of those Roman villas. Finally, there is a last and probably not purely formal device in Charlottesville, though it was exploited by the architect Jefferson to enhance the dramatic beauty of the whole. This is the introduction of two levels on the campus which is laid out in two descending terraces. It is certainly not dictated solely by the natural conditions of the hill, which could easily have been leveled off. On the other hand, in one of his villas Cicero describes two terraces which he calls his upper and lower gymnasia. These two so-called gymnasia were villa gardens in two levels framed by porticoes and serving as abodes for philosophical speculation and dialogues between cultured men. The upper terrace of this villa included a library, as does the upper terrace of the University of Virginia.

Walking from the lower to the upper terrace, the student is drawn toward the Rotunda, which emerges only gradually. Its high stairway is not visible from the far end, concealed by the edge of the upper terrace. As one approaches it, the Rotunda exerts a more and more powerful attraction. Here were the books, the comprehensive source from which knowledge flowed. Jefferson planned to decorate its dome with a representation of the universe by means of a complicated mechanism of movable and changeable stars. The dome was to fulfill the function of a planetarium. It is evident that his plan to make the dome of the Rotunda an observatory of astronomical phenomena was suggested by Dion Cassius, the historian, who is the most important ancient source for the Pantheon in Rome, the model of the Rotunda of Charlottesville. Dion, whom Jefferson read often and put on the list of required readings in history, said that the dome of the Pantheon represented the heavens. However, he did not find in Dion the concept of mechanically moving stars. This he found in Varro's description of the domed rotunda of his aviary; it is the same Roman villa structure from which he had derived the mechanism of a weathervane on the roof connected with a hand on the inner ceiling of the porch in Monticello.

The art of living which had found its physical expression in the Roman villa of old was to Jefferson not merely a private ideal. Its forms inspired the appearance of the great university which was created to direct the mind of American youth toward individual and social ideals of liberty and happiness. To him, personally, during that last decade of his long life, the classics became "sweet composers" to the "rest of the grave." But their sense of freedom, their science, their poetry, their philosophy, their arts, were to inspire future generations of Americans.

CHAPTER 12

The Portico of Learning

TO THOMAS JEFFERSON the classics had been the guiding element of his early schooling. They had become one of the most important tools of the continued self-education which he carried on to the end of his days. Through the classics, he had learned to elaborate his empirical and positivistic understanding of the history of man. He had seen him struggling with evil forces, succumbing to them and standing up against them with human dignity. He had learned to recognize the uniqueness of historical conditions and the relative value of the good that is attainable at any given time and place. He had seen through the blinding glamour of fame and alleged greatness.

In the classics, above all, he had experienced the great manifestations of the natural endowment of man with reason and imagination. Moral sense developed in reasonable terms by Epicurus secured personal happiness for the individual. If one added to that philosophy Christian charity, this world would become a good one to live in. Roman law was the clarifying guide to the practice of justice. Language, the vehicle of ideas, became a stark and excitingly rich reality in the study of Greek. Its richness and euphony and the masterly style of individual expression in ancient poetry and prose offered never-ending, invigorating experiences. Roman architecture, the mature and ductile elaboration of a natural human sense of beauty, furnished an unceasing stimulus to creative imagination. And behind it he had grasped and adapted a personal ideal of the art of living which was classical in origin.

Civilized man had been a free agent in the ancient world, and as such he had achieved all those things. That civilized spirit combined with Christian morality was at hand to lead man into a free and happy world if he would avail himself of both these tools which history had added to his natural endowments. The ancients had been deficient in recognizing the indivisible connection between individual and social happiness. If man was endowed with a social moral sense, the development of civilization would eventually create a balance between true Christian morality and individual happiness. He thought that this development had begun with the American Revolution. That revolution had set man free in an age of enlightenment, cherishing the ideals of ancient civilization and enabling him to know and understand the simple yet sublime teachings of Jesus.

These ideas are the ultimate background of Thomas Jefferson's famous educational enthusiasm and the framework of his plans for public instruction, as well as of his concept of the self-education of the individual. Freedom was the firstborn daughter of science. The diffusion of knowledge would make man free. "And without going into the monitory history of the ancient world, in all its quarters, and at all its periods, that of the soil in which we live and of its occupants indigenous and immigrant, teaches us the awful lesson that no nation is permitted to live in ignorance with impunity." It was on this background that Jefferson conceived of the "charter of modern education" and of the system of primary and secondary schools and universities which is fundamental for the present. To be sure, the time was ripe for such a development. And in the mere appearance of the educational pyramid which Jefferson had advocated since the draft of his Bill for the More General Diffusion of Knowledge (in 1779), the system was not unlike that charted for Prussia a generation later by Wilhelm von Humboldt. It has been suggested that Humboldt was inspired by Jefferson's ideas. And this seems quite possible, in view of the fact that his brother Alexander, the great explorer, was a correspondent of Jefferson's and, of course, owned and knew his *Notes on Virginia* which included a discussion of his educational plans. However that may be, the very foundation of Jefferson's educational pyramid was complete freedom from ecclesiastical influence in all schools of the republic, and he would not have acknowledged the Prussian scheme, which was tied up with monarchical worship and religious instruction, as one likely to secure progress—in spite of its high-minded classical appearance.

Thomas Jefferson was an eclectic in his educational ideas as in every other sphere. But the very organic connection of heterogeneous elements in the sense of a limitless subordination of teaching to freedom was his own. To him the purest republic was the republic of letters. It was more real than any other, and could not bear dictatorship in any form. True, within that republic, too, vested interests threatened thought. "A single priest is more than a sufficient opponent to a whole army," he remarked to Mme. de Staël. And books "have done more towards the suppression of the liberties of man, than all the millions of men in arms of Bonaparte. . . ." Though he feared nothing for the liberty of America from the assaults of force, he was concerned about the influence of books, principles and manners opposed to that liberty. However, inasmuch as man was naturally endowed with reason, by developing his faculties, education would enable him to judge for himself. Education, largely obtained from books, would free him. Education was, to be sure, only a secondary thing. An illiterate "peasant" in America was a Solon compared with the educated French legislators who advanced a law of religious intolerance. "An honest heart being the first blessing, a knowing head is the second." But if education spread, man's natural endowment of reason would secure a majority opinion dictated by sound reasoning. Education furnished tools to be used for that purpose and for the development of social and individual happiness.

Thomas Jefferson's endeavor to make man free and happy through education was opposed to a tradition in which indoctrination with principles of religion and of a stable social order had been the ultimate aim of instruction. Neither did his faith in education imply the goal of producing a standardized type of intellectual and citizen such as had been the ideal of Plato and was more or less that of Humboldt. Nor did he think of any type of instruction as a means to direct or guide the development of the individual, his personality and character, by external influence or counsel. Instruction in all types of schools should simply furnish man with the tools of knowledge. To learn to read, write and figure in the elementary grade was not essentially different from learning languages, arithmetic and English style in the secondary, or from acquiring knowledge in any branch in the highest. Man grew and matured as he acquired more and more knowledge and experience, and he should aim to attain as much as he could at any given stage. Truth, thus experienced, would make him more and more powerful, safe and happy, according to the standards of his time, his surroundings, his personal talent. Knowledge and experience would develop his natural endowment to whatever degree his station and his genius allowed. But the ultimate use of the tools which instruction furnished for him was a matter of his own judgment and decision.

It was no use furnishing tools if man would not avail himself of them. Jefferson's ultimate optimism was the conviction that a wide diffusion of knowledge could not fail to fertilize man's innate instincts for reason, morality and beauty. In restricted societies, such as that of pre-Revolutionary France, knowledge could not be exploited beyond the range of individuals who were aiming to put it to good use for themselves. But the majority of men were endowed with unfailing instincts for reason and morality. Thus a wide diffusion of knowledge would secure social progress according to the law of majority opinion. To be sure, a high degree of knowledge in one direction was sterile unless it was integrated with common sense, reason, a broad social outlook. In early years, he had marked a passage in Middleton's *Life of Cicero* referring to Roman intellectuals: "the more Greek they knew, the greater knaves they were." But the majority of men, he trusted, would direct the use of the tools, which instruction handed to them, in a manner useful both to themselves and to society.

Education thus was nothing but handing on tools to be used by the individual who could take advantage of them to exploit his natural endowments of reason and imagination. As to morality, no special education was needed: Man's moral instinct, freed by reason, would easily embrace the truth to be found in the moral teachings of Jesus and of some philosophers. Man endowed with reason and imagination, however, had to acquire the tools of knowledge in order to use them in action and reflection. Due to the natural endowment of reason, the very process of studying, "the acquisition of science is a pleasing employment." But labor was not only enjoyable, it was a necessity, and pure intuition without knowledge would lead nowhere. "Now men are born scholars, lawyers, doctors; in our day this was confined to poets," he wrote angrily in 1810.

The task of society was to offer knowledge in public schools. By making basic knowledge available in elementary schools, everybody would get the simple tools of reading, writing, arithmetic and history. Only the best talents would proceed to the secondary schools and from there, in turn, only the highest qualified to the university. Thus an aristocracy of talent and virtue would emerge in each generation. He proposed this selection of *aristoi*, instead of the artificial breeding advocated by the old Greek poet Theognis, and the aristocracy of wealth and power of modern times. His scheme of public ward schools of the first degree, district schools for secondary education, and the state university for higher learning is based on this concept. Certain tools furnished by education were so basic that every man had to use them. They were furnished in prescribed and standardized education in elementary schools. The secondary schools, too, were to hand on relatively basic tools, not yet real science. But in the university the student equipped with these tools had reached a stage at which he should follow his own judgment and freely elect what further instruments of knowledge he wished to acquire. After he had left school, he would continue to use them, in his profession, in public life, in his leisure time. It is important to understand the implication of this theory of the gradual equipment of man with knowledge to make him more and more free and, finally, to leave him on his own. In the university every person "who can read, write, and cipher will be free to learn what he chuses . . . without . . . prescribed course. But we shall not teach elementary classics. In that line we shall give only the last critical finishing to those who have been of the highest class of the ordinary academies." In fact, the place Jefferson assigned to the classics within his educational pyramid best illustrates his ideas about the tools of knowledge and their use.

The statement just quoted seems to be at odds with his own profession that he always was "a zealous advocate" of classical learning. Furthermore, it seems to contradict his assertion that the University of Virginia and Harvard University, above all other American institutions of higher learning, would give to the youth of America "a truly classical and solid education." In earlier years he had named classical knowledge as the first in order of the objects of "an useful American education." And when he drew up lists of books

AVIARY IN VARRO'S VILLA RECONSTRUCTED BY ROBERT CASTELL.
SEE pp. 184, 187 f.

MONTICELLO FROM GARDEN SIDE IN 1826. ANONYMOUS WATER COLOUR, PRIVATE COLLECTION.

THE LAWN OF THE UNIVERSITY OF VIRGINIA.

THE LAWN OF THE UNIVERSITY OF VIRGINIA.

for the library of the University of Virginia, he included not less than 409 classical titles as the biggest item in a first library of about 6,800 books. And yet, in an early plan for the university, he did not regard the classics as a field to be taught.

Jefferson's attitude toward the classics in his educational plans seemed puzzling and contradictory to some of his contemporaries. On the other hand, a modern critic has blamed him for inconsistency in granting complete freedom of selective choice in all fields in the university and yet requiring that an examination in Latin be given to all students before they could obtain a degree.

All these seeming contradictions are not contradictions at all. Jefferson considered a thorough training in the classics as indispensable for every well educated American. A "proficiency in these languages which constitute the basis of good education, and are indispensable to fill up the character of a well educated man" was regarded by him as a pure necessity for his time and for America. In fact, this was to him, as to most people of his age, a self-evident axiom of education. It was so much in the nature of an axiom that he forgot to mention the classics when, in a less orthodox way, he stressed the necessity for every educated American to learn French and Spanish. In his early considerations of a school system for Virginia in 1779, he stated: "The learning Greek and Latin, I am told, is going into disuse in Europe. I know not what their manners and occupations may call for; but it would be very ill judged in us to follow their example in this instance."

The source of the seeming contradictions in Jefferson's attitude toward the classics in education is his conviction that the study of the ancient languages was merely a basic tool. As such it had to be acquired early. It was a matter for secondary schools, not for the university. And he justified a sharp distinction in this respect by pointing to the difference in strength of the three Baconian faculties of the human

mind in the various phases of human life. Reason, strengthened by experience, was vigorous in old age, though memory
and imagination might decline. Imagination was stronger in
youth than reason. Memory was the most vigorous faculty in
childhood. "The memory is then most susceptible and tena-
cious of impressions; and the learning of languages being
chiefly a work of memory, it seems precisely fitted to the
powers of this period [the age between eight and fifteen],
which is long enough too for acquiring the most useful languages, anti 'nt and modern. I do not pretend that language
is science. It is only an instrument for the attainment of science." Twenty years later, he justified his omission of the
classics in a first sketch of the fields to be taught in the University of Virginia by exactly the same reason.

After the Revolution, the professorship of Greek and Latin
had been temporarily abolished in William and Mary College, together with that of religion, inasmuch as it was not
the task of a college to teach elementary languages. The secondary schools provided for it while modern languages were
not yet taught in them and were therefore retained in the
curriculum. Jefferson feared that the inclusion of the classics
in the plan of the University might eventually result in con-
verting this department into a grammar school. But these
languages were, nevertheless, "the foundation common to all
the sciences." The place where they should be taught, and
thoroughly taught, was the secondary school, as early as his
Bill for the More General Diffusion of Knowledge, in 1779,
and he did not change this opinion. It was not necessary, he
thought, to acquire a "hypercritical knowledge of the Latin
and Greek languages" in school. What mattered was to "possess a substantial understanding of their authors." One generally learned languages "for the benefit of reading the books
written in them." After having acquired this basic tool and
being capable of reading classical authors, one could proceed
for oneself—and read them. The university provided a super-

structure, while learning Greek and Latin was but a foundation.

Actually, however, practical experience taught that the high standards of proficiency in languages both ancient and modern which Jefferson considered as basic for entrance to his university were not met by secondary school education. The compromise which he reached was that the freshman should use the first year for a finishing touch in the two main fields of secondary education, languages and mathematics. Even so, the entrance requirement to the classical school in the university equaled the standard final requirement for the bachelor's degree in American colleges about thirty years ago. The obligatory examination in Latin which Jefferson introduced before granting a degree to any student was but a further acknowledgment of the fact that secondary schools did not guarantee sufficient proficiency in that language.

Greek and Latin he considered to be "the foundation preparatory for all the sciences." The secondary schools which taught them were a classical "portico of entry to the university," such a portico as surrounded the campus and formed the entrance to the library of the university.

The scheme which Jefferson advocated was conditioned by his age, and even then it was not completely practical, as his own compromise with reality shows. Within the framework of that compromise his personal standards were rather too high even for his day and its schools. And a member of the board of the university protested that "the student should be a better scholar than most of our teachers before he shall enjoy the benefit of classical instruction in the University." However, the fact that spending time on acquiring linguistic knowledge after the age of sixteen, when man has the faculty for studying "sciences," is in a sense a waste, has ever since worried teachers and students of the classics.

It is, of course, futile to ask what Jefferson would have recommended in an age of such different standards as ours. He himself unceasingly insisted that education, like everything else in human institutions, had to follow the changes of civilization and the human mind. His conviction was that, given certain principles, their adaptation to specific conditions of time and space was in any case a matter of compromise. If in view of other requirements the secondary schools had no longer been able to provide for the thorough training in the classics that he assigned to them, he would have looked for a second degree of classical education.

Jefferson's ideas about female education, which were naturally entirely different from those of modern times, may give a hint in that direction. French he considered to be indispensable for the education of both sexes. He did not require training in the classical languages for girls. But he directed his daughters and others to read classical authors in translations. He himself, polyglot as he was, did not know all the languages which contained great books. He did not know Hebrew, for example, and he longed for a translation of the Psalms of such high poetical quality as one of his translations of Horace. And though he advocated the principle of reading originals instead of translations wherever that was possible, and though he was keenly aware of the uniqueness of linguistic expression, he preferred a good translation of a great book to a poor original. "I enjoy Homer in his own language infinitely beyond Pope's translation of him, and both beyond the dull narrative of the same events by Dares Phrygius" (a late antique writer), he stated. And he thought it highly desirable, for instance, to have Epictetus translated into English. In drawing up the reading requirements in history for the University of Virginia, he requested the students to read "Herodotus, Thucydides, Xenophon, Diodorus, Livy, Caesar, Suetonius, Tacitus, and Dion in their originals, if understood, and in translations if not." This was his last word in the matter and opened the road for a wide and expanded reading of translations in the classics in view of the decreasing knowledge of Greek and Latin. And we may assume that this solution, rather than the selection of a few "great" authors of antiquity to be read in English translation, would have been his compromise with the changed conditions of schooling brought about by the industrial age.

For those who knew Greek, he proposed the reading of the New Testament in the original as one of the first exercises, because to him the learning of languages was only the means of securing the great experiences available in books. Therefore the choice of ancient authors to be read in school should be defined not merely, or even primarily, by the need for formal grammatical or stylistic training. The value of the subject matter or the quality of great poetry should determine the selection. For instance, the classical books used by students for learning the languages "can be such as will at the same time impress their minds with useful facts and good principles." Cicero's orations, which had been a mainstay of formal education in Latin since the time of St. Augustine, as they still are today, did not belong to that category. Nobody could profit from the heavy "task work" of understanding the subtleties of arguments presented in the courts of ancient Rome by a naturally biased lawyer. The niceties of his style could not justify spending much time on them, while his philosophical writings contained valuable fruits of ancient thought and his letters were an important source of history.

In reading the ancients for the purpose of acquiring factual information, historical events were, indeed, foremost in importance. In the organization of the university, ancient history was to be taught in conjunction with ancient languages, and modern history in the school of modern languages: "not as a kindred subject but on a principle of economy." The same method of killing several birds with one stone applied to geography. Geography as well as history was to be taught in the department of languages, together with the literature and thought of the respective areas. It may be that this idea of expanding linguistics into general studies of civilization was inspired by the model of a Swiss institution. And in the classical field it had a parallel in the German science of antiquity which developed as a unified cultural science during Jefferson's later lifetime. In the case of geography, it is interesting to note that his inclusion of higher learning in that field into an "area" curriculum was not merely based on the principle of economy—from that point of view geography could have been taught in connection with other fields. Originally, indeed, he had considered it to be a section of natural history; in 1817, the idea of connecting geographical instruction with law and government had occurred to him. Thus he began to stress the relationship between natural and social conditions. The final shift to geographical area training in connection with languages and history marks a clarification in a truly humanistic sense. Man and his use of his natural surroundings, the influence of those surroundings upon him, as well as his cultural activity in them were a unit. Long before the revolution in modern geographical science took place which led to the introduction of the term anthropo-geography, Jefferson forecast such a development.

Man in space and time, his conditions of life, his actions in history, his formation of ideas in languages, thus became in Jefferson's educational plans the center of a related and comprehensive humanistic study. Schools existed to hand tools of understanding to the young. But if schools aimed at making young people free by knowledge, it was up to them to use those tools to their own best advantage.

Jefferson's basic ideas about education—his elaboration of scholastic plans and, especially, his numerous personal directions to young men—are connected with an axiomatic belief in self-education. This belief takes it for granted that in childhood and youth the student will immediately put to use the tools furnished by instruction for expanding his knowledge in independent reading. And it is based on the assumption that, possessed of tools for acquiring knowledge, man will continue to use them to the end of his days. He himself had lived up to the former task in his early years and practiced the latter throughout his life: in science as well as in the humanities and, above all, in the classics.

The purpose of schools was not to give qualifications and degrees after the attainment of which one might discontinue what one had done in school and forget about it. As one continued to use the tools of reading, writing and ciphering, one should continue with the languages, literatures, history, mathematics, natural sciences. Some of these studies would strengthen professional or vocational abilities, as the case might be. Others would make for political wisdom. Still others would give pure and continuous enjoyment, satisfying man's urge for reason, morality and beauty. Together they would make him free and happy, if continually used. The classics were one such tool, and a very important one, to Jefferson. To make it really useful the student had to do a lot of reading by himself in high school and college, in addition to his progressive acquisition of linguistic abilities. And once equipped with the basic linguistic tools, he should proceed during the later years of college to read for himself without losing time in attending classes. The law student should pay special attention to reading ancient historians, moralists and orators, while in training, but he should read poetry, too, as well as mathematics and sciences. History, ethics, politics, economics and belles-lettres—much of it in classical authors —would be a matter of continued private study, while the young man's professional education furnished him with other more specialized tools in addition to those he had acquired previously.

To Thomas Jefferson, school would never be a "finishing" agency. From each stage, man would have to move on in a never ending process of self-education, deliberately using the tools he had acquired. The narrow professional who had but a technical knowledge of his little vocational area was a curse to him. Education had to be broad in order to assure the freedom and happiness of man. "Nothing can be sounder than your view of the importance of laying a broad foundation in other branches of knolege whereon to raise the superstructure of any particular science which one would chuse to profess with credit and usefulness. The lamentable disregard of this since the revolution has filled our country with Blackstone lawyers, Sangrado physicians, a ranting clergy and a lounging gentry, who render neither honor nor service to mankind, and when their country has occasion for scientific services, it looks for them in vain over it's wide extended surface." Not trained by the merely superficial technicalities of Blackstone's textbook, lawyers should acquire an academic training in mathematics and the physical world in addition to their classical schooling. History, the closest adjunct of law, ethics, politics, political economy, belles-lettres and an indefinite "etcetera" should be their concern in continued private reading. Evidently, to enable them to do just that was the value of what he thought to be a "truly classical" training. And he contrasted his "education on a broad scale" with "that of the petty *academies,* as they call themselves, which are starting up in every neighborhood, and where one or two men, possessing Latin and sometimes Greek, a knowledge of the globes, and the first six books of Euclid, imagine and communicate this as the sum of science." Taught in the right way, the classics would be one foundation of a broad education, provided that the instruction obtained in school would enable the student to exploit this tool by continued and expanding reading "at leisure in the progress of life."

The acquisition of the classical languages, to be effected in early years in order to avoid a later waste of time, was a "solid basis for most, and an ornament to all the sciences." To the moralist, these languages furnished ethical writings of high value, and the clergyman should be able to read his Greek and Latin sources. The lawyer needed Latin because of the basic impact of Roman law. In the changing realm of medicine, too, the old ideas of Hippocrates offered concepts still valuable to the modern physician. The statesman would find in ancient history, politics, mathematics, ethics, astronomy, and in ancient expressions of patriotism, a rich source of experience. And while the merchant and the agriculturist could do without classical training, all sciences used classical ideas in their terminology. He concluded these arguments, which have often since been repeated by classicists, by a remarkable statement expressing his ideas about the value of schools for furnishing man with tools which he could use to his advantage: "I know it is often said there have been shining examples of men of great abilities in all the businesses of life, without any other science than what they had gathered from conversations and intercourse with the world. But who can say what these men would not have been, had they started in the science on the shoulders of a Demosthenes or Cicero, of a Locke or Bacon, or a Newton?"

In the same letter, which is in the nature of an apology for the classics, he had stressed their general value for educated men in three respects: These languages had developed a civilized style of speech, and inasmuch as to him as to Locke and the *idéologues* of his age, language was but articulation of ideas, the ancients were the prototype of mental progress. Secondly, their great works in poetry and prose offered unique enjoyment, and if it was luxury, to the Epicurean Jefferson this delight was part of man's happiness. Thirdly, the ancient books were a rich source of knowledge in all fields of the humanities and sciences.

There was then a precious tool at hand in these old books. If one could not read them in the original—and not all men, let alone women, could read them even then—their values could be made available in translations and digests. The freedom, safety and happiness of man, the ultimate aim of education, made it necessary to open to him the experience of history. Jefferson considered the field of Greek and Roman history as the most important area of general history. That is evident both from his own particular preoccupation with ancient history and from his advice to others. Instead of previous religious instruction, his school bill of 1779 proposed to teach the most useful facts of Greek, Roman, European and American history in the elementary schools. In the secondary schools, the prevailing emphasis on Greek and Latin assured a prominent place for ancient history. In the law for the establishment of the University of Virginia, the teaching of history and geography, ancient and modern, is the first objective named. In addition, of course, there was the student's private reading in all grades, and Jefferson judged that there, too, history should be given more time than philosophy and poetry. The Bible should be included in such reading merely as a historical source, along with Livy and Tacitus. In proposed public county libraries, historical books are listed as first in order of importance. Livy, Thucydides, Tacitus, *The Life of Anacharsis* by Barthélemy, Gibbon's *Decline and Fall of the Roman Empire*, Middleton's *Life of Cicero*, were necessary reading matter for young girls.

This preoccupation with history in education, and above all with ancient history, is based on the concept that historical reading provided for extended social human experience and, indeed, was the most direct approach to it. Though history should be presented "in the genuine republican principles of our Constitution" it was not to be used as a moral exercise. It was a means of realistic appraisal of human nature and society. As far as American education was concerned, historical experience would teach all citizens that "until the mass retains sufficient control," oppression and the perpetuation of wealth and power in a ruling class will follow. Historical knowledge would "promote . . . unanimity and perseverance" in the great enterprise of the American experiment in government. "To disdain despair, encourage trial, and nourish hope" were the objectives of writing history, as they were the goal of any political and philanthropic work. The experiences of other times, as he had early remarked in the preamble of the Bill for the More General Diffusion of Knowledge, would protect the American liberties of the people who were their only safe depositories by making them "judges of the actions and designs of men." A comparison of former historical confederations with that of America would "be to the advantage of ours and would increase the veneration of our countrymen for it." On the other hand, experience of the election of magistrates which had led to permanent one-man rule, first in the Roman Empire, would warn of the dangers of re-electing American presidents. Referring to the suppression of a history book in France, he exclaimed: "Is reason to be forever amused with the *hochets* of physical sciences, in which she is indulged merely to divert her from solid speculations on the rights of man, and wrongs of his oppressors?"

Ancient history was his chosen field of social education, as a result of the fact that its relatively free political life, in which feudal and ecclesiastical powers were absent, offered a better field for observation than later history. The dangers inherent in the fundamental character of man and human society could better be explored in that area than elsewhere. And the ancient historians were freer intellectual judges in their presentation of history than the historiographers of later ages.

Opinion, thus formed, was power. In that sense, he thought, education would have been the only means of leading ancient society itself toward truly good government, and this was a lesson to be learned from ancient history, too: that society, in spite of all its civilization, had failed to educate the people. "I do most anxiously wish to see the highest degrees of edu-

cation given to the higher degrees of genius, and to all degrees of it, so much as may enable them to read and understand what is going on in the world, and to keep their part
of it going on right: for nothing can keep it right but their
own vigilant and distrustful superintendence." The principal
aim of general education remained to him to "enable every
man to judge for himself what will secure or endanger his
freedom." History, therefore, was its core, the study of man
in the society of the past, especially in the civilized societies
of the ancients.

If man should avail himself of tools furnished by instruction for the sake of his own freedom, education could not be
entirely compulsory, in Jefferson's opinion. But society might
induce parents to send their children to school by making the
exercise of the full rights of the citizen dependent upon
literacy.

If man carried on for himself, using the tools which he had
acquired, progress would result, not an infinite but an indefinite progress—that is, a never ceasing, dynamic social
progress. Science, the superstructure of education, if it was a
search for truth, was also a never ending, progressive expansion of understanding. The learned, therefore, were the path-
finders of civilization. The "tardy will of governments who
are always, in their stock of information, a century or two behind the intelligent part of mankind," could not secure that
progress. The organization of individuals in learned societies
was called upon to push these tardy governments toward
progress, for example, in the standardization of measures and
weights.

Public education should secure social progress in all realms
and it was, therefore, the very "keystone of the arch of our
government." Yet Jefferson did not imbue it with the power
of a gospel. Its success depended entirely upon the natural,
self responsible desire of the individual for self-education and
upon its fulfillment. To be educated, or rather to educate

oneself perpetually by expanding use of the instruments acquired in schools, was in itself not only power, it was happiness. The individual might find himself torn between circumstances and desire, social duties and personal happiness, in that as in every other respect. He himself offered an example of that. "Nature intended me for the tranquil pursuits of science, by rendering them my supreme delight. But the enormities of the times in which I have lived, have forced me to take a part in resisting them, and to commit myself on the boisterous ocean of political passions." To keep the passions in balance and under control and to secure tranquillity of the mind was the goal of the Epicurean philosophy. "Science" in general, not what is strictly called philosophical speculation, was to Jefferson the antipodes of this boisterous ocean of untrammeled passions. And study of the ancients was foremost among such sciences. It is quite logical, thus, that the "sublime luxury" of reading the classics, which he indulged in so exuberantly, was of the greatest educational value. It at once made the individual happy and tranquil, as did all science. Quoting Cicero and Horace, he explained to the preceptor of Fryeburg Academy in Maine that the ultimate goal of instruction by teachers and of the labors of students was, apart from their social aspects, the true freedom and happiness of the wise man. The possession of science would "above all things render you dear to your friends, and give you fame and promotion in your own country," next to the possession of an honest heart, he admonished young Carr. To the practical politician, mathematics and natural sciences would be but "amusements," while the study of politics, law, rhetoric and history was necessary. But within the framework of Jefferson's philosophy, amusements and luxury in occupations of the mind were part of the natural birthright of man because of his endowment with reason and imagination, and they were to make him individually free and happy.

It is natural that such a concept of self-education, which

combined the luxuries of intellectual amusement with the professional endeavors of the learned, was opposed to single-mindedness. In fact, his requirement of broad public instruction coincides with his idea of the scholar as a broad-minded personality possessed of knowledge beyond his "field." To Jefferson, a professor "knowing nothing but his own profession" and lacking broad culture was no good, and he would have been shocked by the often unqualified modern worship of the specialist. But even within the professional sphere, his viewpoint, which was largely that of his age, required a breadth of knowledge which has been made impossible by modern scientific development. In the classics, more than anywhere else, that breadth of knowledge was necessary. The professor of classics in his university had to teach Latin, Greek, Hebrew, rhetoric, belles-lettres, ancient history and ancient geography. This vast extent, paralleled though not quite equaled by the requirements for other professors, is balanced by a teaching schedule which is surprisingly limited. Every professor was to teach only six hours during the week, in three sessions, one on each second day. Jefferson's concept of the time a good, broad-minded teacher needed for his research and preparation is remarkable.

He evidently was deeply aware of the necessity of having instructors who were themselves not mere machines of information but men who were continually engaged in the never ending process of self-education.

The Greeks, as the first civilized nation, "presented examples of what man should be." In an overstatement pardonable in view of the circumstances of an election campaign in the year 1800, he proclaimed the Greek ideal as that of future America. Progress, he said, he expected "to be made here, under our democratic stimulants, on a great scale, until every man is potentially an athlete in body and an Aristotle in mind." Knowledge was an achievement of the ancients and an inheritance from them. And "knolege is power, knolege is safety . . . knolege is happiness." It was for America to keep alive the flame of civilization which could spread its light only in a free society of self-reliant individuals. As the mists of political reaction and obscurantism spread over post-Napoleonic Europe, he thought of Italy and of the poor Greeks whose desire for freedom might be thwarted. The world seemed dark to him when he approached his eightieth year and the opening of his university which was to be the classically shaped source of what he called a truly classical education. This university was part of America's work for the sake of the freedom and happiness of men everywhere: "I shall not die without a hope that light and liberty are on steady advance. We have seen, indeed, once within the records of history, a complete eclipse of the human mind continuing for centuries. And this, too, by swarms of the same northern barbarians, conquering and taking possession of the countries and governments of the civilized world. Should this be again attempted, should the same northern hordes, allured again by the corn, wine, and oil of the south, be able again to settle their swarms in the countries of their growth, the art of printing alone, and the vast dissemination of books, will maintain the mind where it is, and raise the conquering ruffians to the level of the conquered, instead of degrading these to that of their conquerors. And even should the cloud of barbarism and despotism again obscure the science and liberties of Europe, this country remains to preserve and restore light and liberty to them."

NOTES

The notes on the following pages, by and large, are limited to Jefferson's statements referred to or quoted in the text, and to sources on which the analysis of his ideas is based. Only particularly relevant bibliography for general or special problems has been added. In selecting this bibliography from the immense mass of previous writings on Jefferson, the author has aimed at acknowledging his indebtedness to the ideas of others and at stating opinions regarding specific problems which diverge from those he himself has formed.

The following abbreviations are used throughout:

> M. *The Writings of Thomas Jefferson.* Definitive Edition by Andrew A. Lipscomb and Albert Ellery Bergh. Issued under the Auspices of the Thomas Jefferson Memorial Association, 20 volumes, Washington, D.C., 1905.

> F. *The Writings of Thomas Jefferson.* Collected and Edited by Paul Leicester Ford, 10 volumes, New York and London, 1892–1899.

> F'. Typewritten copy of Jefferson manuscripts made by Paul Leicester Ford, and available in the Manuscript Room of the New York Public Library.

> L.B. *The Literary Bible of Thomas Jefferson.* His Commonplace Book of Philosophers and Poets, with an introduction by Gilbert Chinard, Baltimore, 1928.

> C.P.B. *The Commonplace Book of Thomas Jefferson.* A Repertory of His Ideas on Government, with an introduction and notes by Gilbert Chinard. (*The Johns Hopkins Studies in Romance Literatures and Languages.* Extra Vol. 2), Baltimore, 1926.

> Randall: Henry S. Randall, *The Life of Thomas Jefferson.* 3 volumes, New York, 1858.

All other titles referred to are given without abbreviation in the notes to each chapter.

The notes list sources in the order in which they are used or

*quoted in each paragraph of the text. Each note contains the refer-
ences for an entire paragraph even if that paragraph continues on
the following page or pages. The numbering of paragraphs refers
to the beginning of each paragraph on a specific page. Hence the
latter part of a paragraph continued from a preceding page is included in the notes to that page.*

Introduction

Page   1, par. 2: John Dewey, *The Living Thoughts of Thomas
Jefferson,* New York, 1940, p. 4.

Page   2, par. 7: Gilbert Chinard, *Thomas Jefferson. The Apostle
of Americanism,* 2nd ed., Boston, 1939.—"Civilization":
Charles Beard, *The Mississippi Valley Historical Re-
view,* XXX, 1943, pp. 161f.
Jefferson as amateur; A. J. Nock, *Jefferson,* Washington,
D. C., 1926. What Jefferson was not: H. J. Coolidge,
Thoughts on Thomas Jefferson, Boston, 1936.

Page   3, par. 1: Woodrow Wilson, quoted by: James Truslow
Adams, *The Living Jefferson,* New York, 1936, Motto.

Page   5, par.1: For a masterly characterization of this side of
Goethe, the reader may be referred to André Gide's essay
in *The Kenyon Review,* Spring issue, 1944, pp. 161f.
Jefferson's own statement, *see below,* p. 207.
par. 2: Gilbert Chinard (*The American Scholar,* I, 1932,
p. 134) refrained from calling Jefferson a humanist because of the obvious difference of his outlook from that
of the "humanists" of the present day. Lewis Mumford,
The South in Architecture, New York, 1941, pp. 43f. has
rightly stressed Jefferson's descendance from Renaissance
humanism. Louis B. Wright ("Thomas Jefferson and the
Classics," *Proceedings of the American Philosophical Society,* LXXXVII, pp. 223f.) has more specifically related
this tradition to Jefferson's studies of the ancient world.
This fine paper which became available to me only after
the completion of the manuscript, touches on many
aspects which are discussed in the following essays. Generally, in writings on Jefferson, his amazing interest in
the classics has not been sufficiently considered. This
neglect has been largely caused by the failure of the edi-
tors of his writings to list names and subject matter of
this kind in the indices.

Apart from the articles by Chinard and Wright, few special contributions related to Jefferson's studies of the classics have been made: Th. Fitzhugh, *Letters of Thomas Jefferson concerning Philology and the Classics* (Reprinted from *University of Virginia Alumni Bulletin*, 1918–9 and 1919), Charlottesville, 1919; Gilbert Chinard, "Thomas Jefferson as a Classical Scholar," *The Johns Hopkins Alumni Magazine*, XVIII, 1929–30, pp. 291f.

Chapter 1

Page 9, par. 1: 1200 letters: Letter to J. W. Eppes, Jan. 1822, *Scribner's Magazine*, XXXVI, 1904, p. 585.

Page 10, par. 3: Letter to Thomas Cooper, Jan. 16, 1814, M. XIV, p. 60.
Letter to Edward Everett, Aug. 30, 1805, F'. III, p. 160: "The common brand of philosophers seem to write only for one another."

Page 11, par. 1: For Jefferson's aversion to systems, *see below*, chap. 5.
Garden Book: *Thomas Jefferson's Garden Book, 1766–1824.* Annotated by E. M. Betts *(Memoirs of the American Philosophical Society, XXII)*, Philadelphia, 1944.
Commonplace Books: L.B. and C.P.B., *see above*, p. 211.
Collection of Laws: Letter to George Wythe, Jan. 16, 1796, M. IX, pp. 319f.
Randolph G. Adams, *Three Americanists*, Philadelphia, 1939, p. 75.
Organization of Library: *Catalogue of the Library of the United States*, Washington, 1815; *Catalogue. President Jefferson's Library*. By N. P. Porr, Washington, 1829. *See:* Roy J. Honeywell, *The Educational Work of Thomas Jefferson (Harvard Studies in Education, XVI)*, Cambridge, Mass., 1931, pp. 211f.
Linné's classification: Letter to John Manners, Feb. 22, 1814, M. XIV, pp. 97f.

Page 12, par. 2: Homer: Note on the flyleaf of Jefferson's copy of Thomas Blackwell's *An Enquiry into the Life and Writings of Homer;* Francis W. Hirst, *Life and Letters of Thomas Jefferson*, New York, 1926, p. 506; Adrienne Koch, *The Philosophy of Thomas Jefferson*, New York, 1943, p. 128.

Page 13, par. 1: Letter to Dr. Wistar, March 20, 1791, M. VIII, p. 151.
Letter to John Adams, May 17, 1818, M. XV, p. 169; F. X, p. 108.
par. 2: F. IX, p. 480 note: Honeywell, *op. cit.*, pp. 217f.

Chapter 2

Page 15, par. 2: See his excerpts in original languages in the *Literary Bible* and the *Commonplace Book*, as well as the requirements of the letter to a student of law, *see above*, pp. 13f.; *see also*, letters to Peter Carr, Aug. 10, 1787, M. V, p. 84; F. IV, pp. 427f., and to Edmund Randolph, Feb, 3, 1794, M. IX, p. 280.

Page 16, par. 1: Jefferson's libraries: *see above*, note to p. 11, 1; Francis W. Hirst, *Life and Letters of Thomas Jefferson*, New York, 1926, pp. 502f.; W. D. Johnston, *History of the Library of Congress*, Vol. 1, Washington, D.C., 1904; Randolph G. Adams, *Three Americanists*, Philadelphia, 1939, pp. 69f.; *Thomas Jefferson, 1743–1943*. A Guide to the Rare Books, Maps and Manuscripts exhibited at the University of Michigan, Ann Arbor, 1943, pp. 21f.

Books owned by Jefferson's father: *Virginia Magazine*, X, 1902–3, p. 391. For relatively extensive collections of classical books in pre-Jeffersonian Virginia, see: G. K. Smart, "Private Libraries in Colonial Virginia," *American Literature*, X, 1938–9, pp. 37f.; Louis B. Wright, *The First Gentlemen of Virginia*, San Marino, 1940, pp. 140f.; *idem*, "The Classical Tradition in Colonial Virginia," *Papers of the Bibliographical Society of America*, XXXIII, 1939, pp. 85f.

According to the Catalogue of 1815 Jefferson's first library contained, aside from better known authors, editions of Celsus, Berossus, Manetho, the Chronicum Alexandrinum, Ptolemæus Hephæstion, Byzantine historians, and Orosius. Here as elsewhere the ancient texts are overwhelmingly represented in the original and there are but few translations. In the rich section on modern and medieval history (with the exception of British history) few original sources appear in contrast with the section on antiquity. Dioscurides and Theophrastus are included in the botanical collection; Alexander of Aphrodisias, Boethius, Demetrius Cydonius, "Cebes," Hier-

ocles, Ocellus, and Timœus occur along with the standard philosophers; editions of the Church Fathers are
numerous. In the geographical section one finds along
with Strabo and Mela, Dionysius the Perihegete, So-
linus, and the Itinerarium Antoninum. The sections on
poetry and oratory are exhaustive. Collections of fragments, epigrams, etc., are included. Standard authors
are often represented in two, three, or even four editions.
Classical and mathematical books retained in 1815: Letter to S. H. Smith, Sept. 21, 1814, M. XIV, p. 193; F. IX,
p. 487.
For the later library, *see* the Sales Catalogue of 1829 (*see
above,* note to p. 11, 1).

Page 17, par. 1: O. W. Long, *Thomas Jefferson and George Ticknor,* Williamstown, Mass., 1933, pp. 11f., 16f., 18f. *See
also,* Edith Philips, *Louis Hue Girardin and Nicholas
Gouin Despiof and Their Relations with Thomas Jefferson (The Johns Hopkins Studies in Romance Literatures and Languages.* Extra Vol. III), Baltimore, 1926.
par. 2: Long, *op. cit.,* pp. 16, 19f.
For Jefferson's critical knowledge of editions of classical
authors, see the interesting letter to Messrs. Wells and
Lilly (1818) in: *Thomas Jefferson. Correspondence,
Printed from the Originals in the Collection of William
K. Bixby,* edited by W. Ch. Ford, Boston, 1912, p. 238.
par. 3: The Latin phrases mean: "explanation of interpreters, insertion of scribes, additions by smatterers,
brought about by a stupid and barbarian man." Long,
op. cit., p. 16.
Letter to Edward Everett, Feb. 24, 1823, M. XV, p. 413;
compare, on late Greek usage of words, letter to F. W.
Gilmer, Oct. 14, 1817, *Correspondence of Thomas Jefferson and Francis Walker Gilmer,* edited by R. B. Davis,
Columbia, 1946, p. 55.

Page 18, par. 1. Long, *op. cit.,* p. 16.
Dictionaries: Letter to John Waldo, Aug. 16, 1813,
M. XIII, p. 340; letter to John Adams, Aug. 15, 1820,
M. XV, p. 273. The reacquisition of these dictionaries,
which he certainly did not own in more than one copy
before 1815, results from the fact that they occur in both
of his library catalogues (*see above,* note to 1, p. 11).
Criticism of the quality of dictionaries: Daniel Webster,

Private Correspondence, edited by F. Webster, I, Boston, 1857, p. 373.

Use of dictionaries: Letter to Edward Everett, Feb. 24, 1823, M. XV, p. 413.

Ticknor's observations: Long, *op. cit.,* pp. 34f.

Page 19, par 1: Letter to ———, Oct. 25, 1825, M. XVI, pp. 124f. Gibbon: *ibid.;* letter to Joel Barlow, Dec. 25, 1808, M. XII, p. 217.

Page 20, par. 1: Letters to John Adams, Aug. 15, 1820, M. XV, p. 275, and Jan. 24, 1814, M. XIV, pp. 75f.

For Brucker-Enfield, *see:* Gilbert Chinard, "Jefferson Among the Philosophers," *Ethics, LIII,* 1942–3, pp. 263f.

par. 2: Plato: *see below,* pp. 84f.

Plato's Republic: Letter to John Adams, July 5, 1814, M. XIV, pp. 147f.; F. IX, p. 462. Timeus: Letter to William Short, Aug. 4, 1820, M. XV, p. 258.

par. 3: Screw of Archimedes: Letter to Isaac McPherson, Aug. 13, 1813, M. XIII, pp. 329f., 332.

"Batture": M. XVIII, pp. 62f.; *see below,* pp. 62f.

Page 21, par. 1: M. XVIII, pp. 414f.; *see below,* p. 102. Chastellux died in 1788, therefore the letter to him cannot be as late as assumed in M.

par. 2: Letter to Priestley, April 9, 1803, M. X, pp. 374f.; F. VIII, pp. 224f.

Page 22, par. 1: *See below,* pp. 137f.

par. 2: *See below,* pp. 57f.

Letter to John Adams, March 21, 1819, M. XV, pp. 181f.

par. 3: Letter to Madison of July 19, 1788, M. VII, pp. 77f. At the same time he offered his own diplomatic services for procuring a vocabulary of an allegedly surviving Punic language from northern Africa. Letter to Edward Rutledge, July 18, 1788, M. VII, pp. 8of.; F. V, p. 41; *see below,* p. 58.

Page 23, par. 1: Letter to Joseph Coolidge, Jr., Jan. 15, 1825, M. XVIII, pp. 336f.

Page 24, par. 1: Letter to Volney, April 20, 1802, F'. II, p. 196. Pyramid and "Cleopatra": *Niles Register, XI,* 1816–17, pp. 317f.; *see also,* Paul Wilstach, *Jefferson and Monticello,* New York, 1925, p. 108.

Blue Ridge mountain: Randall, III, pp. 338, 436; Sarah N. Randolph, *The Domestic Life of Thomas Jefferson,* 3d ed., Cambridge, Mass., 1939, p. 316.

par. 2: Indian mound: *Notes on Virginia*, M. II, pp. 134f.; F. III, pp. 198f. *See*, K. Lehmann-Hartleben. "Thomas Jefferson Archæologist," *American Journal of Archæology*, XLVII, 1943, pp. 161f., with bibliography to which add: the fine article "Thomas Jefferson Field Archæologist," by A. D. Frazer in *The Four Arts, Dedicated to Artistic Virginia, II*, 1935, pp. 3f. (which had escaped my attention previously).

Architectural studies: Fundamental: Fiske Kimball, *Thomas Jefferson, Architect*, Boston, 1916. All later studies and references are based on this magnificent and penetrating work. For Jefferson's books on ancient architecture, *see* especially, pp. 34f., 90f.

For Jefferson's interest in ancient sculpture and his books, *see:* Fiske Kimball, "Jefferson and the Arts," *Proceedings of the American Philosophical Society,* LXXXVII, 1943, pp. 238f., especially, p. 241; A. Hyatt Mayor, "Jefferson's Enjoyment of the Arts," *The Metropolitan Museum of Art, Bulletin*, II, 1943, pp. 140f.

Page 25, par. 1: John Adams's amazing statement is found in a letter to the sculptor Binon (Feb. 7, 1819) reprinted in *Life Masks of Noted Americans of 1825 by John H. I. Browere*, Catalogue, M. Knoedler and Company, New York, 1940 (to plate 2). This letter contains the lapidary phrase: "I would not give sixpence for a picture of Raphael or a statue of Phidias."

Ticknor: *Life, Letters and Journal of George Ticknor*, I, Boston, 1876, p. 348; *see*, H. B. Adams, *Thomas Jefferson and the University of Virginia* (U.S. Bureau of Education. *Circular of Information*, No. 1, 1888. *Contributions to American Educational History*, No. 2) Washington. D. C., 1888, p. 124.

Page 26, par. 1: *See*, Kimball's article, quoted above, note to p. 24, 2. "Cleopatra": note to p. 24. 1. Jefferson's pictures, *see also, Catalogue of Valuable Oil Paintings, many of them by the old masters, and all choice pictures being the Collection of the late President Jefferson to be sold at Auction on Friday, July 19, At Mr. Harding's Gallery, School St.*, Boston, 1833 (photostat copy in New York Public Library). In the preface it is said that Trumbull assisted Jefferson with his purchases.

par. 3: Architecture: *see above*, note to p. 24, 2 and in

addition: *Fiske Kimball, Domestic Architecture of the American Colonies and of the Early Republic,* New York, 1922; *Idem., American Architecture,* Indianapolis, 1928, chap. 7, pp. 69f.; Thomas T. Waterman, *The Mansions of Virginia,* 1706-1776, Chapel Hill, 1946, pp. 341f.; *see below,* chaps. 10 and 11 with notes.

Desgodets: edition of 1682, plates 111f.135, compare: I. T. Frary, *Thomas Jefferson Architect and Builder,* Richmond, 1931, plates 11, 12, 14, 15, 19.

Details of Pantheon: Desgodets, plates 1f.; Fréart, English edition of 1707, plates 21, 23, 25, 43, 45.

Southern France: Letter to the Comtesse de Tessé, March 20, 1787, M. VI, pp. 103, 106. *See also,* letter to William Short, March 29, 1787, *William and Mary College Quarterly,* ser. 2, XI, 1931, p. 247.

Page 27, par. 1: *See,* S. K. Padover, *Jefferson,* London, 1942, p. 148; Gilbert Chinard, *Thomas Jefferson, The Apostle of Americanism,* 2nd ed., New York, 1939, p. 170 for disappointment with the travel notes. See, in general, Edward Dumbaud, *Thomas Jefferson American Tourist,* Norman, 1946, with good remarks about this problem, pp. 152f.

Memoranda taken on a Journey from Paris into the Southern Parts of France and Northern of Italy, in the year 1787, M. XVII, pp. 153f.; Dumbaud, *op. cit.,* pp. 83f. The building in Vienne, called by Jefferson a sepulchral monument, is now generally assumed to belong to the decoration of the Roman Circus there. M. XVII, pp. 167f.

Bordeaux: *ibid.,* p. 221.

Bricks for the Capitol: Letter to Johnson, Stuart and Carroll, March 8, 1792, M. XIX, p. 90. From the divergence of measurements given for Roman bricks in the *Memoranda* and in this letter, and from the more detailed character of the latter, one may conclude that Jefferson had more specific notes on his measurements, aside from the published memoranda, and that he consulted them.

Page 28, par. 1: Letter to the Comtesse de Tessé, March 20, 1787, M. VI, p. 106.

Page 29, par. 1: Letter to George Wythe, Sept. 16, 1787, M. VI, p. 297; F. IV, pp. 442f.

The Camp of Varus: *Memorandums on a Tour from Paris to Amsterdam, Strassburg, and back to Paris,* M. XVII, p. 253; Dumbaud, *op. cit.,* pp. 110f.

Page 30, par. 1: Letter to William Short, Sept. 20, 1788, M. VII, p. 148; F. V, p. 51.

par. 2: Goethe's visit to Pompeii: Entry in his *"Italienische Reise,* March 11, 1787.

Letter to George Wythe, Sept. 16, 1787, M. VI, p. 297; F. IV, p. 442. Compare also, letter to Maria Cosway, July 1, 1787, Helen Duprey Bullock, *My Head and My Heart,* New York, 1945, p. 68; letter to Gaudenzio Clerici, Aug. 15, 1787, Dumbaud, *op. cit.,* p. 146.

Letter to William Short, Dec. 8, 1788, M. VII, p. 235.

Letter to Ticknor's father, written in 1817: O. W. Long, *Thomas Jefferson and George Ticknor,* Williamstown, Mass, 1933, p. 20, note 1. See also below, p. 57.

Chapter 3

Page 32, par. 2: For the seventeenth and early eighteenth century classical tradition in Virginia, *see:* Louis B. Wright, *Proceedings of the American Philosophical Society,* LXXXVII, 1943, pp. 223f. with bibliography; *see also above,* note to p. 16, 1, and *The Secret Diary of William Byrd of Westover, 1709–1712,* edited by L. B. Wright and Marin Tinling, Richmond, Va., 1941.

Maury's servants: Marie Kimball, *Jefferson. The Road to Glory. 1743–1776,* New York, 1943, p. 37.

Names of horses: Randall, I, p. 69; *Scribner's Magazine,* XXXVI, 1904, p. 576.

The inscription *Hilaritas sapientium et bonæ vitæ proles* in the Apollo room: Marie Kimball, *op. cit.,* p. 61.

Ships: Letter to Madison, Feb. 7, 1783, M. IV, pp. 430f.; F. III, pp. 300f.; *Autobiography,* M. I, p. 90; F. I, p. 85.

Pantops: *see below,* note to p. 182, 2.

Names for new territories: F. III, pp. 409f.; Gilbert Chinard, *Thomas Jefferson, The Apostle of Americanism,* 2nd ed., Boston 1939, p. 149; *Thomas Jefferson, 1743–1943.* A Guide to the Rare Books, Maps and Manuscripts exhibited at the University of Michigan, Ann Arbor, 1943, pp. 13f.

Houdon's monument: Letter to Madison, Feb. 8, 1786, M. V, pp. 280f.

The Emblem of Virginia: Letter to Henry Lee, June 28, 1793, F. VI, pp. 320f.

Page 34, par. 1: Letter to Priestley, Jan. 27, 1800, M. X, p. 147; F. VII, p. 414.

Letter to John Brazier, Aug. 24, 1819, M. XV, p. 209.

Memories of his grandchildren: Randall, I, p. 18.

par. 2: Douglas and Maury: *Autobiography*, M. I, p. 3; F. I, p. 3.

Page 35, par. 1: Letter to Priestley, quoted above, p. 34, 1.

School bill for Virginia: *Notes on Virginia*, Query XIV, M. II, p. 203; F. III, pp. 251f.

Letter to Peter Carr, Aug. 19, 1785, M. V, pp. 84f.

Page 37, par. 1: Letter to Monsieur de Crève-Cœur, Jan. 15, 1787, M. VI, pp. 53f.

Page 38, par. 1: The reference at the beginning of the paragraph is to the distorted interpretation by Otto Vossler, *Die Amerikanischen Revolutionsideale in ihrem Verhaeltnis zu den Europaeischen* (*Historische Zeitschrift*, Beiheft, XVII), Munich, 1929, p. 125.

George Wythe's education: Marie Kimball, *op. cit.*, p. 74, quoting an English traveler of 1760.

Paris: Letter to Madison, Sept. 1, 1785, M. V, p. 109 (compare, letters to Edmund Randolph, Sept. 20, 1785, M. V, p. 138, and Aug. 3, 1787, M. V, p. 220; letter to Ticknor, 1816, O. W. Long, *Thomas Jefferson and George Ticknor*, Williamstown, Mass., 1933, p. 16).

Letter to Ralph Izard, July 17, 1788, M. VII, p. 71.

par. 2: Ch. H. Sherrill, *French Memoires of Eighteenth Century America*, New York, 1915, pp. 232f.

Page 39, par. 1: Letter to John Bannister, Oct. 15, 1785, M. V, pp. 185f.

Notes on Virginia, Query XV, M. II, p. 209; F. III, p. 255 (compare, his advice to J. W. Eppes, July 28, 1787, M. VI, p. 190).

par. 2: Attic Societies: Letter to L. H. Girardon, Jan. 15, 1815, M. XIV, pp. 231f.

George Wythe: *Notes for the biography of George Wythe*, M. I, pp. 166f.

Legal documents: John Patton, "College Days of Thomas Jefferson," *The Atlantic Monthly*, XXIX, 1872, pp. 32f.

Page 40, par. 1: Aversion to grammar: *see below*, pp. 79f.

Page 41, par. 1: Letter of John Adams to Jefferson, July 9, 1813,

M. XIII, pp. 302f. The Greek words mean "Concerning the composition of nouns."

par. 2: John Bernard, *Retrospections of America, 1779–1811*. Edited by B. Bernard, New York, 1887, p. 238. Marie Kimball, *op. cit.*, p. 116. *See below,* pp. 146f.

Page 42, par. 1: John Bernard, *l.c.;* Marie Kimball, *op. cit.,* p. 117.

par. 2: *Literary Bible: see above,* p. 211. The present author, though at times dissenting from Professor Chinard's interpretations, wishes to state his fundamental indebtedness to this edition and that of the *Commonplace Book.* These critical editions have provided him with the most important material, apart from Jefferson's letters. The reader may also be referred to the fine use Marie Kimball has made of these editions (*op. cit.,* pp. 84f.) and to her invaluable contributions to the chronology of the entries, and to Professor Chinards' own discussion, *Thomas Jefferson, op. cit.,* pp. 21f. *See below,* pp. 138, 148. For the practice of commonplacing at the time, *see,* N. G. Goodman, *Benjamin Rush,* Philadelphia, 1934, p. 7.

Herodotus, *History,* Book II, chap. 104, L.B., p. 39; *idem.,* Book II, chap. 123, *ibid.; idem,* Book IV, chapters 84-5 *ibid.*

Pope's *Essay on Man, ibid.* pp. 130f.

Bolingbroke: *ibid.,* pp. 65f.; *see also* Gilbert Chinard, "Jefferson Among the Philosophers," *Ethics,* LIII, 1942–3, p. 256.

Cicero's *Tusculan Dialogues, ibid.,* pp. 72f.

Euripides' tragedies, *ibid.,* pp. 83f.; *Hecuba,* 1.844, compare C.P.B., p. 96, No. 557, note; *see below,* pp. 50f.

Page 44, par. 2: Homer, *Iliad,* IV, 447f.; XIII, 130, L.B., p. 191; *see below,* p. 147.

Patrick Henry: *Autobiography,* M. I, p. 5; F. I, p. 6; *ibid.,* M. I, p. 55; *see below,* pp. 93, 147.

Page 45, par. 1: Compare, Chinard, *Thomas Jefferson, op. cit.,* pp. 21f.

Page 46, par. 1: Letter to a law student: *see above,* p. 13 with note.

Reading: Marie Kimball, *op. cit.,* pp. 80f.

Adam Dickson, *The Husbandry of the Ancients,* 2 vols., Edinburgh, 1788.

See Roy J. Honeywell, *The Educational Work of Thomas*

Jefferson (Harvard Studies in Education, XVI), Cambridge, Mass., 1931, p. 218.

Chapter 4

Page 47, par. 2: *See,* for 18th century approaches to history, the fine essays by J. B. Black, *The Art of History,* London, 1926.

Notes on Virginia, M. II; F. III, pp. 69f.

Page 48, par. 1: *Commonplace Book: see above,* p. 211 and note to p. 42, 2.

Simon Pelloutier, *Histoire des Celtes,* and *Histoire des Galates,* Le Haye, 3 vols., 1740–1750; Chinard, C.P.B., pp. 21f., 168f., notes to entries 696f.

Page 49, par. 1: Jefferson's criticism, especially: entries 697, 698, pp. 160f., 701, pp. 176f., 705, p. 173, 709 and 711, pp. 176f.

Page 50, par. 1: For Lord Kames, *see:* Gladys Bryson, *Man and Society, The Scottish Inquiry of the Eighteenth Century,* Princeton, 1945.

Euripides: C.P.B., p. 96, note to 557; *see above,* p. 42 with note; Tacitus, *ibid.,* p. 226, 755.

Stanyan, Temple, *Grecian History down to the Death of Philip of Macedon,* London, 1739; Chinard, C.P.B., pp. 22, 181f.

Montesquieu, *ibid.,* pp. 31f, 275f.; *see below,* pp. 83f.

Voltaire, *ibid.,* pp. 334f.

Calendar, *ibid.,* pp. 339f.

Church Fathers, *ibid.,* pp. 343f.; *see,* for the use of these excerpts, Jefferson's *Notes on Religion* from 1776, F. II, pp. 92f.

Page 51, par. 1: *Literary Bible: see above,* pp. 42f., with notes.

par. 2: Architecture: *see,* especially, Fiske Kimball's works quoted to pp. 24 and 26. For the early period, *see also* the good account by Marie Kimball, *Jefferson. The Road to Glory. 1743–1776,* New York, 1943, pp. 147f.

Notes on the Garden and Burial Place: Randall, I, p. 60; *Thomas Jefferson's Garden Book, 1766–1824.* Annotated by E. M. Betts (*Memoirs of the American Philosophical Society,* XXII), Philadelphia, 1944, pp. 25f.

Cato and Varro: *see below,* p. 74: Pliny the Younger, *see below,* pp. 61f., 179f.

Robert Castell, *The Villas of the Antients Illustrated,*

London, 1728; Fiske Kimball, *Thomas Jefferson Architect*, Boston, 1916, p. 92. For Monticello and Roman villas, *see below*, chap. 11.

Page 53, par. 1: Slavery: M. II, pp. 197f.; F. III, pp. 247f.

par. 2: Epigram for his sister, Randall I, p. 41:

> *Ah, Joanna, puellarum optima,*
> *Ah, aevi virentis flore praecepta,*
> *Sit tibi terra levis;*
> *Longe, longeque valeto!*

Inscription on tombstone for Mrs. Jefferson: Homer, *Iliad*, XXII, ll. 389/90 (transl. Lang-Leaf-Myers). *See,* the comments of George Tucker *The Life of Thomas Jefferson*, Philadelphia, 1837, I. p. 159 note; Randall, I, p. 138; Gilbert Chinard, *Thomas Jefferson. The Apostle of Americanism*, 2nd ed., Boston, 1939, p. 138; Marie Kimball, *op. cit.*, p. 186; S. K. Padover, *Jefferson*, London, 1942, p. 111.

For skepticism about translations, *see below*, pp. 102f.

Page 55, par. 3 *See,* for Paris, in general, the entertaining account of Helen Duprey Bullock, *My Head and My Heart*, New York, 1945.

For monuments in France, *see above*, pp. 27f.

Clérisseau, *Monuments de Nismes (Antiquités de la France*, Première Partie), Paris, 1778.

For Clérisseau: U. Thieme, *Allegemeines Lexikon der Bildeorden Künstler*, VII, Leipzig, 1912, pp. 91f.

For the Capitol in Richmond, *see,* Fiske Kimball's works: "Thomas Jefferson and the First Monument of Classical Revival in America," *Journal of the American Institute of Architects*, III, 1915, pp. 371f., 421f., 473f. Reprint, pp. 1f.; *idem,* "Thomas Jefferson and the Origins of the Classical Revival in America," *Art and Archaeology*, I, 1915, pp. 219f; *Thomas Jefferson Architect*, Boston, 1916, pp. 41f.

Exhibition in Paris: *Autobiography*, M. I., p. 68; F. I., p. 64.

See also, An Account of the Capitol of Virginia, M. XVII, pp. 353f.

Page 56, par. 1: Houdon: Gilbert Chinard and F. H. Taylor, *Houdon in America (Historical Documents, Institut Francais de Washington*, cahier 4), Baltimore, 1930.

David: Letter to Madame de Breham, March 14, 1787, M. VII, p. 308; F. V, p. 90; *see* Gilbert Chinard, *Trois Amitiés Francaises de Jefferson,* Paris, 1927, p. 42.

Wedgwood: Letter to Jay, Jan. 9, 1787, M. VI, p. 46; the Wedgwood plaque on the mantel of the dining room in Monticello with "antique" Muses: Fiske Kimball, *Domestic Architecture of the American Colonies and the Early Republic,* New York, 1922, p. 256, Fig. 215; I. T. Frary, *Thomas Jefferson Architect and Builder,* Richmond, 1931, pl. 17.

Trumbull: Original letter (it seems to be unpublished) to James Barbour, Jan. 19, 1817, in the New York Public Library, James Barbour File; *see also,* Daniel Webster, *Private Correspondence,* edited by F. Webster, I, Boston, 1857, p. 372; Dumbaud, *op. cit.,* pp. 136f.; Bullock, *op. cit.,* passion; and, for Houdon and Trumbull, Fiske Kimball, "The Life Portraits of Jefferson and their Replicas," *Proceedings of the American Philosophical Society,* LXXXIII, 1940, pp. 499f.

Jean Jacques Barthélemy, *Voyage du Jeune Anacharsis,* Paris, 1787.

Letter to Dr. Currie, Dec. 20, 1788, M. VII, p. 240; letter to Madison, Jan. 12, 1789, M. VI, pp. 269f. F. V, p. 65; letter to Doctor Willard, March 24, 1789, M. VII, p. 325; Jefferson's personal acquaintance with Barthélemy: Randall, I, p. 437; Gilbert Chinard, *Thomas Jefferson, op. cit.,* p. 165.

"Correct" classical scholars: *see above,* p. 35 with note.

Classical education in France: *see above,* p. 38 with note.

Decay of monuments in Provence: Letter to the Comtesse de Tessé, March 20, 1787, M. VI, pp. 103f.

Page 57, par. 1: Modern Greek: *see above,* p. 22 with note.

Desire to go to Greece: *see above,* pp. 30f.

Accentuation: *see above,* p. 21, with note 1.

The language of Homer: Letter to George Wythe, Sept. 16, 1787, M. VI, p. 299; F. IV, pp. 444f.

par. 2: Jefferson told Ticknor later he had planned to go to Italy, Sicily, and Greece after his hoped for return to France: *Life, Letters and Journals of George Ticknor,* I, Boston, 1876, p. 35; compare, above, p. 30; *see also,* letter to Trumbull, Oct. 13, 1786, Dumbaud, *op. cit.,* p. 138.

Page 58, par. 1: Moral and ethical ideas, *see below,* pp. 112f., 137f. Perversion of Christianity, *see below,* pp. 84f.
Especially important during this period were, his conversations with Benjamin Rush: Letter to him, April 21, 1803, M. X, pp. 379f.; F. VIII, p. 223.
par. 2: Letter to Moses Robinson, March 23, 1801, M. X, p. 237.
Indians and Carthaginians: Letter to Edward Ruthledge, July 18, 1788, M. VII, pp. 8of.; F. V., p. 41; *see above,* p. 23.
World-wide comparative linguistics: Letter to John Sibley, May 27, 1805, M. XI, pp. 79f.

Page 59, par. 1: Septuagint: Letter to Charles Thompson, Dec. 25, 1808, M. XII, p. 217; F. IX, p. 234.
Reading: Letter to John Adams, May 17, 1818, M. XV, p. 169; F. X, p. 108; Letter to William Short, Oct. 31, 1819, M. XV, p. 221; F. X, p. 145.

Page 60, par. 1: The documents for Jefferson's extensive reading in the last years of his life will, in part, appear in the Second and Third Sections of this book. A full account will be possible only after a complete publication of his writings. Gray's visit in 1814: Francis C. Gray, *Thomas Jefferson in 1814.* Being an account of a visit to Monticello, Virginia. With notes and introduction by H. S. Rowe and T. Jefferson Coolidge, Jr., Boston, 1924, p. 68.
Ticknor: Life, etc., *op. cit.,* p. 349.
Tragedians: Randall, III, pp. 346, 539.
Pliny: Th. Fitzhugh, "Letters of Thomas Jefferson Concerning Philology and the Classics" (Reprinted from *University of Virginia, Alumni Bulletin,* 1918-9), Charlottesville, 1919, p. 22.

Page 62, par. 1: Pliny the Younger, *Epistles,* II, 17, 8.
Poplar Forest library: Randall, III, pp. 344f.; Dumbaud, *op. cit.,* pp. 191f.; Bedford trip: Letter to Joseph Milligan, Apr. 6, 1816, M. XIV, p. 459.
par 2: Opinion on the "Batture": M. XVIII, pp. 1f., *see above,* pp. 2of.
University of Virginia, *see below,* chapters 10 to 12.
par. 3: Letter to John Adams, May 5, 1817, M. XV, pp. 110f.
Giuseppe Micali, *L'Italia avanti il dominio dei Romani,* 4 vols., Florence, 1810.

Page 63, par. 1: *Summum bonum,* the "greatest good": Letter to John Melish, Jan. 13, 1813, M. XIII, p. 213; F. IX, p. 377.

For Epicureanism and Christianity, *see below,* pp. 39f.

Jefferson Bible: M. XX, Appendix; Randolph G. Adams, *Three Americanists,* Philadelphia, 1939, pp. 8of.

Socrates and Jesus: *see below,* pp. 137f.

par. 2: Linguistic studies, *see above,* pp. 17f.

The letter referred to: Letter to————, Feb. 20, 1825, M. XVI, pp. 107f.

Page 65, par. 1: Letter to John Brazier, Aug. 24, 1819, M. XV, p. 208. Letter to Girardon, Aug. 26, 1820, E. Philips, *Louis Hue Girardin and Nicholas Gouin Dufief and Their Relations with Thomas Jefferson (The Johns Hopkins Studies in Romance Literatures and Languages,* Extra Volume III), Baltimore, 1926, p. 41.

Letter to John Adams, Sept, 8, 1817, M. XV, p. 137; compare, the letter to J. Correa de Serra, Nov. 25, 1817, M. XV, p. 154.

Letter to W. B. Giles, Dec. 26, 1825, M. XVI, p. 150; F. X, p. 357.

par. 2: Randall, III, pp. 505f.

Letter to John Adams, July 5, 1814, M. XIV, p. 150; F. IX, p. 464.

Letter to Charles Thompson, Jan. 9, 1816, M. XIV, p. 385; F. X, p. 5

Page 66, par. 1: Many statements on which these essays are based are taken from the correspondence of Jefferson and Adams in their old age. This correspondence is available only in the editions of the complete works, since the selection published by Paul Wilstach, *Correspondence of John Adams and Thomas Jefferson, 1812–1826,* Indianapolis, 1925, is rather superficial and not representative.

Chapter 5

Page 71 par. 1: Jefferson fond of paradox: *Life, Letters and Journals of George Ticknor,* I, Boston 1876, p. 34.

par. 2: "Antediluvian topics," *see above,* p. 65.

"Learned lumber": Letter to Fulwar Skipwith, Aug. 3, 1771, M. IV, p. 237; F. I, p. 396.

His granddaughter's recollections: Randall, III, p. 346.

par. 3: *See below,* pp. 203f. Bolingbroke, in his *Letter*

on the Study and Use of History of 1735 (which early
influenced Jefferson, *see above,* p. 43) outspokenly
stresses the didactic importance of modern history: *The
Works of Lord Bolingbroke,* II Philadelphia, 1841, pp.
171f. In Voltaire's (*see,* J. B. Black, *The Art of History,*
London, 1926, pp. 29f.) as well as in Schiller and Herder's
historical research, the emphasis on modern rather than
antique history is evident. *See also above,* p. 47f.

Page 72, par. 1: Letter to Volney, Jan. 8. 1797, M. IX, p. 365.
Letter to Nathaniel Macon, Jan. 12, 1819, M. XV, p.
179; F. X, pp. 120f.
Letter to John Brazier, Aug. 24, 1819, M. XV, p. 209.
par. 2: For Jefferson's philosophical thought, its connection with and difference from that of various schools
of his century, *see* the very valuable dissertation of
Adrienne Koch, *The Philosophy of Thomas Jefferson,*
New York, 1943; *see also,* Gilbert Chinard, "Jefferson
among the Philosophers," *Ethics, LIII,* 1942-3, pp. 255f.
Ecclecticism: Koch, *op. cit.,* pp. 4f.; *see also,* James
Truslow Adams, *The Living Jefferson,* New York, 1936,
pp. 78f.; *see below,* p. 164.
For Lord Kames, *see above,* p. 50 with note. Cicero: *see*
the references in the register at the end.
In general, the influence on young Jefferson of the Stoic
compound in Cicero's writing has been overemphasized
by modern interpreters, such as Professor Chinard and
Dr. Koch.

Page 73, par. 1: Letter to F. A. Van der Kemp, March 22, 1812,
M. XIII, p. 135.
par. 2: Bill for the More General Diffusion of Knowl-
edge: F. II, p. 221: compare, *Notes on Virginia,* Query
XIV, M. II, p. 207; F. III, pp. 252f.; *see below,* p. 113f.
Letter to David Ramsay, Aug. 4, 1787, M. VI, p. 226, and
letter to Benjamin Hawkins, Aug. 4, 1787, M. VI, p. 232;
F. IV, p. 426.

Page 74, par. 1: Adam Dickson, *The Husbandry of the Ancients,*
2 vols., Edinburgh, 1788.
Roy J. Honeywell, *The Educational Work of Thomas
Jefferson (Harvard Studies in Education,* XVI,) Cambridge, Mass., 1931, p. 218. Cato and Varro are used in
his discussion on slavery in the *Notes on Virginia, see
below,* p. 111.

Books used for agriculture: Randall, II, p. 303; M. L. Wilson, "Thomas Jefferson Farmer," *Proceedings of the American Philosophical Society,* LXXXVI, 1943, p. 218. For his library classification *see above,* pp. 16f. with notes; Honeywell, *op. cit.,* pp. 211f.

Cookbooks: Marie Kimball, *Thomas Jefferson's Cook Book,* Richmond, 1941, p. 9.

Page 75, par. 1: Southern France: *see above,* pp. 26f., 55f.

Letter to T. L. Shippen, Sept. 29, 1788, M. VII, pp. 153f.

Page 76, par. 1: Euripides, *Hippolytus,* ll, 189f., L. B., p. 103, Letter to John Adams, March 14, 1820, M. XV, p. 241. (For his empiricism, Jefferson explicitly refers in this letter to Locke.)

Cicero: Chinard, L. B., p. 17; *idem, Thomas Jefferson, The Apostle of Americanism,* 2nd, ed., Boston, 1939, p. 23.

On Jefferson's skepticism: Koch, *op. cit.,* pp. 89f.

"ignorance" etc. Letter to the Rev. Mr. White, Apr. 25, 1812, *Missouri Historical Society, Glimpses of the Past,* III, 1936, p. 117.

Comte: Gilbert Chinard, *Jefferson et les idéologues,* Baltimore, 1925, p. 285; *The Mississippi Valley Historical Review,* XXX, 1943, pp. 184f.; *Ethics,* l. c., pp. 267f.

Page 77, par. 1: Letter to John Adams, Oct. 14, 1816, M. XV, p. 75.

Letter to John Rutledge, Sept. 9, 1788, M. VII, p. 138.

par. 2: Euripides, *Phoenician Women,* ll. 469f., L. B., p. 97.

Tacitus: C. P. B., p. 226, No. 755; *see,* Gilbert Chinard, *The Correspondence of Jefferson and Du Pont de Nemours,* Baltimore, 1931, p. LX.

Twelve Tables: C. P. B., p. 294, No. 800.

"Batture": M. XVIII, pp. 1f.; *see above,* pp. 20f, 62.

Page 78, par. 1: Geology: Letter to Thomas Cooper, Aug. 6, 1810, M. XII, p. 401; Honeywell, *op. cit.,* pp. 116f.; *Thomas Jefferson's Correspondence. Printed from the Originals in the Collection of William K. Bixley,* edited by W. Ch. Ford, Boston, 1916, p. 268.

Political Economy and Medicine: *ibid,* p. 286; *see,* Gilbert Chinard, *Correspondence, op. cit.,* pp. 1f.

Medicine: Skepticism about medical theory was repeatedly expressed in Jefferson's letters. *See,* especially:

Letters to Benjamin Rush, Aug. 17, 1811, M. XIII, p. 75;
F. IX, p. 328; to John Crawford, Jan. 2, 1812, M. XIII,
pp. 117f.; to Dr. Wheaton, Feb. 14, 1812, M. XIII, pp.
133f.; to Benjamin Rush, March 6, 1813 (*vis medicatrix
naturae*), M. XIII, p. 223; to Thomas Cooper, Oct. 7,
1814, M. XIV, p. 200 ("Perhaps I should concur with you
in excluding the theory [not the practice] of medicine.");
to John Brazier, Aug. 24, 1819, M. XV, p. 210 (Hippocrates): to Caspar Wistar, June 21, 1807, F. IX, p. 81.
Compare, Randall, III, p. 514.

For medical theories in post-Revolutionary America, *see,*
N. G. Goodman, *Benjamin Rush,* Philadelphia, 1934,
pp. 229f.

His surgical ability: Sarah N. Randolph, *The Domestic
Life of Thomas Jefferson,* 3rd. ed., Cambridge Mass.,
1939, p. 282.

Vaccination: Henry A. Martin, "Jefferson as a Vaccina-
tor," *North Carolina Medical Journal,* VII, 1881, pp. 1f.
John Millar, *Observations on the Change of Public
Opinion in Religion, Politics, Medicine,* 2 vols., London,
1805. (*Catalogue of the Library of the United States,*
Washington 1815, chapter 10.) The author of this book,
the first edition of which appeared with a slightly different title in 1770, is not identical with the better known
lawyer-philosopher of the same name.

See also below, p. 129.

Page 79, par. 1: *See above,* pp. 19f.

Voltaire: C. P. B., p. 335, No. 853.

Allegorical interpretation: Letter to John Adams, Oct.
14, 1816, M. XV, p. 74.

par. 2: Letter to Charles Thompson, Sept. 20, 1787,
M. VI, p. 312; F. IV, p. 447.

par. 3: *See,* in general, Albert C. Baugh, "Thomas
Jefferson Linguistic Liberal," *Studies for William A.
Read.* Edited by N. M. Caffee and T. A. Kirby, Louisiana
University, 1940, pp. 88f.; H. C. Montgomery, "Thomas
Jefferson as a Philologist," *American Journal of Phi-
lology,* LXV, 1944, pp. 367f.; for interest in Indian lan-
guages, *see also,* Mabel Morris, "Jefferson and the Lan-
guages of the American Indians," *Modern Language
Quarterly,* VI, 1945, pp. 31f. *See below,* pp. 96f., 101f.,
148f.

Page 80, par. 1: Baugh, *op. cit.*, pp. 100f.

Letter to John Waldo, Aug. 16, 1813, M. XIII, p. 339.

par. 2: *See,* in general: H. C. Mencken, *The American Language,* 4th ed., New York, 1938, and *Supplement,* I, New York, 1945 (Index, under Jefferson, for Jefferson's own part in the actual development of an American language).

Letter to John Waldo, Aug. 16, 1813, M. XIII, p. 340.

Smetlege, *Nouveau Dictionnaire français contenant les expressions de nouvelle création du Peuple francais. Ouvrage additional au Dictionnaire de l'Académie francaise.*

See below, pp. 150f.

Neology and Greek: Letter to John Adams, Aug. 15, 1820, M. XV, pp. 272f.; compare, letter to Joseph Milligan, April 6, 1816, M. XIV, pp. 463f., and Baugh, *op. cit.,* p. 105.

Page 81, par. 1: Letter to Edward Everett, Feb. 24, 1823, M. XV, pp. 414f.

Letter to Madison, Dec. 12, 1811, quoted by Baugh, *op. cit.,* p. 104.

Connecticut Latin: *see above,* p. 65.

Page 82, par. 1: Pelloutier: *see above,* pp. 48f.; C. P. B., p. 175.

par. 2: Letter to F. W. Gilmer, June 7, 1816, M. XV, pp. 23f.; F. X, pp. 31f.

Page 83, par. 1: Excerpts from Montesquieu: C. P. B., pp. 257f.; *see above,* p. 50.

Democracy and size of territory: *ibid.,* p. 267 with comment by Chinard; Marie Kimball, *op. cit.,* p. 212 has suggested instead that Montesquieu's admiration of British institutions was responsible for Jefferson's antipathy. This may well be the case and this emotional reaction of Jefferson may have caused him to single out Montesquieu's system as a target of attack as his anticlericalism was in the background of his attacks of the "speculations" of Plato.

Page 84, par. 1: Plato: Louis B. Wright, "Thomas Jefferson and the Classics," *Proceedings of the American Philosophical Society,* LXXXVI, 1943, p. 229. The principal passages directed against Plato are found in these letters: to John Adams, July 5, 1814, M. XIV, pp. 147f.; F. IX, pp. 462f.; to William Short, Oct. 31, 1819, M. XV, pp. 219f.; F. X, pp. 143f., and Aug. 4, 1820, M. XV, pp. 258f. *See below,* p. 118, and note to p. 132, par. 1. The Fact that Lucretius was concerned solely with "natural philosophy" constituted a factor in Jefferson's neglect of him. *See: Memoirs of John Quincy Adams,* edited by Ch. F. Adams, I, Philadelphia, 1874, p. 472; Claude G. Bowers, *Jefferson in Power,* Boston, 1936, p. 48 (a discussion with Jefferson, concerning Epicureanism).

Page 85, par. 1: Letter to Benjamin Rush, April 21, 1803, M. X, p. 383; F. VIII, pp. 223f.

Letter to Salma Hales, July 26, 1818, F'V, p. 79.

Letter to Benjamin Waterhouse, June 26, 1822, F. X, p. 219.

Chapter 6

Page 87, par. 2: Bolingbroke: *see above,* pp. 43, 72 with notes. *See also,* Marie Kimball, *Thomas Jefferson. The Road to Glory 1743–1776.* New York, 1943, p. 124. Originals and "compilers". Letter to———, Oct. 25, 1825, M. XVI, p. 124.

Page 88, par. 1: Letter to Peter Carr, Aug. 10, 1787, M. VI, pp. 258f.; F. IV, pp. 430f. For Bolingbroke's influence on Jefferson, in this respect, *see* Gilbert Chinard, *Thomas Jefferson. The Apostle of Americanism,* 2nd. ed., Boston, 1939, p. 21. *Syllabus of an Estimate of the Merit of the Doctrines of Jesus Compared with Those of Others,* in letter to Benjamin Rush, April 21, 1803, M. X, p. 383; F. VIII, p. 227.

Locke: C. P. B., pp. 386f.

Jefferson Bible: *above,* p. 63, with note to par. 1.

Page 89, par. 2: The preference for the authors mentioned can be concluded from the various references to them in Jefferson's later writings. *See,* the register at the end of this book.

Polybius: Th. Fitzhugh, "Letters of Thomas Jefferson Concerning Philology and the Classics." Reprinted from *University of Virginia, Alumni Bulletin,* 1918–9. Charlottesville, 1919, p. 22.

Letters of Cicero: *see below,* pp. 115f.

Letters of Pliny: *see above,* pp: 60f. with note.

Washington's archive: Letter to William Johnson, June 12, 1823, M. XV, p. 442.

Page 90, par. 1: Letter to the Editor of the *Journal de Paris*, Aug. 29, 1787, M. XVII, pp. 148f.; F. X, p. 228.

Page 91, par. 1: Carthage: *see above,* pp. 62f. with note.

Panegyric biography: Randall, III, p. 506.

Livy and Diodorus: Letter to William Short, Aug. 4, 1820, M. XV, p. 257.

Fictive speeches: Letters to John Adams, Aug. 10, 1815, M. XIV, p. 343; F. IX, p. 527, and May 5, 1817, M. XV, p. 111; letter to G. A. Otis, Dec. 25, 1820, M. XVIII, p. 306.

par. 2: Tomb of Virgil: *see above,* pp. 29f.

Château of Nymwegen: *Memorandum on a tour from Paris to Amsterdam, Strassburg and back to Paris,* M. XVII, p. 252.

Scrapbook from poems: The editor, John W. Wayland ("The Poetical Tastes of Thomas Jefferson," *The Sewanee Review,* XVIII, 1910, pp. 285f.) has not correctly understood the character of this collection, it seems to me.

Augustus: *see below,* p. 117.

Page 92, par. 1: Letter to S. A. Wells, June 23, 1819, F. X, p. 133 note.

David's picture: Edith Philips, *Louis Hue Girardin and Nicholas Gouin Dufief and Their Relations with Thomas Jefferson (The Johns Hopkins Studies in Romance Literatures and Languages,* Extra Vol. III), Baltimore, 1926, p. 44. My colleague Walter Friedlaender tells me that the reference can only be to the painting "The Sons of Brutus," and to the women represented there. This picture caused much excitement when it was exhibited in 1787 during Jefferson's stay in Paris: Helen Duprey Bullock, *My Head and My Heart,* New York, 1945, p. 77.

Portraits: should have modern, not ridiculous antique dresses, letter to Washington, Aug. 14, 1787, M. VI, p. 275; Letter to William Short, Aug. 25, 1790, *William and Mary College Quarterly,* ser. 2, XII, 1932, p. 301; however, later, he preferred Roman toga and colossal size for a statue to be made by Canova, letter to Nathanial Macon, Jan. 22, 1816, M. XIV, pp. 408f.

See, in general: Gilbert Chinard and F. H. Taylor, *Houdon in America (Historical Documents,* Institut

Francais de Washington, cahier 4), Baltimore, 1930; A. Hyatt Mayor, "Jefferson's Enjoyment of the Arts" (*The Metropolitan Museum of Art, Bulletin,* December, 1943), p. 141.

For Bacon, Locke, Newton, *see below,* pp. 120f.

Monticello: Randall, III, pp. 337, 522; Sarah N. Randolph, *The Domestic Life of Thomas Jefferson,* 3rd. ed., Cambridge, Mass., 1939, p. 268; *Life, Letters and Journals of George Ticknor,* I, Boston, 1876, pp. 34f.

Page 93, par. 2: Patrick Henry: *see above,* p. 45.

Arnold—Xenophon: Letter to John Page, Dec. 10, 1775, M. IV, p. 253; F. I, p.·496.

Adams—Themistocles: Letter to John Adams, May 27, 1813, M. XIII, p. 249.

British and Persian kings: Letter to Levi Lincoln, Aug. 25, 1811, M. XIII, p. 82.

Burr—Catalina: *The Anas,* Oct. 22, 1806, M. I, p. 460; F. I, p. 318; letter to John Langdon, Dec. 22, 1806, M. XIX, p. 157.

Napoleon—Alexander: Letter to John Langdon, March 5, 1810, M. XII, p. 374.

Caesar: Roy J. Honeywell, *The Educational Work of Thomas Jefferson (Harvard Studies in Education,* XVI), Cambridge, Mass., 1931, p. 229.

Rienzi: Letter to F. A. Van der Kemp, May 1, 1817, F. X, p. 78 note.

par. 3: C. P. B., pp. 181f.

Page 94, par. 1: England—Carthage: Letter to F. C. Gray, March 4, 1815, M. XIV, p. 271; letter to John Langdon, March 5, 1810, M. XII, p. 375.; letter to William Duane, Nov. 13, 1810, M. XII, p. 433; F. IX, p. 287.

Hamiltonians: Letter to J. W. Eppes, Sept. 11, 1813, M. XIII, p. 361; F. IX, pp. 395f.; letter to Albert Gallatin, Oct. 16, 1815, M. XIV, p. 356.

Balance of powers: Letter to C. W. F. Dumas, May 6, 1786, M. V, p. 310.

Greeks: Letter to John Adams, Nov. 25, 1816, M. XV, p. 85.

Page 95, par. 3: The "Batture": M. XVIII, pp. 30f.

Anglo-Saxon precedent: *see,* James Truslow Adams, *The Living Jefferson,* New York, 1936, p. 58.

Napoleon: Letter to T. M. Randolph, Feb. 2, 1800, M. X, p. 150; F. VII, p. 422.

Page 96, par. 1: Linguistics: *see above,* pp. 17f., 63f., 79f., *see below,* pp. 101f.

Anglo-Saxon: E. A. Allen, "Thomas Jefferson and the Study of English," *The Academy* (Syracuse) IV, 1889, pp. 1f.; A. C. Baugh, *op. cit.,* pp. 90f.

Modern Greek: *see above,* pp. 22, 57.

Letter to John Page, Aug. 20, 1785, M. V, pp. 89f.; *see also,* letter to Monsieur Le Vavasseur, March 23, 1808, M. XII, p. 20.

Letter to George Wythe, Sept. 16, 1787, M. VI, p. 299; F. IV, p. 445.

Page 97, par. 1: Letters to John Adams, March 21, 1819, M. XV, pp. 181f., and to N. F. Moore, Sept. 22, 1819, M. XV, pp. 216f. Compare Chapter III of the *Essay on Anglo-Saxon,* M. XVIII, pp. 372f.

Already in 1785 he considered the Italian pronunciation of Latin to be more correct: Letter to John Bannister Jr., Oct. 15, 1785, M. V, p. 185.

Page 98, par. 1: Italian Latin: *see below,* pp. 182f.

Martha Jefferson's Livy: Sarah N. Randolph, *op. cit.,* pp. 84f., (p. 92).

Letter to Peter Carr, Aug. 10, 1787, M. VI, p. 256; F. IV, p. 428.

par. 2: Fight against purism: *see above,* pp. 79f.

Dialects: *see below,* p. 103.

Dialectic regeneration: H. E. Shepherd, "Thomas Jefferson as a Philologist," *American Journal of Philology,* III, 1882, pp. 211f.; Honeywell, *op. cit.,* p. 114. *See also,* his interest in Provençal dialect: Letter to William Short, March 29, 1787, *William and Mary College Quarterly,* ser. 2, XI, 1931, pp. 247f.

Exaggerations: Baugh, *op. cit.,* pp. 95f. (The passage quoted is found on p. 97.)

Page 99, par. 2: Letter to Priestley, March 21, 1801, M. X, p. 229; F. VIII, p. 22.

Montesquieu: C. P. B., p. 281, No. 792; *see,* Chinard, *ibid.* p. 37.

Adrienne Koch, *The Philosophy of Thomas Jefferson,* New York, 1943, pp. 129f.

"Cloudless sky": Letter to Volney, Feb. 8, 1805, M. XI, p. 64.

A poet: Letter to William Short, May 21, 1787, *William and Mary College Quarterly*, 2nd ser., XI, 1931, p. 339.

Page 100, par. 1: Koch, *op. cit.*, pp. 40f.

Letter to Thomas Law, June 13, 1814, M. XIV, p. 143; compare, the letter to John Adams, Oct. 14, 1816, M. XV, p. 76.

Letter to T. M. Randolph, Jr., July 6, 1787, M. VI, p. 165; F. IV, p. 403.

Contract theory: Koch, *op. cit.*, pp. 140f.

Louisiana: H. J. Coolidge, *Thoughts on Thomas Jefferson*, Boston, 1936, p. 27.

Page 101, par. 1: Indians: Letters to John Adams, June 11, 1812, M. XIII, pp. 156f.; F. IX, pp. 355f., and May 27, 1813, M. XIII, pp. 246f.

par. 4: Language: *see above,* pp. 17f., 63f., 79f., 96f., *see below,* pp. 151f.

Difference of English from Greek and Latin, especially: letter to Joseph Coolidge, Jr., Jan. 15, 1825, M. XVIII, p. 335.

Letter to Herbert Croft, Oct. 30, 1798, M. XVIII, p. 361. *Essay on Anglo-Saxon,* p. 1, M. XVIII, p. 365; compare *below,* p. 116.

Page 102, par. 1: *Thoughts on English Prosody. An Essay on the Art of Poesy,* M. XVIII, pp. 414f.; *see above,* p. 21 with note.

par. 2: Locke: *Essay on Knowledge,* III, chap. 5, 8.

Translations never adequate: Letter to Destutt de Tracy, Jan. 26, 1817, M. XIII, p. 14; F. IX, pp. 305f.; letter to Joseph Milligan, Oct. 25, 1818, M. XIX, p. 263.

Homer: Gilbert Chinard, *The Correspondence of Jefferson and Du Pont de Nemours,* Baltimore, 1931, p. 28.

Writing in a foreign language: Letter to Du Pont de Nemours, Dec. 31, 1815, M. XIV, p. 372.

Epitaph for Jane Jefferson: *see above,* p. 53 with note.

Page 103, par. 1: Dialects: *see above,* p. 98.

Languages of social groups and Indians: Letter to Peter Wilson, Jan. 20, 1816, M. XIV, pp. 401f.

par. 2: Religious dogmas: Letter to Thomas Leiper, Jan. 21, 1809, M. XII, pp. 236f.; F. IX, p. 238; letter to James Fishback, Sept. 27, 1809, M. XIV, p. 315.

par. 3: Montesquieu: C. P. B., p. 281, No. 792.
Letter to John Quincy Adams, Nov. 1, 1817, M. XV, p. 145.
Superstructure of law: *The Batture at New Orleans,* chapter on Chancery Jurisdiction, M. XVIII, p. 120; *see below,* pp. 132f.
Lycurgus and Solon: Letter to William Lee, Jan. 16, 1817, M. XV, p. 101.

Page 104, par. 1: Montesquieu: *see above,* pp. 83f. with notes.
par. 2: Euripides, *Medea,* l. 298.
French Revolution: *see,* the fine résumé of Jefferson's attitude by James Truslow Adams, *The Living Jefferson,* New York, 1936, pp. 189f.
South American republics: Letter to Du Pont de Nemours, April 24, 1816, M. XIV, pp. 487f.; F. X, pp. 23f.
Letter to Madame de Staël, Sept. 6, 1816, M. G. Kimball, "Unpublished Correspondence of Mme. de Staël with Thomas Jefferson," *North American Review,* CCVIII, July–December, 1918, p. 71.

Page 105, par. 1: The phrase quoted in the text is used in connection with Destutt de Tracy's Treatise on Political Economy: Letter to Joseph Milligan, April 6, 1816, M. XIV, p. 461.

Chapter 7

Page 106, par. 1: *See,* Gilbert Chinard, "Thomas Jefferson as a Classical Scholar," *The American Scholar,* I, 1932, p. 137.
par. 2: John Bernard, *Retrospections of America. 1797–1811,* edited by B. Bernard, New York, 1887, p. 138.

Paage 107, par. 1: Euripides, *Orestes,* l. 1, 115, L. B.
Christianity, especially: Letter to Samuel Kercheval, Jan. 19, 1810, M. XII, p. 345; letter to John Adams, Oct. 13, 1813, M. XIII, p. 389.
Priests: Letter to H. G. Spafford, Jan. 10, 1816, F. X, pp. 12f.
Letter to Madison, Jan. 1, 1797, M. IX, pp. 359f.; F. VII, p. 100.

Letter to Walter Jones, March 31, 1801, M. X, p. 256; compare, letter to Du Pont de Nemours, April 24, 1816, M. XIV, p. 492; F. X, pp. 22f.

Page 108, par. 1: Letter to the Emperor of Russia, April 19, 1806, M. XI, p. 105; F. VIII, pp. 440f.

Letter to John Wilson, Aug. 17, 1813, M. XIII, p. 348; F. IX, p. 403.

Letter to Du Pont de Nemours, Nov. 29, 1813, M. XIX, p. 200.

par. 2: Danger of reversals: Letter to F. A. Van der Kemp, March 22, 1812, M. XIII, p. 136.

Southern France: Letter to the Comtesse de Tessé, March 20, 1787, M. VI, p. 106.

Letter to Benjamin Waterhouse, June 26, 1822, M. XV, p. 383; F. X, p. 220.

For Plato, *see above*, pp. 84f.

Page 109, par. 1: Letter to John Adams, June 27, 1813, M. XIII, pp. 279f. Compare, the letters to: La Fayette, Nov. 4, 1823, M. XV, p. 492; F. X, pp. 280f.; Henry Lee, Aug. 10, 1824, M. XVI, p. 74; F. X, pp. 317f.; William Short, Jan. 8, 1825, M. XVI, p. 96; F. X, pp. 334f.

par. 2: Letters of John Adams to Jefferson, July 9, 1813, M. XIII, pp. 302f.; *The Works of John Adams*, edited by Ch. F. Adams, X, Boston, 1856, pp. 49f., and July 13, 1813, M. XIII, pp. 306f.; *Works of John Adams, ibid.*, pp. 52f.

Letter to John Adams, Oct. 28, 1813, M. XIII, pp. 394f.; F. IX, pp. 424f.

Page 110, par. 1: Prisoners of war: Adrienne Koch, *The Philosophy of Thomas Jefferson*, New York, 1943, pp. 18f.

Exposition of infants: Letter to David Williams, Nov. 14, 1803, M. X, p. 430.

Patria potestas: An Act for Establishing Elementary Schools, appended to letter to J. C. Cabell, Sept. 9, 1817, M. XVII, p. 423, note.

Fathers selling children: Letter to J. W. Eppes, Sept. 11, 1813, M. XIII, p. 357; F. IX, pp. 396f.

Ancient Slavery: *Notes on Virginia*, Query XIV, M. II, pp. 197f.; F. III, pp. 246f.

Page 111, par. 1: Report of 1818, preparing the University of Virginia: *see,* Roy J. Honeywell, *The Educational Work*

of Thomas Jefferson (Harvard Studies in Education,
XVI), Cambridge, Mass., 1931, p. 256.

Greek and Roman militia: Letter to Monroe, Jan. 1,
1815, M. XIV, p. 227; F. IX, p. 497.

Letter to Thomas Cooper, Sept. 10, 1814, M. XIV, pp.
184f.

Page 112, par. 1: Religion and poetry: Hymn of Cleanthes, letter to John Adams, Oct. 13, 1813, M. XIII, p. 392.

Literary Bible: see above, pp. 42f. with notes.

Voltaire: *see above,* p. 79.

Letter to James Smith, Dec. 8, 1822, M. XV, p. 408.

Letter to Benjamin Rush, April 21, 1803, M. X, p. 381;
F. VIII, pp. 223f. (*Syllabus of an Estimate of the Merit
of the Doctrines of Jesus Compared with Those of
Others.*)

Shaftsbury: *Notes on Religion,* F. II, p. 95; *see below,*
p. 130.

par. 2: Koch, *op. cit.,* chap. 4, especially, pp. 31f.; *see
below,* pp. 136f.

See, particularly, the letter to Priestley, April 9, 1803,
M. X, pp. 374f.; F. VIII, pp. 224f.

Letter to Edward Dowse, April 19, 1803, M. X, pp. 376f.

Syllabus, op. cit., M. X, pp. 381f.; F. VIII, pp. 223f.

Speculative philosophy: Letter to John Adams, Oct. 13,
1813, M. XIII, pp. 390f.

Stoics: Letter to William Short, Oct. 31, 1819, M. XV,
p. 219; F. X, pp. 143f.

Page 113, par. 1: Letter to John Norvell, June 14, 1807, M. XI,
p. 223; F. IX, p. 72.

Value of historical studies: *see above,* p. 73.

Letter to A. Coray, Oct. 31, 1823, M. XV, pp. 480f.

Internal strife: Letter to Robert Williams, Nov. 1, 1807,
M. XI, p. 390.

Greek republics: Letter to Ellridge Gerry, June 11,
1812, M. XIII, pp. 162f.

Eternal wars: *Anas,* Preface, M. I, pp. 266f.

Letter to John Adams, Sept. 28, 1787, urging a study of
former confederations which would indicate the superiority of the American confederacy, M. VI, pp. 321f.

Page 114, par. 1: Letter to I. H. Tiffany, Aug. 26, 1816, M. XV,
p. 65; F. IX, p. 360.

Page 115, par. 1: C.P.B., pp. 212 (No. 754), 296 (No. 803).

Notes on Virginia, Query XIII, M. II, p. 177; F. III, p. 234.

Letters of Cicero: Letter to John Adams, Dec. 10, 1819, M. XV, pp. 233f.; F. X, pp. 152f. Jefferson seems not to have taken special interest in Angelo Mai's discovery of Cicero's *Republic*—though he received a copy of the edition from Gilmer in 1823: *Correspondence of Thomas Jefferson and Francis Walker Gilmer, 1814–1826,* edited by R. B. Davis, Columbia, 1946, pp. 76f.

Lack of political courage: Letter to Samuel Brown, July 14, 1813, M. XIII, p. 311.

Provincial government: Letter to the Comtesse de Tessé, March 20, 1787, M. VI, p. 106; compare, above, pp. 93f. with note.

Page 117, par. 1: The traditional respect for such "great men" is stated and not questioned, for example, by Middleton in the preface to his *History of the Life of Marcus Tullius Cicero,* though the author pleads for equal evaluation of such a different type of man as Cicero. Jefferson, too, read this book, then and afterwards very popular, and incidentally recommended it to students.

"Puny heroes": Letter to the Comtesse de Tessé, cited in the preceding note.

Philip of Macedon: Letter to John Adams, Nov. 25, 1816, M. XV, p. 85.

Alexander: Letter to John Langdon, March 5, 1810, M. XII, p. 374.

Cæsar: Letter to J. C. Cabell, Feb. 2, 1816, M. XIV, p. 422.

Augustus: Letter to Nathaniel Macon, Jan. 12, 1819, M. XV, p. 179; F. X, p. 120.

Further comparisons, *see above,* pp. 93f.

Kings: Letter to John Langdon (*see above*), M. XII, pp. 375f.

Alexander of Russia: Randall, III, p. 170.

Page 118, par. 1: Jefferson's reading of Cato's book on agriculture results from the use he made of that source regarding slavery in the *Notes on Virginia: see above,* pp. 111. *Notes on the Biography of George Wythe,* appended to letter to John Saunderson, Aug. 31, 1820, M. I, p. 169.

par. 2: For Plato, *see above,* pp. 84f.

St. Paul: Letter to William Short, April 13, 1820, M. XV,
p. 245.

Page 119, par. 2: Louis B. Wright's statement (*op. cit.*, p. 228)
that Jefferson "disliked" Cicero's style, is not correct.

Father of oratory and philosophy: Letter to A. J. Cook,
Jan. 21, 1816, M. XIV, pp. 404f.

Comparison with Demosthenes: Letter to John Adams,
July 5, 1814, M. XIV, p. 148; F. IX, p. 463.

Forensic oratory: Letter to J. W. Eppes, Jan. 17, 1810,
M. XII, p. 343; F. IX, p. 267; letter to G. W. Summers
and J. B. Garland, Feb. 27, 1822, M. XV, p. 353.

Cicero, an accomplice of the Stoics: Letter to Charles
Thompson, Jan. 9, 1816, M. XIV, p. 386; F. X, p. 6; letter to William Short, Oct. 31, 1819, M. XV, p. 219; F. X,
p. 143. *See* Gilbert Chinard, "Jefferson among the Philosophers," *Ethics*, LIII, 1942/3, p. 265.

Dilettantism: Letter to Du Pont de Nemours, Dec. 31,
1815, M. XIV, p. 372.

Patriotism: Letter to John Adams, Dec. 10, 1819, M. XV,
pp. 233f.; F. X, pp. 152f.

Jefferson's realistic judgment is very different from the
résumé on Cicero's character at the end of Middleton's
biography which, though intended to be objective, is
much more favorable. *See also below*, pp. 151f., 199.

Page 120, par. 1: Jacob Burckhardt, *Weltgeschichtliche Betrach-
tungen* (English translation: *Force and Freedom*), New
York, 1943, chap 5, pp. 301f.

Cicero, *Tusculan Dialogues*, I, 45, 109, L.B., p. 77.

"Seeds of genius": Letter to William Duane, Aug. 4,
1812, M. XIII, p. 180; F. IX, p. 365.

Jefferson and Hamilton: Letter to Benjamin Rush, Jan.
16, 1811, M. XIII, p. 4; F. IX, p. 296.

Page 121, par. 2: Against despair: Letter to F. A. Van der Kemp,
March 22, 1812, M. XIII, p. 136.

Evils producing good: Letter to Benjamin Rush, Sept.
23, 1800, M. X, p. 173; F. VII, p. 458.

par. 3: Euripides, *Orestes*, ll. 1545f., L.B.

Cicero, *Tusculan Dialogues*, III, 1, 1, L.B.; *see* Koch, *op.
cit.*, pp. 22, 45f., 116f.; *see below*, pp. 131f.

Science and bad social conditions: Letter to Monsieur
Paganel, April 15, 1811, M. XIII, p. 37.

Science progressive: Letter to John Adams, June 15, 1813, M. XIII, p. 255; F. IX, p. 387.

Violence, etc.: Letter to Samuel Knox, Feb. 12, 1810, M. XII, pp. 360f.

Dreams of the future: Letter to John Adams, Aug. 1, 1816, M. XV, p. 59; *see* chap. 12.

Chapter 8

Page 125, par. 1: *See above,* pp. 15f.

par. 2: Letter to William Duane, April 4, 1813, M. XIII, p. 230.

Page 126, par. 1: Letter of John Adams to Jefferson, June 28, 1812, M. XIII, p. 288; *Works of John Adams,* edited by Ch. F. Adams, X, Boston 1856, p. 19.

Good principles: *see below,* p. 199.

Scientific studies: Letter to T. M. Randolph, Jr., July 6, 1787, M. VI, p. 166; F. IV, p. 404.

"Sublime luxury": Letter to Priestley, Jan. 27, 1800, M. X, pp. 146f.; F. VII, p. 414.

par. 2: "Civilized and learned": Letter to J. W. Eppes, Sept. 11, 1813, M. XIII, p. 357; F. IX, p. 396 note.

par. 3: Dark Ages: Letter to Madison, Aug. 28, 1789, M. VII, p. 449; F. V, p. 111.

"Gothic ignorance": Letter to Count Dugnani, Feb. 14, 1816, M. XIX, p. 259; letter to Priestley, Jan. 27, 1800, M. X, p. 148; F. VII, p. 414.

Barbaric invasion: *see,* the excerpt from William Robertson's *History of the Reign of the Emperor Charles V with a View of the Progress of Society from the Subversion of the Roman Empire to the Beginning of the Sixteenth Century,* 1769 (reprinted in Philadelphia, 1770), C.P.B., p. 235, No. 761.

Greece: Letter to Dr. Stiles, July 17, 1785, M. V, p. 39. Compare letter to John Page, Aug. 20, 1785, M. V, p. 89. Letter to A. Coray, Oct. 31, 1823, M. XV, pp. 481, 490.

Page 127, par. 1: Letters: to Major L'Enfant, April 10, 1791, M. VIII, p. 163; to Madison, Sept. 1, 1785, M. V, p. 110, Feb. 8, 1786, M. V, p. 282, Sept. 20, 1785, M. V, p. 135; to Edmund Randolph, Sept. 20, 1785, M. V, p. 138. *See* Fiske Kimball, *Thomas Jefferson and the First Monument of Classical Revival in America* (Reprinted from

Journal of the American Institute of Architects, III), 1915, p. 13.

par. 2: Romantic garden: Marie Kimball, *Jefferson. The Road to Glory, 1743–1776,* New York, 1943, pp. 161f.

Novels: Letter to Nathaniel Burwell, March 14, 1818, M. XV, p. 166; F. X, pp. 104f.

Don Quixote ranked with Homer, Virgil, Dante, Corneille, Shakespeare and Milton: Randall, III, p. 346.

Romantic novels, *ibid.* I, p. 448. A letter to Maria Cosway, April 24, 1788, shows Jefferson's appreciation of Sterne's *Tristram Shandy* (Helen Duprey Bullock, *My Head and My Heart,* New York, 1945, p. 92).

Page 128, par. 1: For the political worship of antiquity, *see:* Harold T. Parker, *The Cult of Antiquity and the French Revolutionaries,* Chicago, 1937.

Winckelmann: *Catalogue of the Library of the United States,* Washington, 1815, chap. 31; *see also,* Fiske Kimball, "Jefferson and the Arts," *Proceedings of the American Philosophical Society,* LXXXVII, 1943, p. 241.

For Clérisseau, *see above,* pp. 55f.

For Jefferson's "Romanism" in architecture, *see* Fiske Kimball, "Thomas Jefferson and the Origin of the Classical Revival in America," *Art and Archæology,* I, 1915, p. 227; *idem, Thomas Jefferson Architect,* Boston, 1916, pp. 63, 80f.; *see below,* pp. 148f.

par. 2: Freedom in antiquity: Letter to I. M. Tiffany, Aug. 26, 1816, M. XV, p. 65; Letter to Benjamin Galloway, Feb. 2, 1812, M. XIII, p. 130; letter to John Adams, Jan. 22, 1821, M. XV, p. 308; F. X, p. 185.

Page 129, par. 1: Letter to Francois D'Ivernois, Feb. 6, 1795, M. IX, pp. 297f.; F. VII, pp. 2f.

Letter to A. Coray, Oct. 31, 1823, M. XV, p. 490.

Letter to Thaddeus Kosciusko, Feb. 26, 1810, M. XII, pp. 369f.

Letter to John Brazier, Aug. 24, 1819, M. XV, pp. 209f.; for medicine, *see above,* p. 78.

Euclid: Letter to John Adams, Jan. 21, 1812, M. XIII, p. 124; F. IX, p. 334; Oct. 14, 1816, M. XV, p. 76.

Page 130, par. 1: Letter to Ralph Izard, Sept. 26, 1785, M. V, p. 153.

par. 2: *See above,* pp. 121f., p. 112 with note.

par. 3: Homer, *Odyssey*, XVII, l.323, *Notes on Virginia*, Query XIV, M. II, p. 199; F. III, p. 249.

Literary Bible, see above, pp. 42f.

Moralizing history: *see above* pp. 125f.; letter to Anne Cary Bankhead, Dec. 8, 1808, M. XVIII, p. 255.

Page 131, par. 1: Liberty, truth, probity, honor: Letter to Du Pont de Nemours, April 24, 1816, M. XIV, p. 490; F. X, p. 24.

par. 2: For "moral sense, *see,* in general: Adrienne Koch, *The Philosophy of Thomas Jefferson,* New York, 1943, pp. 15f.

Euripides, *Hippolytus,* line 380, L.B.

Cicero, *see above,* p. 121 with note; *see also,* Gilbert Chinard, "Jefferson among the Philosophers," *Ethics,* LIII, 1942–3, p. 257.

Lord Kames' influence on Jefferson: Koch, *op. cit.,* p. 45; Chinard, *op. cit.,* pp. 258f.

Letter to John Adams, Oct. 14, 1816, M. XV, p. 76.

Page 132, par. 1: τὸ καλόν at once the "beautiful" and "good," a central term of Platonic philosophy: Letter to Peter Carr, Aug. 10, 1787, M. VI, p. 257; F. IV, p. 429; an early anti-Platonic statement, compare above, pp. 84f.

Letter to Thomas Law, June 13, 1814, M. XIV, p. 139.

par 2: Letter to Mrs. Cosway (known as the *Dialogue between Head and Heart*), Oct. 12, 1786, M. V, p. 443; F. IV, p. 319; Helen Duprey Bullock, *op. cit.,* pp. 29f. Jefferson's reluctant statement, in his letter to Richard Price, Feb. 7, 1788, M. VI, p. 424, admitting "morality to be the child of understanding rather than of the senses," remains singular.

Library classification, *see above,* p. 11 with note.

par. 3: Letter to F. W. Gilmer, June 7, 1816, M. XV, pp. 23f.; F. X, pp. 31f.

Legal superstructures: *see above,* p. 104.

Imperfections of ancient society: *see above,* pp. 110f.

Page 133, par. 1: Solon, *see above,* p. 118.

Roman law: *see above,* p. 95; *The Batture at New Orleans,* M. XVIII, pp. 35f.

Report relative to negotiations with Spain to secure the free navigation of the Mississippi, and a port on the same, March 18, 1792, II, 3, M. III, p. 180; F. V, pp. 469f.; letter to John Brazier, Aug. 24, 1819, M. XV, p. 210.

Page 134, par. 1: Letter to William Canby, Sept. 18, 1813, M. XIII, p. 377.

par. 2: Library classification, *see above,* p. 11 with note.

Ancient religion, *see above,* p. 112.

On Jefferson's religious opinions: G. H. Knoles, "The Religious Ideas of Thomas Jefferson," *The Mississippi Valley Historical Review,* XXX, 1943, pp. 187f.

Cicero, *Tusculan Dialogues,* I, 13, 30, L.B., p. 73.

Trinity: Letter to William Canby, Sept. 13, 1813, M. XIII, p. 378.

Letter to Thomas Withermore, June 5, 1822, M. XV, p. 374.

Page 135, par. 1: *Notes on Virginia,* Query XVII, M. II, p. 221; F. III, p. 264; *see above,* the excerpt from Shaftsbury, p. 112.

Page 136, par. 1: Reformation: Letter to Salma Hales, July 26, 1818, F' V, p. 79.

New Testament: Letter to John Brazier, Aug. 24, 1819, M. XV, p. 209. In the catalogue of that part of his library which he sold to Congress, not less than eleven editions of the Greek New Testament are listed, in addition to several others that he certainly retained: *Catalogue of the Library of the United States,* Washington, 1815, chap. 17.

Letter to William Short, April 13, 1820, M. XV, pp. 244f.

Morality: Letter to Thomas Law, June 13, 1814, M. XIV, p. 139; ———— of Jesus: Letter to Edward Dowse, April 19, 1803, M. X, p. 377.

Page 137, par. 1: *See above,* p. 112, with note to par. 2.

Socrates: Letter to William Short, Aug. 4, 1820, M. XV, p. 258.

Ancient moralists: Letter to John Brazier, Aug. 24, 1819, M. XV, p. 209.

Literary Bible: see above, pp. 42f.

Libraries, *see above,* pp. 16f.

Letter to Peter Carr, Aug. 19, 1785, M. V, p. 85.

Syllabus of moralists: *see above,* pp. 21f., 63f.

Letters to: Priestley, April 9, 1803, M. X, pp. 374f.; F. VIII, pp. 224f.; Benjamin Rush, April 21, 1803, M. X, pp. 379f.; F. VIII, pp. 223f., with appended *Syllabus of*

*an Estimate of the Merit of the Doctrines of Jesus, com-
pared with Those of Others.*
par. 2: *See above,* p. 113.
Syllabus, op. cit., M. X, p. 382; F. VIII, pp. 225f.
Page 138, par. 1: Letter to John Adams, Oct. 13, 1813, M. XIII,
p. 391.
Letter to Edward Dowse, April 19, 1803, M. X, p. 377.
Syllabus, op. cit., I, 1.
Egotism: Letter to Thomas Law, June 13, 1814, M. XIV,
p. 140.
Euripides, *Medea,* 1.86, L.B., p. 99.
par. 2: Eclecticism: *see above,* pp. 72f.; Koch, *op. cit.,*
p. 8.
Platonism: *see above,* pp. 84f.; George Wythe, Marie
Kimball, *op. cit.,* p. 74.
Against Stoicism: Letter to William Short, Oct. 31, 1819,
M. XV, p. 219; F. X, pp. 143f.
Page 139, par. 1: For Jefferson's interpretation of Epicureanism,
see Gilbert Chinard, *Thomas Jefferson, The Apostle of
Americanism,* 2nd ed., Boston, 1939, pp. 521f., where,
however, the fact that contrary to popular conceptions,
Jefferson's interpretation is close to the genuine teach-
ing of that school does not emerge clearly. *See also,*
Koch, *op. cit.,* p. 42, note 8.
Horace, *Satires,* II, 7, 11.82–7, L.B.; letter to A. J. Cook,
Jan. 21, 1816, M. XIV, p. 405.
Page 140, par. 1: Stoic criticism of Epicureanism, *see above,* p.
138, note to par. 2.
Cicero, *see above,* pp. 119f.
Hamilton: *see* James Truslow Adams, *The Living Jef-
ferson,* New York, 1936, p. 242.
Letter to Charles Thompson, Jan. 9, 1816, M. XIV, p.
386; F. X, p. 6.
Summum bonum, the supreme good and the goal of Epi-
curean behavior: Letter to John Melish, Jan. 13, 1813,
M. XIII, p. 213; F. IX, p. 377; letter to John Stevens,
Nov. 23, 1818, *Missouri Historical Society, Glimpses of
the Past,* III, 1936, p. 122; letter to John Adams, June
27, 1813, M. XIII, p. 279; *see above,* p. 63.
Page 141, par. 1: Materialism: *see* Koch, *op. cit.,* pp. 34f., 95f.;
letter to A. B. Woodward, March 24, 1824, M. XVI, pp.
18f.

"I feel," etc.: Letter to John Adams, Aug. 15, 1820, M. XV, p. 273.

"Jesus," etc.: letters to: Thomas Cooper, Aug. 14, 1820, M. XV, p. 266; John Adams, Aug. 15, 1820, M. XV, pp. 274f., and April 11, 1823, M. XV, pp. 425f.; A. B. Woodward, cited above. *See also,* letter to F. A. Van der Kemp, Feb. 9, 1818, F' V, pp. 52f.

par. 2: Letter to William Short, Oct. 31, 1819, M. XV, p. 222; F. X, p. 1.

Letter to John Adams, April 8, 1816, M. XIV, p. 467.

Letter to William Short, cited, p. 198, *see* the *Syllabus of the Doctrines of Epicurus,* appended to this letter.

Chapter 9

Page 143, par. 2: Declaration of Independence: Carl Becker, *The Declaration of Independence,* 2nd ed., New York, 1942; letter to James Mease, Sept. 26, 1825, M. XVI, p. 123; F. X, p. 346.

Jesus: Letter to William Short, Oct. 31, 1819, M. XV, p. 221; F. X, p. 145.

Cicero: Letter to John Adams, Dec. 10, 1819, M. XV, p. 233; F. X, p. 15.

Tacitus: *see above,* p. 81.

Page 144, par. 1: Letter to Thomas Law, June 13, 1814, M. XIV, p. 140.

Letter to Priestley, Jan. 27, 1800, M. X, p. 147; F. VII, pp. 413f.

Page 145, par. 2: Early excerpts: *see above,* pp. 42f.

Pragmatism: Letter to Robert Skipworth, Aug. 3, 1771, M. IV, pp. 237f.; F. I, pp. 396f.

Letter to Charles E. Brown, Jan. 15, 1800, F' I, p. 336.

Letter to A. J. Cook, Jan. 21, 1816, M. XIV, p. 405.

Page 146, par. 1: Empiricism: *see above,* chap. 5.

par. 2: *See above,* p. 42 with note.

Late reading: Randall, I, p. 28: III, pp. 346, 539.

Terence: L. B., pp. 123f., 195; *see* the letters to: ———, June 8, 1778, M. IV, p. 39; F. II, p. 156; Edmund Randolph, Aug. 3, 1787, M. VI, p. 219; Madison, Aug. 16, 1807, M. XI, p. 326; F. IX, p. 124.

Page 147, par. 1: Homeric character of Indians: Appendix to *Notes on Virginia,* 5, M. II, p. 274.

Homeric simile, *see above,* pp. 44f.

The woodcutter on Mt. Ida: Letter to John Adams, June 27, 1813, M. XIII, p. 279.

Thoughts on English Prosody. An Essay on the Art of Poesy, M. XVIII, p. 448; compare, for Homeric rhythm, letter to John Adams, March 21, 1819, M. XV, p. 184; *see also* his dedication of a copy of Homer to Mme. de Tot (Nov. 28, 1786) with "the few rules of Greek prosody which must be indispensably known" (Edward Dumbaud, *Thomas Jefferson American Tourist,* Norman, 1946, p. 95, note 37).

Autobiography, M. I, p. 55; F. I, p. 6; *see above,* pp. 44, 93.

Psalmist: Letter to John Adams, Oct. 13, 1813, M. XIII, p. 392.

Page 148, par. 1: Romanism in architecture: *see above,* p. 128, with note.

"Logic": *see above,* pp. 79f., 96f., 101f.; Adrienne Koch, *The Philosophy of Thomas Jefferson,* New York, 1943, pp. 108f.

Letter to J. E. Denison, Nov. 9, 1825, M. XVI, p. 133.

Greek "least useful": Letter to J. W. Eppes, July 28, 1787, M. VI, p. 190; positive value: letters to John Brazier, Aug. 24, 1819, M. XV, p. 208; N. F. Moore, Sept. 22, 1819, M. XV, p. 228; John Waldo, Aug. 16, 1813, M. XIII, p. 341.

Madison: *Autobiography,* M. I, p. 61; F. I, p. 57.

Page 149, par. 1: Letter to Waldo, quoted in the preceding note.

Compare: Letter to John Adams, Aug. 15, 1820, M. XV, p. 272; *Essay on the Anglo-Saxon Language,* chap. 4, M. XVIII, pp. 378f.

Ablative: Letters to Edward Everett, Feb. 24, 1823, M. XV, p. 413, and March 27, 1824, M. XVI, pp. 20f.; *Essay,* l.c.

English: *ibid.,* M. XVIII, p. 365.

French: Letter to John Adams, cited above, M. XV, p. 272.

Page 150, par. 1: Dual: *Essay, op. cit.,* chap. 4, 3, M. XVIII, pp. 379f.

Letter to John Waldo, cited above, M. XIII, pp. 339f.

par. 2: Letter to John Adams, Aug. 22, 1813, M. XIII, p. 350; F. IX, pp. 412f.

Page 151, par. 1: *Thoughts on English Prosody*, chapter on "The length of Verse," M. XVIII, p. 441.

Letter to E. Everett, Febr. 24, 1823, M. XV, p. 414.

par. 2: *See:* Gilbert Chinard, *Thomas Jefferson, The Apostle of Americanism*, 2nd ed., Boston, 1939, p. 77.

Singularity of languages: *see above*, pp. 101f.

Letter to Peter Carr, Aug. 19, 1785, M. V, p. 85.

Bolingbroke—Cicero: Letter to Francis Eppes, Jr., Jan. 19, 1821, M. XV, pp. 305f.; F. X, p. 183; letter to J. G. Jefferson, April 14, 1793, M. XIX, p. 104; letter to G. W. Summers and J. B. Garland, Feb. 27, 1822, M. XV, p. 353; letter to John Adams, July 5, 1814, M. XIV, p. 148; F. IX, p. 463; *see above*, pp. 119f.

Forensic oratory: "Course of Reading for a law student," Roy J. Honeywell, *The Educational Work of Thomas Jefferson (Harvard Studies in Education,* XVI), Cambridge, Mass., 1931, p. 220.

"Batture": M. XVIII, pp. 128f. (section on the responsibility of a public functionary).

Cicero: *see above*, pp. 119f.; *see below*, p. 199.

Page 152, par. 1: Letter to John Brazier, Aug. 24, 1819, M. XV, p. 208.

Letter to David Harding, April 20, 1824, M. XVI, p. 30; compare the letter to J. W. Eppes, Jan. 17, 1810, M. XII, p. 343; F. IX, p. 267.

Letter to Summers and Garland, quoted in the preceding note.

Letter to John Adams, July 5, 1818, M. XIV, p. 148; F. IX, p. 463.

Before 1815, Jefferson himself owned at least three editions of Isocrates: *Catalogue of the Library of the United States*, Washington, 1815, chap. 40.

Page 154, par. 1: For Tacitus, *see above*, pp. 81, 125, 131.

par. 2: Winckelmann, *see above*, pp. 55, 128.

Chapter 10

Page 156, par. 1: For basic bibliography, *see above*, notes to pp. 24 par. 2, 26 par. 3. Add: Lewis Mumford, *The South in Architecture*, New York, 1941, pp. 43f; Nancy Noland, "Jefferson and Palladio," *Vassar Journal of Undergraduate Studies*, XVI, 1943, pp. 1f.; H. Montgomery, "The Architect of the American Republic," *The Classical Weekly*, XXXIX, 1945, pp. 74f.

Page 157, par. 2: France: *see* Fiske Kimball, *Thomas Jefferson and the First Monument of the Classical Revival in America* (Reprinted from *Journal of the American Institute of Architects*, III, 1915), p. 12.

Page 158, par.1: Oratory: *see above*, pp. 151f.

Plan for governor's palace: Fiske Kimball, *Domestic Architecture of the American Colonies and of the Early Republic*, New York, 1922, p. 152, Fig. 114; for the date, *see:* Thomas T. Waterman, *The Mansions of Virginia, 1706–1776*, Chapel Hill, 1946, pp. 394f.

Capitol of Virginia: *see above*, pp. 55f., 128.

Notes on Virginia, Query XV, M. II, pp. 211f.; F. III, pp. 257f.

Page 159, par. 1: Sculptures: Fiske Kimball, "Jefferson and the Arts," *Proceedings of the American Philosophical Society*, LXXXVII, 1943, pp. 241f.; *see above*, p. 26.

Trajan's Column: a column of 200 feet in height, with an interior staircase (doubling the size of the prototype), planned by Jefferson, Kimball, *Thomas Jefferson Architect*, pp. 27, 130.

Washington monument, Randall, II, p. 200.

Monument of Lysikrates: Letter to Robert Mills, March 3, 1826 (photostat in the Manuscript Collection of the New York Public Library, Jefferson File), Marie Kimball, *Jefferson. The Road to Glory, 1743–1776*, New York, 1943, p. 323, note 43.

Traveling Notes for Rutledge and Shippen, June 3, 1788, M. XVII, p. 292.

Jefferson's interest in Art: *see above*, pp. 25f.; John Adams, *ibid.*, p. 27.

University of Virginia: *see below*, pp. 185f.; letter to W. C. Nicholas, April 2, 1816, M. XIV, p. 453; letter to Henry Tazewell, Nov. 1825, *New York Times*, April 26, 1931.

Page 160, par. 1: Approval of centuries, *see above*, p 158.

Dignity of the state: Kimball, *Thomas Jefferson Architect*, pp. 41f.

Capitol and White House: Letter to Major L'Enfant, Apr. 10, 1791, M. VIII, p. 163. Fiske Kimball remarks that Jefferson also submitted anonymously a plan of a Palladion Villa Rotunda for the White House.

Letter to B. H. Latrobe, July 12, 1812, M. XIII, p. 179.

Page 162, par. 1: Direct use of monuments and "literal" classicism: Kimball, *Thomas Jefferson Architect*, pp. 42, 60, 70, 78; *idem., Domestic Architecture*, p. 260.

Empiricism and positivism: *see above*, chap. 5.

Singularity: *see above*, pp. 101f.

Books: above, pp. 24f., with notes.

Original sources: *see above*, pp. 87f.

Page 163, par. 2: Kimball, *Thomas Jefferson Architect*, pp. 60, 161.

Page 164, par. 1: Eclecticism: *see above*, pp. 72f.

Montesquieu: *see above*, pp. 83f.

par. 2: For the Capitol of Virginia, *see above*, pp. 55f. with notes.

Conflict with Clérisseau: Kimball, *Thomas Jefferson and the First Monument, op. cit.*, pp. 13f.

An Account of the Capitol of Virginia, M. XVII, pp. 353f.

Outer pilasters: Kimball, *Thomas Jefferson Architect*, p. 43.

Fréart: *see above*, p. 27 with note.

Pantheon-Library: Kimball, *op. cit.*, p. 78.

Page 165, par. 1: Kimball, *op. cit.*, pp. 45f.

Letters to Madison, Sept. 20, 1785, M. V, pp. 135f., and Edmund Randolph, Sept. 20, 1785, M. V, pp. 138f.

Grandeur, simplicity, beauty: Letter to David Stuart, Jan. 31, 1793, M. IX, p. 17.

University of Virginia: Letter to ———, Nov. 24, 1821, M. XVIII, p. 315; letter to Henry Tazewell, Nov. 1825, *New York Times*, April 26, 1931.

"Ineffable majesty": Letter to Nathaniel Macon, Jan. 22, 1816, M. XIV, p. 410.

Capitals: *Autobiography*, M. I, p. 68; F. I., p. 64.

Page 166, par. 1: Jefferson and Palladio: Kimball, *Thomas Jefferson Architect*, pp. 22f.

Innate taste: above, pp. 144f.

Page 167, par. 1: *Autobiography*, M. I, p. 68; F. I, pp. 63f.

An Account of the Capitol of Virginia, M. XVII, p. 353.

Letter to———, Nov. 24, 1821, M. XVIII, p. 315.

Octagon: Kimball, *op. cit.*, p. 71; *idem, Domestic Ar-*

chitecture, pp. 175f.; *see also,* Clay Lancaster, "Some Octagonal Forms in Southern Architecture," *The Art Bulletin,* XXVIII, 1946, pp. 103f. Professor Kimball suggested dependence of Jefferson on a rather different plan of Inigo Jones's. Inspiration from the "Tower of the Winds" in Athens seems more likely, especially in view of the fact that Jefferson first intended to use this octagonal form not for Poplar Forest, but for Pantops: the farm for which he had invented a Greek name meaning "Lookout," *see above,* p. 33, below, p. 182. Another conspicuous octagonal building that Jefferson might have had in mind is the Roman "Tour Magne" at Nîmes which he must have seen.

Page 168, par. 1: Letter to Robert Mills, March 3, 1826, photostat in the Manuscript Collection of the New York Public Library, Jefferson File. *See also,* letter to Maria Cosway, Oct. 24, 1822, Helen Duprey Bullock, *My Head and My Heart,* New York, 1945, p. 182.

Original plan for University: *see below,* p. 186.

Monticello: *Niles Weekly Register,* XI, 1816/7, p. 318.

Page 169, par. 1: For the Pavillions of the University, *see:* H. B. Adams, *Thomas Jefferson and the University of Virginia* (U. S. Bureau of Education, *Circular of Information,* No. 1, *Contributions to American Educational History,* No. 2), Washington, D. C., 1888.

Kimball, *Thomas Jefferson Architect,* pp. 76f.; Ph. A. Bruce, *History of the University of Virginia 1819–1919,* I, New York, 1920, p. 244.

Page 170, par. 1: Kimball, *op. cit.,* p. 70.

par. 3: Singularity of linguistic expression: *see above,* pp. 98f.

Library, details: John S. Patton, *Jefferson, Cabell and the University of Virginia,* New York, 1906, p. 187.

Page 172, par. 1: Monument of Lysikrates: *see above,* p. 159.

Governor's palace: *see above,* p. 158.

Octagon: *see above,* p. 167.

Kimball, *op. cit.,* pp. 80f.; *idem,* "Thomas Jefferson and the Origin of the Classical Revival in America," *Art and Archaeology,* I, 1915, p. 227.

Latrobe and Jefferson: Kimball, *Thomas Jefferson, Architect,* pp. 63f.

Page 173, par. 2: Jefferson's philhellenism: *see above,* pp. 154f.
Clérisseau, *see above,* pp. 55f.
Southern France, *see above,* pp. 27f.
Maison Carrée: Letter to the Comtesse de Tessé, March 20, 1787, M. VI, pp. 102f.
French "Romanism": Kimball, *op. cit.,* pp. 80f.; also, Montgomery, *op. cit.,* p. 77, who adds a bewildering remark about Jefferson's "greater familiarity with Latin literature."

Page 175, par. 3: Letter to the Comtesse de Tessé, March 20, 1787, M. VI, p. 104.

Chapter 11

Page 177, par. 1: "Art of Living": Kimball, *Thomas Jefferson, Architect,* Boston, 1916, p. 59.

Page 178, par. 1: The affinity of the American to the ancient scene has been noted by Gilbert Chinard, "Thomas Jefferson as a Classical Scholar," *The American Scholar,* I, 1932, p. 136; *see also,* James Truslow Adams, *The Living Jefferson,* New York, 1936, p. 45; 'Louis B. Wright, "Thomas Jefferson and the Classics" *Proceedings of the American Philosophical Society,* LXXXVII, 1943, p. 227f.

Page 179, par. 2: Pliny's *Letters,* apart from the two famous architectural descriptions of his Tuscan and Laurentine villas (*Epistles,* II, 17 and V, 6) contain minor descriptions: *see,* Karl Lehmann-Hartleben, *Plinio il Giovane, Lettre Scelte,* con commento archeologico, Florence, 1936, pp. 42f. For life on Roman villas, in addition to the material quoted there, *see,* especially the letters describing the life of Pliny himself and that of *Spurima* (*Epistles,* I, 9; III, 1; ix, 15, 16, 36). For the continuous interest in Pliny's villas since the Renaissance and the architectural reconstructions of them, *see,* Helen Tanzer, *The Villas of Pliny the Younger,* New York, 1924.
Letter to Thaddeus Kosciusko, Feb. 26, 1810, M. XII, p. 369.
Students: *see also, Jefferson and His Unknown Brother Randolph.* Twenty-eight Letters, with an introduction by Bernard Megs, Charlottesville, 1942, p. 14.

La Rochefoucauld-Liancourt: Randall, II, pp. 302f.

Daniel Webster, *Private Correspondence,* edited by F. Webster, I, Boston, 1857, p. 365.

Ticknor's description of a visit to the Madisons at Montpelier: *Life, Letters and Journals of George Ticknor,* I, Boston, 1876, p. 347.

Page 180, par. 1: For Cicero and Horace, *see* the register at the end of this book.

Pliny: Fitzhugh, *op. cit.,* p. 22.

Cicero L. B.

Horace, *Epodes:* II, L.B.

Page 181, par. 1: Burial ground: Randall, I, pp. 60f.

"Elegant arts": Letter to Benjamin Rush, Sept. 23, 1800, M. X, p. 173; F. VII, p. 459.

Vice-presidency: Letter to Benjamin Rush, Jan. 22, 1797, M. IX, p. 374; F. VII, p. 114.

Page 182, par. 1: As yet we have no satisfactory book on the Roman villa. For architectural features the reader may consult: K. Swoboda, *Roemische Villen und Romanische Palaeste,* Vienna, 1919; for gardens, Pierre Grimal, *Les Jardins Romains,* Paris, 1943. For Cicero's villas, *see* O. E. Schmidt, "Cicero's Villen," *Neue Jahrbuecher fuer das Klassische Altertum,* III, 1889, pp. 328f., 426f.; for Pliny, *see above,* note to p. 179 par. 2. From the eighties on, if not much earlier, Jefferson owned the remarkable work for its time by Robert Castell, *Villas of the Antients,* London, 1728. It has a motto from Horace, refers to Varro (*see,* Fig. IX), and deals for the most part with the villas of Pliny and their reconstruction.

par. 2: Monticello's situation: Marie Kimball, *Jefferson. The Road to Glory, 1743–1776,* New York, 1943, p. 148, and Fiske Kimball, "Romantic Classicism in Architecture," *Gazette des Beaux Arts,* 1946, p. 106, explain it as an expression of preromantic sentiment for landscape, which certainly is an emotional motive involved but hardly sufficient to explain the decision to build the main mansion instead of a hermitage on top of a hill.

Aloofness: James Truslow Adams, *The Living Jefferson,* New York, 1936, p. 44; *see also,* Paul Wilstach, *Jefferson and Monticello,* New York, 1925, p. 24.

Pantops. *see above,* pp. 33, 167, note to par. 1. Italian-Latin: *see above,* pp. 96, 98.

Page 183, par. 1: Early sketches: Kimball, *Thomas Jefferson Architect,* p. 121, Fig. 12; Marie Kimball, *op. cit.,* p. 151. Outbuildings and porticoes: *ibid.,* p. 154.

Diaetae: Karl Lehmann-Hartleben, *Plinio, op. cit.,* p. 46, note to l.53.

par. 2: Features of remodeled Monticello: Kimball, *Domestic Architecture,* pp. 79f., 189f.; *idem, Thomas Jefferson Architect,* pp. 27, 58.

Crytoporticus: *see,* I. T. Frary, *Thomas Jefferson Architect and Builder,* Richmond, 1931, pl. 24; Karl Lehmann-Hartleben, *op. cit.,* p. 46, note to l.70. The Roman crytoporticus was vaulted—a fact which is not indicated in the literary sources—and this is the only difference from Jefferson's scheme. I hesitate to connect the observation towers planned by Jefferson (Kimball, *Thomas Jefferson Architect,* p. 27, Figs. 38, 39) with the *turres* of Roman villas (Lehmann-Hartleben, *op. cit.,* p. 46, note to line 53; Grimal, *op. cit.,* pp. 276f.).

Page 184, par. 1: Pond and cisterns: Edwin M. Betts and Hazlehurst B. Perkins, *Thomas Jefferson's Flower Gardens at Monticello,* Richmond, 1941, pp. 28f.

Aviary: Isaac Weld, *Travels Through the States of North America,* 4th edition, I, 1807, p. 207. Varro's aviary was discussed in Castell's book (*see above,* note to p. 182, par. 1 Fig. IX).

Pigeon towers: Kimball, *Thomas Jefferson Architect,* p. 133, Fig. 63. Pigeon towers with openings under the roof are described as typical of the Roman villa by Varro. Weather vane and clock: *see,* Karl Lehmann, "The Dome of Heaven," *The Art Bulletin,* XXVII, 1945, p. 20, note 173. In Varro's villa this is found in the aviary mentioned above; *see also,* Fig. IX.

par. 2: *See above,* p. 175.

Page 185, par. 1: University of Virginia: *see above,* pp. 168f. Sketch for lawn: William A. Lambeth and Werner H. Manning, *Thomas Jefferson as an Architect and a Designer of Landscapes,* Boston, 1913, pls. 8–9; *see above,* p. 183.

par. 2: Academic village: Kimball, *Thomas Jefferson Architect,* p. 190.

Library: Letter to Henry Tazewell, Jan. 5, 1805, *New York Times*, April 26, 1931.

Students: *see above*, p. 180.

par. 3: *See* the letter to Benjamin Rush, Sept. 23, 1800, M. X, p. 173. Against education in cities, *see also*, Eduard Dumbaud, *Thomas Jefferson American Tourist*, Norman, 1946, pp. 207f.

Original plan: Lambeth-Manning, *op. cit.*, pp. 35f.; *see above*, p. 168.

Page 186, par. 1: Kimball, *Thomas Jefferson Architect*, p. 80. *Diaetae: see above*, p. 183.

Cicero's two gymansia, Academy and Lyceum, the upper one provided with a library: Cicero, *Tusculan Dialogues*, II, 9. This book of Cicero's was familiar to Jefferson from his student days: *see above*, pp. 42f.

Page 187, par. 1: Dome of the Library-Pantheon: Lehmann, *op. cit.*, pp. 22, 25f. Add to the bibliography given there the facsimile reproduction of Jefferson's sheet of instructions, Lambeth-Manning, *op. cit.*, pl. 7.

Varro: *see above*, p. 184.

Page 188, par. 1: Letter to John Brazier, Aug. 24, 1819, M. XV, p. 209; compare, also, letter to William Short, Oct. 31, 1819, M. XV, p. 221; F. X, p. 145.

Chapter 12

Page 190, par. 1: *See,* especially, chap. 8.

Civilization has been defined as the common denominator of Jefferson's concerns by Charles A. Beard, *The Mississippi Valley Historical Review*, XXX, 1943, pp. 161f.

For Jefferson's belief in the development of morality in history, *see* Adrienne Koch, *The Philosophy of Thomas Jefferson*, New York, 1943, pp. 15f.

par. 2: Belief in progress of education: Koch, *op. cit.*, pp. 178f.

Freedom: *see above*, chap. 8. *See also*, H. M. Kallen, "The Arts and Thomas Jefferson," *Ethics*, LIII, 1942/3, pp. 278f.

Report to the Literary Board: William A. Lambeth and Werner H. Manning, *Thomas Jefferson as an*

Architect and a Designer of Landscapes, Boston, 1913, p. 72.

"Charter of modern public education": Gilbert Chinard, *Correspondence of Jefferson and Du Pont de Nemours,* Baltimore, 1931, pp. XCIf.

The best synthesis of Jefferson's educational ideas is found in Roy J. Honeywell, *The Educational Work of Thomas Jefferson (Harvard Studies in Education,* XVI), Cambridge, Mass., 1931; *see also,* Louis B. Wright, "Thomas Jefferson and the Classics," *Proceedings of The American Philosophical Society,* LXXXVI, 1943, pp. 226f.

Humboldt: John C. Henderson, *Thomas Jefferson's Views on Public Education,* New York, 1890, pp. 2f.

Page 191, par. 1: Republic of letters: Letter to Noah Webster, Dec. 4, 1790, M. VIII, p. 111; F. V, p. 254.

Letter to Mme. de Staël, Sept. 6, 1816, M. G. Kimball, "Unpublished Correspondence of Mme. de Staël with Thomas Jefferson," *The North American Review,* CCVIII, July-December, 1918, p. 71.

Letter to H. G. Spafford, March 17, 1814, M. XIV, p. 120; compare, regarding Hume, letters to John Adams, Nov. 25, 1816, M. XV, p. 86, and Oct. 25, 1825, M. XVI, p. 125.

Letter to William Rutledge, Feb. 2, 1788, M. VI, p. 418; F. V, p. 5.

"An honest heart," etc.: Letter to Peter Carr, Aug. 19, 1785, M. V, p. 84.

Page 192, par. 2: France: *see above,* p. 122.

Middleton: Fr. W. Hirst, *Life and Letters of Thomas Jefferson,* New York, 1926, p. 507.

Page 193, par. 1: Moral instinct: *see above,* pp. 131f.

Letter to Peter Carr, Aug. 19, 1785, M. V, p. 82.

Letter to John Tyler, May 26, 1810, M. XII, p. 393; F. IX, p. 277 note.

par. 2: Aristocracy of talent and virtue: Letter to John Adams, Oct. 28, 1813, M. XIII, pp. 394f.; F. IX, pp. 424f.

University: Letter to Judge Bland, June 26, 1821, Th. F. Fitzhugh, *Letters of Thomas Jefferson Concerning Philology and the Classics.* Reprinted from *University of Virginia, Alumni Bulletin,* 1918–9, Charlottesville, 1919, pp. 6of.

Page 194, par. 1: Letter to Thomas Cooper, Oct. 7, 1814, M. XIV, p. 200.

Randall, III, p. 522.

Letter to John Bannister, Oct. 15, 1785, M. V, p. 186.

Books for the University: Honeywell, *op. cit.,* p. 86.

Early curriculum plan: Letter to Priestley, Jan. 18, 1800, M. X, pp. 140f.; F. VII, pp. 407f.

Page 195, par. 2: Honeywell, *op. cit.,* p. 159.

Report on a Meeting of the Visitors of the University, Oct. 4, 1824, M. XIX, p. 444.

Letter to William Rives, Sept. 18, 1811, F' IV, pp. 103f.

Notes on Virginia, Query XIV, M. II, p. 205; F. III, p. 253.

par. 3: *Ibid.,* M. II, pp. 205f.; F. III, p. 253.

Letter to Priestley, Jan. 27, 1800, M. X, p. 146; F. VII, pp. 413f.

Page 196, par. 1: *Notes on Virginia,* Query XV, M. II, pp. 209f.; F. III, p. 256.

Honeywell, *op. cit.,* p. 254.

Letter to Priestley, cited in the preceding note; letter to John Brazier, Aug. 24, 1819, M. XV, pp. 208f.; letter to J. W. Eppes, July 28, 1787, M. VI, p. 190; *Notes on Virginia,* Query XIV, M. II, p. 203; F. III, pp. 251f.

"Hypercritical knowledge": Letter to Thomas Cooper, Oct. 7, 1814, M. XIV, pp. 200f.

Letter to————, Feb. 20, 1825, M. XVI, p. 107.

Page 197, par. 1: Letter to J. P. Emmer, May 2, 1826, M. XVI, pp. 169f.; *see,* Honeywell, *op. cit.,* p. 115; above, pp. 65f.

Fitzhugh, *op. cit.,* pp. 61f.; Honeywell, *op. cit.,* p. 219.

Report, op. cit., M. XIX, p. 444.

par. 2: Letter to W. C. Nicholas, April 2, 1816, M. XIV, pp. 451f.; compare, Honeywell, *op. cit.,* p. 254.

par. 3: Hirst, *op. cit.,* pp. 551f.

Ph. A. Bruce, *History of the University of Virginia, 1819–1919,* II, New York, 1920, pp. 81f.

Page 198, par. 1: Female education: Letter to Nathaniel Burwell, March 14, 1818, M. XV, pp. 165f.; F. X, pp. 104f.; *see above,* pp. 98f.

Translations: Letter to John Adams, Oct. 13, 1813, M. XIII, p. 393. *See above,* p. 98.

Pope: Letter to Priestley, Jan. 27, 1800, M. X, p. 147; F. VII, p. 414.

Epictetus: Letter to William Short, Oct. 31, 1819, M. XV, p. 221; F. X, p. 144.

Student's reading: Letter to————, Oct. 25, 1825, M. XVI, 125.

Page 199, par. 1: New Testament: Letter to J. W. Eppes, May 3, 1818, *Scribner's Magazine,* XXXVI, 1904, p. 578; *see above,* pp. 88f.

Cicero's orations: Letter to J. W. Eppes, Jan. 17, 1810, M. XII, p. 343, F. IX, pp. 267f.; compare, above, pp. 119f., 151f.

par. 2: Honeywell, *op. cit.,* pp. 123, 159.

Page 201, par. 1: Independent reading: Letter to Thomas Cooper, Aug. 14, 1820, M. XV, pp. 264f.

Letters to Peter Carr, Aug. 19, 1785, M. V, pp. 82f., and Aug. 10, 1787, M. VI, pp. 256f.; F. IV, pp. 427f.

Law student: *see above,* pp. 13f.

Letter to William Rives, Sept. 18, 1811, F' IV, pp. 103f.

par. 2: Letter to Rives, cited in the preceding note.

Letter to John Adams, July 5, 1814, M. XIV, pp. 150f.; F. IX, p. 464.

Letter to ————, Oct. 25, 1825, M. XVI, p. 124. *See below,* pp. 206f.

Page 202, par 1: Letter to John Brazier, Aug, 24, 1819, M. XV, pp. 207f.

Page 203, par. 1: *See above,* pp. 72f.

par. 2: A Bill for the More General Diffusion of Knowledge, F. II, pp. 220f.; *Notes on Virginia,* Query XIV, M. II, pp. 204f.; F. III, pp. 251f.

An Act for Establishing Elementary Schools, Sept. 9, 1817, M. XVII, p. 436.

Private reading: Letter to Peter Carr, Aug. 19, 1785, M. V, p. 86.

Bible: Letter to Peter Carr, Aug. 10, 1787, M. VI, pp. 258f.; F. IV, pp. 429f.; *see above,* pp. 88f.

Public Libraries: Letter to John Wyche, May 19, 1809, M. XII, p. 282.

Reading for girls: Sarah N. Randolph, *The Domestic Life of Thomas Jefferson,* 3rd. ed., Cambridge, Mass., 1939, pp. 84, 151, letter to Anne Cary Bankhead, Dec. 8, 1808, M. XVIII, p. 255.

Page 204, par. 1: Letter to F. A. Van der Kemp, March 22, 1812, M. XIII, p. 357; letter to Robert Skipworth, Aug. 3, 1771, M. IV, p. 239; F. I, p. 398.

Bill for the More General Diffusion, etc., F. II, pp. 220f.

Letter to John Adams, Sept. 28, 1787, M. VI, pp. 321f.; F. IV, p. 455.

Letter to Madison, Dec. 20, 1787, M. VI, p. 389; F. IV, pp. 477f.

Letter to Monsieur Paganel, April 15, 1811, M. XIII, p. 37.

Page 205, par 1: *See above,* pp. 125f.

par. 2: "Opinion is power and that opinion will come": Letter to John Adams, Jan. 11, 1816, M. XIV, p. 396; compare, below, p. 209.

Letter to John Adams, Dec. 10, 1819, M. XV, p. 234; F. X, pp. 151f., *see above,* pp. 115f.

Letter to Mann Page, Aug. 30, 1795, M. IX, p. 306; F. VII, p. 24.

Letter to John Tyler, May 26, 1810, M. XII, p. 393; F. IX, p. 277 note.

Page 206, par. 1: An Act for Establishing Elementary Schools, note to 5–6, M. XVII, pp. 423f.

par. 2: Honeywell, *op. cit.,* p. 251.

Letter to Robert Patterson, Sept. 11, 1811, M. XIII, p. 83.

par. 3: Letter to John Adams, Oct. 28, 1813, M. XIII, p. 401; F. IX, p. 428.

Letter to Du Pont de Nemours, March 2, 1809, M. XII, p. 260.

Epicureanism: *see above,* pp. 139f.

"Sublime luxury": Letter to Priestley, Jan. 27, 1800, M. X, pp. 146f.; F. VII, pp. 413f.

Letter to A. J. Cook, Jan. 21, 1806, M. XIV, pp. 403f.

Letter to Peter Carr, Aug. 19, 1785, M. V, p. 82.

Page 207, par. 1: *See above,* pp. 199f.

Honeywell, *op. cit.,* p. 88.

Meeting of the Visitors, l. c., M. XIX, p. 440.

Page 208, par. 2: Letter to A. Coray, Oct. 31, 1823, M. XV, p. 481.

Henry Adams, *History of the United States of America during the First Administration of Thomas Jefferson,* I, New York, 1921, p. 179 (statement of 1800).

"Knowledge is power": Letter to George Ticknor, Nov. 15, 1817, Honeywell, *op. cit.*, p. 146; *see above,* p. 205 and note to par. 2.

Letter to John Adams, Sept. 12, 1821, M. XV, p. 334.

Indices

I. GENERAL

II. ANCIENT AUTHORS

III. JEFFERSON'S WRITINGS

The numbers in parentheses refer to pages of the text in which statements based on the respective documents cited in the notes are made.